LONDON CLUBS

LONDON CLUBS

THEIR HISTORY & TREASURES

By

RALPH NEVILL

LONDON : CHATTO & WINDUS

MCMLXIX

Published by
Chatto & Windus Ltd
40-42 William IV Street
London WC2

*

Clarke, Irwin & Co Ltd
Toronto

First Published 1911
This Edition reprinted 1969

SBN 7011 1520 3

Printed in Great Britain by
William Lewis (Printers) Ltd
Cardiff

NOTE

THE Author wishes to acknowledge the valuable assistance he has received from several Secretaries of Clubs mentioned in this volume, particularly Captain CHARLES PERCY SMITH, who supplied him with information of considerable interest.

CONTENTS

CHAPTER I

CHAPTER II

CHAPTER III

CHAPTER IV

CHAPTER V

CHAPTER VI

CHAPTER VII

CHAPTER VIII

CHAPTER IX

CHAPTER X

CHAPTER XI

LIST OF ILLUSTRATIONS

LONDON CLUBS

CHAPTER I

THE ORIGIN OF CLUBS IN COFFEE-HOUSES AND TAVERNS

THE modern club, with its luxuries and comforts, has its origin in the tavern and coffee-house of a long-past age. The resorts in question have long since entirely changed their character, although they were once important features of London life, and were used by all classes for purposes of conviviality and conversation.

The appellation "club" seems to have come into use at the time when coffee-houses began to be popular in London. The first notable London club, of course, was the Mermaid, in Broad Street, which was supposed to have been founded by Raleigh, and which was the reputed scene of many witty combats between Shakespeare and Ben Jonson. The latter himself originated another club—the Apollo—which had its meetings at the Devil Tavern, near Temple Bar.

In course of time many landlords perceived the advantage which would accrue to their business from the setting apart of special rooms for privileged

1

customers ; and gradually a number of fairly
exclusive clubs came into being.

Thus Tom's, a coffee-house till 1764, in that year,
by a guinea subscription, was easily converted into
a fashionable club. In the same way White's
and the Cocoa-tree changed their character from
chocolate-house to club. When once a house had
customers enough of standing and good repute,
well acquainted with each other, it was quite worth
while to purchase the power of excluding all but
subscribers, and to turn the place into a club ; for b
such a proceeding undesirable characters, who cou
obtain constant admission to an open house, we
at once kept outside the doors.

The evolution of the modern club has been s
simple that it can be traced with great ease. Firs
the tavern or coffee-house, where a certain number
of people met on special evenings for purposes
of social conversation, and incidentally consume
a good deal of liquid refreshment; then the
beginnings of the club proper—some well-known
house of refreshment being taken over from the
proprietor by a limited number of clients for their
own exclusive use, and the landlord retained as
manager ; and finally the palatial modern club, not
necessarily sociable, but replete with every comfort,
and owned by the members themselves. In such
places, however, the old spirit of club-life is generally
lost. Dr. Johnson, for example, can be imagined
passing through the portals of one of these huge
buildings, and saying : " Sir, this may be a palace,
but it is no club." There is no doubt that in a great
measure he would be right.

It is believed that the first house in Pall Mall ever used as a club was No. 86, originally built for Edward, Duke of York, brother of George III. It was opened as a " subscription house," and called the Albion Hotel towards the end of the last century.

In the early part of the eighteenth century there were said to be no fewer than 2,000 coffee-houses in London. Every profession, trade, class, party, had its favourite coffee-house. The lawyers discussed law or literature, criticized the last new play, or retailed the legal scandal at Nando's or the Grecian, not very far away from the Temple. At such places the young bloods of the Inns of Court paraded their gowns in the morning, and swaggered in their lace coats and Mechlin ruffles at night, after the theatre. City men met to discuss the rise and fall of stocks, and to settle the rate of insurance, at Garraway's or Jonathan's; parsons exchanged University gossip or discussed points of theology at Truby's or at Child's, in St. Paul's Churchyard; whilst military men mustered to grumble over their grievances at Old or Young Man's, near Charing Cross. The St. James's and the Smyrna were the headquarters of the Whig politicians, whereas the Tories frequented the Cocoa-tree or Ozinda's, in St. James's Street; Scotchmen had their house of call at Forrest's, Frenchmen at Giles's or Old Slaughter's, in St. Martin's Lane; the gamesters shook their elbows in White's and the chocolate-houses round Covent Garden; and the leading wits gathered at Will's, Button's, or Tom's, in Great Russell Street, where, after the theatre, there was piquet and the best of conversation till midnight. At all these places, except a few of the most aristocratic coffee or chocolate houses of the West End, smoking was allowed.

Many of these old taverns must have been exceedingly comfortable places, and the few which survive have an especial charm. They carry one's thoughts irresistibly to the days when Dr. Johnson blew his cloud by the side of an old-fashioned fireplace, and occasionally floored some unhappy wight with the sledge-hammer of his conversation.

One of the last, if not the last, hostelries, which still retains its ancient appearance, is the Cheshire Cheese. This well-known house is half-way up Fleet Street, on the northern side. It remains, I believe, substantially as it was when, seven years after the Restoration, it was rebuilt on the site of that older Cheshire Cheese where Shakespeare and many other Elizabethan wits were wont to meet.

Ben Jonson was a frequent visitor, and here occurred his dispute with Sylvester as to which of them could make the best couplet in the shortest time. The latter began :

> " I, Sylvester,
> Kiss'd your sister."

The other's retort was :

> " I, Ben Jonson,
> Kiss'd your wife."

" But that's not rhyme," said Sylvester. " No," said Jonson, " but it's true."

The original courtyard of the Cheshire Cheese is

now roofed over with glass, and here may be seen some interesting old prints. These include two by H. Bunbury—"A City Hunt" and "Hyde Park, 1780"; while others are, "Destruction of the Bastille, July 14, 1789," after a painting by H. Singleton, and a line engraving by James Heath, from a painting by F. Wheatley of "The Riot in Broad Street on the 17th of June, 1773."

Dr. Johnson is supposed to have passed many an evening here, and from his time down to the present day unbroken links of tradition connect the Cheshire Cheese of the twentieth century with the Cheshire Cheese of the eighteenth.

The seat on which legend reports that the redoubtable lexicographer sat is one of the most treasured relics of the dining-room. Above it hangs a copy of the famous portrait by Sir Joshua Reynolds, now preserved in the National Gallery. Underneath may be read the following inscription: "The Favourite Seat of Dr. Johnson. Born 18th Septr., 1709. Died 13th Decr., 1784. In him a noble understanding and a masterly intellect were united with grand independence of character and unfailing goodness of heart, which won the admiration of his own age and remain as recommendations to the reverence of posterity. 'No, Sir! there is nothing which has yet been contrived by man by which so much happiness has been produced as by a good tavern.'—JOHNSON."

A number of quaint pictures and prints are to be found scattered over the house.

Upstairs is another copy of Sir Joshua's oil-painting of the Doctor. This, it is said, dates back to Johnson's time, and was painted in order that it might adorn the room at the Mitre, in Chancery Lane, where the club founded by Dr. Johnson first held its meetings. Dr. Johnson's Mitre has long since been pulled down, but the club he founded still exists, and it meets several times a year in what was formerly the coffee-room. This is now known as " William's room," on account of the portrait of William Simpson which hangs over the fireplace. William began to be a waiter at Ye Olde Cheshire Cheese Chop-house in 1829, and his portrait, as the inscription below says, "was subscribed for by the gentlemen frequenting the coffee-room, and presented to Mr. Dolamore (the landlord) to be handed down as an heirloom to all future land-lords of 'Ye Olde Cheshire Cheese,' Wine Office Court, Fleet Street." The name of the artist is unknown.

In the opposite room is a picture of another waiter—a portrait of Henry Todd, as the inscription informs us, who commenced as waiter at Ye Olde Cheshire Cheese February 27, 1812. It was painted by Wageman, July 1827, and "subscribed for by the gentlemen frequenting the coffee-room, and presented to Mr. Dolamore (the landlord) in trust to be handed down as an heirloom to all future landlords of the Old Cheshire Cheese, Wine Office Court, Fleet Street."

Besides being the meeting-place of the Mitre Club, the Cheshire Cheese is used by a number of clubs resembling somewhat those which were so popular with a long-vanished generation. These are : The Johnson Club, founded about twenty-five years ago; the Sawdust Club, founded 1906; "Ourselves," founded 1897; St. Dunstan's, founded 1890; the Rump Steak Club; the Dickens Club. The Johnson Club is literary and social in character, and consists of thirty-one members, who sup together annually on or about December 13th, the anniversary of the Doctor's death. Various other meetings are held throughout the year.

The Doctor was certainly the most typical clubman of a past age, and his name is connected with quite a number of social clubs which held their meetings at coffee-houses and taverns. Indeed, no more clubbable man than the writer of the famous Dictionary ever lived; but, then, sociability was the main object of the clubs of his day, whereas the modern tendency is more towards comfort and efficient management than anything else. In most large modern clubs quite a number of members are totally unknown to their fellows, and there is no reason why a member should speak to anyone at all unless he wishes to do so. The majority of the larger modern clubs are in reality merely comfortable caravanserais — hotels receiving a certain number of selected visitors who recognize no social obligations within the club walls except such as regulate ordinary civilized behaviour.

Dr. Johnson founded several social clubs at the taverns and coffee-houses which he loved to frequent. One of these was the King's Head, Ivy Lane, Paternoster Row, a famous beefsteak house, and here he spent every Tuesday evening in conversation with the members of a social club of his own foundation.

At the Queen's Arms, in St. Paul's Churchyard, the Doctor in later years founded a club of a similar sort, and Boswell records that he was also desirous of having a City club, the members of which he suggested that Boswell should collect. " Only," added the great lexicographer, " don't let there be any patriots."

Yet another club instituted by Dr. Johnson was one which met thrice a week at the Essex Head, in Essex Street, Strand, at the time when that tavern was kept by Samuel Greaves—an old servant of Mr. Thrale's. Failure to attend was penalized by a fine of twopence.

The Mitre Tavern in Fleet Street, so often referred to by Boswell, was Dr. Johnson's favourite supper-place, and here was planned the celebrated tour to the Hebrides. It is interesting to remember, in this connection, that Chamberlain Clarke, who died in 1831, aged ninety-two, was the last survivor of those friends with whom Dr. Johnson forgathered at the Mitre.

Peele's Coffee-house, at Nos. 177, 178, Fleet Street, which afterwards became a tavern, was also supposed to have been a haunt of Dr. Johnson, whose portrait, painted on the keystone of a chimney-piece, for years after his death formed one of the attractions of the house. The artist was supposed to have been Sir Joshua Reynolds. Peele's was once noted for its collection of old newspapers. Here were preserved files from the following dates : The *Gazette*, 1759 ; *Times*, 1780 ; *Morning Chronicle*, 1773; *Morning Post*, 1773; *Morning Herald*, 1784; *Morning Advertiser*, 1794.

Nearly every literary man of that time had his favourite coffee-house.

George's, at No. 213 Strand, near Temple Bar, was the resort of Shenstone, who found it an economical place. Probably it was for this reason that the eccentric Sir James Lowther, a very rich man, but penurious, also went there. On his first visit he got the proprietors to change a piece of silver in order to pay twopence for his coffee. A few days later he returned expressly to tell the woman that she had given him a bad halfpenny, and demanded another in exchange for it.

Clients of this coffee-house could read pamphlets and papers for a very moderate subscription.

London hours were very different in those days. Three o'clock, or at latest four, was the dining hour of the most fashionable people, for in the country no such late hours had been adopted. In London, therefore, the men began to assemble soon after six at the coffee-house they frequented—unless, indeed, they were setting in for hard drinking, which seems to have prevailed much less in private houses than in taverns.

The conversation varied in different coffee-houses. In those about the Temple, legal matters formed the principal subject of discussion. On the other hand, at Daniel's, the Welsh coffee-house in Fleet Street, it was mostly of births, pedigrees, and descents; Child's and the Chapter, upon glebes, tithes, advowsons, rectories, and lectureships; North's, undue elections, false pollings, scrutinies, and the like; Hamlin's, infant baptism, lay ordination, free-will, election, and reprobation; Batson's, the prices of pepper, indigo, and saltpetre ; and all those about the Exchange, where the merchants met to transact their affairs, were in a perpetual hurry about stock-jobbing—cheating, and tricking widows and orphans, and committing spoil and rapine on the public, malicious people said.

In some coffee-houses and taverns political feeling ran high. One noted chop-house near Holborn lost its business owing to the democratic character of a number of its frequenters, and eventually had to be shut up. A new landlord, however, seeking to restore its prosperity, exhibited the sign of the King's Head, referring to which a friend said to him: " Do you think your new sign will keep away old customers ? Why, there is not one of them but would like as much as ever to have a chop at the King's Head."

The Chapter Coffee-house in Paternoster Row, an ancient building with low rooms and heavy beams, was in the eighteenth century the resort of all the booksellers and publishers ; and the literary hacks, the critics, and even the wits, used to go there in search of ideas or employment. This was the place about which Chatterton wrote, in those delusive letters he sent to his mother at Bristol, while he was starving in London. The Chapter also retained traditions of Oliver Goldsmith.

In later years it became the tavern frequented by University men and country clergymen who were up in London for a few days, and, having no private friends or access into society, were glad to learn what was going on in the world of letters.

from the conversation which they were sure to hear in the coffee-room.

At one time leather tokens were issued by the proprietor ; and the Chapter was noted for being entirely managed by men, no women servants being kept.

In the north-east corner of the coffee-room was a box known as the Witenagemote, which in the early morning was occupied by a group of individuals nicknamed the Wet Paper Club. The name was derived from their habit of opening the papers as soon as these were brought in by the newsman, and reading them before they were dried by the waiter ; a dry paper was regarded as a stale commodity. In the afternoon another party enjoyed the wet evening papers.

A gentleman who was considered a fixture in this box was Mr. Hammond, a Coventry manufacturer, who evening after evening, for nearly forty-five years, was always to be found in the same place, and during the entire period was well known for his severe and often able comments on the events of the day. Here he pontificated throughout the days of Wilkes, of the American War, and of the French War, and, being on the side of liberty, was constantly in opposition to almost everyone else.

The Chapter continued to be a coffee-house up to 1854, when it became a tavern.

The Royal Exchange was the resort of all the trading part of the City, foreign and domestic, from half an hour after one till near three in the afternoon ; but the better sort generally met in the

Exchange Alley a little before, at three celebrated coffee - houses called Garraway's, Robin's, and Jonathan's. In the first the people of quality who had business in the City, and the most considerable and wealthy citizens, congregated. In the third met buyers and sellers of stock.

The Royal Exchange Coffee-house resembled a gaming-house more than anything else, being full of gamesters, with the same sharp, intent looks, with the difference only that there it was selling of Bank stock, East India, South Sea, and lottery tickets, instead of the cards and dice dear to ordinary gamblers.

The British Coffee-house in the West End was much frequented by Scotchmen, whilst a mixture of all sorts went to the Smyrna, not very far away. There were other little coffee-houses much frequented in this neighbourhood—Young Man's for officers, Old Man's for stockjobbers, paymasters, and courtiers, and Little Man's for sharpers. Here there were two or three faro tables upstairs.

After the theatre fashionable men went to Tom's and Will's Coffee-houses, where they played piquet and indulged in conversation. Here you might see blue and green ribbons and stars sitting familiarly with private gentlemen, and talking with the same freedom as if they had left their quality and degrees of distance at home — a sight which amazed foreigners not used to the liberty of speech permitted in England.

A favourite resort of literary men was the Percy Coffee-house in Rathbone Place, Oxford Street. This was used by Thomas Byerley and Joseph

Robertson, who together produced the " Percy Anecdotes " in 1820, writing as Sholto and Reuben Percy. A large sum was realized by the work in question, which began in 1820 and ran into forty-four parts.

The West End coffee-houses were often disturbed by the eccentricities of the " bloods." A wild band, for instance, frequented the Royal Chocolate-house in St. James's Street, where on one occasion a dispute at hazard produced a quarrel, which became general throughout the room ; and, as they fought with their swords, three gentlemen were mortally wounded. The affray was at length ended by the interposition of the Royal Guards, who were compelled to knock the parties down indiscriminately with the butt-ends of their muskets, as entreaties and commands were of no avail. On this occasion a footman of Colonel Cunningham's, greatly attached to his master, rushed through the swords, seized and literally carried him out by force without injury.

Lord Camelford, of duelling notoriety, one evening entered the Prince of Wales Coffee-house, Conduit Street, and, as was his usual custom, sat down and began to read the papers. A dashing fellow, and in his own opinion a first-rate blood, happening to come in, threw himself on the opposite seat of the same box, and, in a consequential tone, bawled : " Waiter ! bring me a pint of madeira and a couple of wax candles, and put them in the next box." He then drew over to himself Lord Camelford's candles, and began to read, which proceeding merely caused his lordship to look indignant, whilst he continued reading his paper. The waiter soon reappeared, and announced the completion of the gentleman's commands, who immediately lounged round to his own box. Lord Camelford, having now finished his paragraph, called out, in a mimicking tone: "Waiter! bring me a pair of snuffers." These being quickly brought, his lordship laid down his paper, walked round the table at which the " blood " sat, snuffed out both the candles, and retired to his seat. Boiling with rage and fury, the indignant beau roared out: "Waiter, waiter! who the devil is this fellow that dares to insult a gentleman? What is he? What do they call him?" "Lord Camelford, sir," replied the other in a tone scarcely audible. The coxcomb, horror-struck at the name of the dangerous nobleman, said tremblingly, "What have I to pay?" and, on being told, quietly laid down his money and sneaked away, leaving his madeira untasted.

Disturbances were frequently caused in coffee-houses by dashing bucks who attempted either to dominate or to upset the domination of others. At the west end of Cecil Court, in St. Martin's Lane, there existed, towards the end of the reign of George II, Pon's Coffee-house, much frequented by foreigners of distinction, officers, and men about town. In the course of time the foreigners began to dominate this place, always contriving to get one of themselves into the chair, and occupying special seats which were kept for them alone. This created much ill-feeling, and at length reached the ears of the celebrated Lord Tyrawley, at that time a gay spark about town. Discussing the foreign ascendancy which prevailed in this place, Lord Tyrawley said, in his vigorous way: " It is all your own fault.

The Frenchmen see you are afraid of them, and therefore behave with insolence. I am sure they are cowards, and if I was in the company I would undertake to insult the lot with impunity, and leave the room without being questioned or prevented by any one of them." This led to a conversation, which ended in a bet that Lord Tyrawley would carry his threat into execution, and on an appointed day he proceeded to action.

Having made arrangements with a confederate, his lordship entered the room in time enough to take his seat in the president's chair unquestioned, according to the law of the place. Afterwards the confederate, pretending to be a stranger, seated himself unnoticed, in the same manner, in the deputy chairman's place at the bottom. As the Frenchmen dropped in, one by one, they were surprised to perceive the posts of honour thus unusually occupied. They whispered and muttered to each other as their numbers increased, but at last took their seats anywhere they could. In tones of discontent, deep but not loud, one whispered to his neighbour: "Connaissez-vous celui-là?" pointing to the new president. "Non." "Ni l'autre?" "Non." "Ni moi, non plus; ma foi, c'est singulier! Ah! les drôles! Eh bien, tout-à-l'heure le président viendra, et alors nous verrons comme tout cela va finir!" At last the French president arrived, and, finding the post of honour unexpectedly filled by the two dashing officers of rank, quietly took his seat, like his countrymen, where he could find it. The others, who were interested in the scene, seated themselves at the lower end of the table, whilst the few French who had come early seated themselves as near to the new president as they could.

The two intruders enjoyed the scene in secret, but behaved with politeness and affability to all, in their respective circles, till at last dinner was served. Lord Tyrawley formally did the honours—tasted the soup, put on a critical look, and asked those who were near him to taste, and favour him with their opinions. They were surprised at his assurance, but several tasted, and said simultaneously, "Assez bien—comme à l'ordinaire—qu'en pensez-vous?" and so on. Lord Tyrawley then exclaimed : "It is most execrable stuff, and only fit to be placed before pigs! Waiter" (the man crept forward trembling), "what do you bring this stuff here for?" The astonished servant looked silently towards the Frenchmen, in the hopes of catching a hint, when Tyrawley, in a rage, vociferated: "Don't answer me, sir! take it away, and bring me the next dish—take it away instantly, I say!" So saying, he seized his own plate in both hands, raised it above his head, and then dashed it with all his force, with its flat bottom, into the midst of the soup, which spread, in a circular sheet, upon the table and the clothes of all who sat at that end of it. The Frenchmen started with horror and surprise, springing from their seats to save their clothes, while his confederate jumped up, exclaiming: "What do you mean by that, sir?" "I mean to say," said Lord Tyrawley, with provoking coolness, "the soup is very bad." "Nonsense, sir," said the apparently enraged deputy chairman; "you have insulted every man here, and I will see that you give me immediate satisfaction." "Oh, sir," said the Peer, very coolly, "if you are for that sport, I will indulge you at once." So saying, each took down his hat and sword with great dignity, and, the challenger strutting after the challenged, both descended into the courtyard. The bespattered foreigners, finding a duel was in progress, crowded the window for good places to see the sight, till it was quite full. The combatants took their ground, drew, and began a very furious-looking assault; one fought retreating, the other pushing him back till they were at the end of the court in St. Martin's Lane, when they took off their hats, bowed gracefully to the astonished Frenchmen, and walked away arm in arm, laughing and kissing their hands to the company they had left, leaving them to enjoy their spoiled dinner and well-greased clothes as they were best able.

The great dread of the peaceful citizens who frequented taverns and coffee-houses was an incursion by members of the clubs known as Bold Bucks and Hell-Fires—for the most part composed of deliberately abandoned villains. The Bold Bucks were given up to licentiousness of an unbridled kind; blind and bold love was their motto, and their main object seems to have been the assimilation of man to brute.

The Hell-Fires, as may be gathered from their appellation, aimed at an even more transcendent malignity, and derided the forms of religion as a trifle.

A regular code of etiquette was observed at coffee-houses. At most of these, though not at the fashion-

able West End ones, a penny was usually laid on the
bar on entering, which entitled the guest to the use
of the room and of the news-sheet.   Every rank of
life, except perhaps the very lowest, was represented
at one or other of these houses.   Men met there
to transact business, talk politics, discuss the latest
play or poem, to play dice or cards.   To one man
the coffee-house was an office for business, where
he received, and from which he dated, his letters;
to another, a place in which to push his fortunes
among patrons ; to most, a lounging-place in which
to discuss the news and pass away the time.   The
advertisements of the day are full of allusions to
them.   One gentleman loses his watch or his sword,
and will give a reward if they are returned to Tom's
or Button's, " and no questions asked."   Another,
one Brown, " late City Marshall," will settle all
affairs that he had in his hands while holding that
office, if the persons interested will repair to " Mr.
Gibbon's Coffee House at Charing Cross."

The first coffee-house—that is, the first house
where coffee was sold to the public in England—is
said to have been the George and Vulture, in
George Yard, Lombard Street, a house still in
existence.

About 1652 a Turkey merchant, Mr. Edwards
by name, is supposed to have brought to London
from Smyrna a Ragusan youth, Pasqua Rosee by
name, specially to prepare coffee for him every
morning.   This servant he eventually allowed to
sell the new-fashioned infusion publicly, and eventually the Ragusan established the first coffee-house
in London, at St. Michael's Abbey, Cornhill, under

the title of Pasqua Rosee's Inn, afterwards known to fame as the George and Vulture.

The old Rainbow in Fleet Street, now known as Groom's, was the second coffee-house; but the owner of the Rainbow apparently did not purvey a very attractive form of the new beverage, for he was indicted by the Vestry for selling " a strong drink called Coffee which annoyed the neighbourhood by its evil smell."

Curiously enough, both houses, Groom's and the George and Vulture, now belong to the same proprietor, Mr. John Gardner, who, when he recently puchased the lease of the former, also acquired the original coffee-making recipe.

As a coffee-house the George and Vulture was a well-known resort of poets, wits, and satirists. The servants appear to have been very enterprising in attracting customers, for they would rush out and seize passers-by, crying: " Coffee, sir; tea, sir! Walk in and try a fresh pot !"

At the George and Vulture, Swift discussed the South Sea Bubble with his friends. Here, too, came Richard Estcourt, of Drury Lane, and founded the first Beefsteak Club. At a later period this coffee-house, on account of its sign, was especially popular with patriotic clubs. Amongst its patrons were Addison and Steele, whilst Daniel Defoe seems also to have been a visitor.

In Georgian days the old coffee-house became one of the most popular resorts of John Wilkes, and there also went Hogarth and other well-known men of the day, whilst members of the Hell-Fire Club were constant though unwelcome visitors.

In later times Charles Dickens immortalized the George and Vulture by making it an abode of Mr. Pickwick and Sam Weller; the old hostelry was also selected by the great novelist as being the place where subpœnas were served on Mr. Pickwick's friends in the famous case of Bardell and Pickwick. Dickens's affection for " the George " is now perpetuated by the City Pickwick, a social club which holds its meetings there.

Dickens is supposed to have obtained the idea for the name of Tom Pinch from Dr. Pinche's school, which in early Victorian days occupied the site of the Deutsche Bank, close to the George and Vulture, in George Yard. Sir Henry Irving was a pupil here, as was that still surviving legal luminary, Sir Edward Clarke.

Another resort full of old-world memories— the London Coffee-house, on Ludgate Hill, where John Leech's father and grandfather were proprietors—occupied a Roman site. In 1800, behind this house, in a bastion of the City Wall, was found a sepulchral monument, dedicated to a faithful wife by her husband, a Roman soldier. Here also were found a fragment of a statue of Hercules and a female head. In front of the coffee-house, immediately west of St. Martin's Church, stood Ludgate.

This coffee-house was within the rules of the Fleet Prison ; and in the coffee-house were " locked up " for the night such juries from the Old Bailey Sessions as could not agree upon verdicts. In later days it became a tavern.

A curious incident once occurred in this house.

Mr. Broadhurst, the famous tenor, by singing a high note caused a wineglass on the table to break, the bowl being separated from the stem. Brayley, the topographer, was present at the time.

Lloyd's, now such a well-known institution, originated in a coffee-house of that name, which flourished as early as the very beginning of the eighteenth century.

Lloyd's Coffee-house was originally in Lombard Street, at the corner of Abchurch Lane, subsequently in Pope's-head Alley, where it was called " New Lloyd's Coffee-house "; but on February 14, 1774, it was removed to the north-west corner of the Royal Exchange, where it remained until the destruction of that building by fire. When the Royal Exchange was rebuilt, special rooms were set aside for Lloyd's, which assumed the form in which it flourishes to-day.

Lloyd's, as a place for insuring ships, was at first started by an astute individual who saw the possibilities of a meeting-place for underwriters and insurers of ships' cargoes.

As early as the year 1740, it is recorded that Mr. Baker, Master of Lloyd's Coffee-house, in Lombard Street, waited on Sir Robert Walpole with the news of Admiral Vernon's capture of Portobello. This was the first account received thereof, and, as it proved to be true, Sir Robert was pleased to order Mr. Baker a handsome present.

Another resort, somewhat similar to Lloyd's, was Garraway's Coffee-house—the first place where tea was sold in England. It was during the time of the South Sea Bubble that this became the scene of great mercantile transactions. The original proprietor was Thomas Garway, tobacconist and coffee-man. He issued the following curious circular: "Tea in England hath been sold in the leaf for six pounds, and sometimes for ten pounds the pound weight, and in respect of its former scarceness and dearness, it hath been only used as a regalia in high treatments and entertainments, and presents made thereof to princes and grandees till the year 1651. The said Thomas Garway did purchase a quantity thereof, and first publicly sold the said tea in leaf and drink, made according to the directions of the most knowing merchants and travellers into those eastern countries; and upon knowledge and experience of the said Garway's continued care and industry in obtaining the best tea, and making drink thereof, very many noblemen, physicians, merchants, and gentlemen of quality, have ever since sent to him for the said leaf, and daily resort to his house in Exchange Alley, aforesaid, to drink the drink thereof; and to the end that all persons of eminence and quality, gentlemen and others, who have occasion for tea in leaf, may be supplied, these are to give notice that the said Thomas Garway hath tea to sell from ' sixteen to fifty shillings per pound.'"

In 1673 there were some great sales of wine at Garraway's. These took place " by the candle "— that is, by auction while an inch of candle burnt. In the *Tatler*, No. 147, we read : "Upon my coming home last night, I found a very handsome present of French wine left for me, as a taste of 216 hogsheads, which are to be put to sale at £20 a hogshead,

at Garraway's Coffee-house, in Exchange Alley,"
etc. A sale by candle is not, however, by candlelight, but during the day. Such sales took place
by daylight, and at the commencement of the sale,
when the auctioneer had read a description of the
property and the conditions on which it was to be
disposed of, a piece of candle, usually an inch long,
was lit, the last bidder at the time the light went
out being declared the purchaser.

Garraway's was famous for its sandwiches and
sherry, pale ale, and punch. The sandwich-maker,
it was said, occupied two hours in cutting and
arranging the sandwiches before the day's consumption commenced. The sale-room was on the first-
floor, with a small rostrum for the seller, and a few
rough wooden seats for the buyers. Sales of
drugs, mahogany, and timber, were its speciality
in the fifties of the last century, when twenty or
thirty property and other sales sometimes took place
in a day. The walls and windows of the lower room
were covered with sale placards—unsentimental
evidences of the mutability of human affairs.

In 1840 and 1841, when the tea speculation was
at its height, and prices were fluctuating sixpence and
eightpence per pound on the arrival of every mail,
Garraway's was frequented every night by a host of
the smaller fry of dealers, and there was much more
excitement than ever occurred on 'Change when the
most important intelligence arrived. Champagne
flowed, and everyone ate and drank, and went, as
he pleased, without the least question about the
bill ; yet everything was paid, though such a state
of affairs continued for several months.

At one time many taverns were the meeting-places of "mug-house clubs," amusing resorts where gentlemen, lawyers, and tradesmen used to meet in a great room, seldom under a hundred in number.

Such assemblies usually had a president, who sat in an armchair some steps higher than the rest of the company, to keep the whole room in order. A harp played all the time at the lower end of the room ; and every now and then one or other of the company rose and entertained the rest with a song, some being good singers. Here nothing was drunk but ale, and every gentleman had his separate mug, which he chalked on the table where he sat, as it was brought in. A free - and - easy atmosphere pervaded the place, and everyone did and said exactly what he pleased.

A number of these "mug-house clubs" were to be found in Cheapside and its vicinity, and others about Covent Garden, a district which formerly abounded in well-known coffee-houses. In the eighteenth century, in Russell Street alone, were three of the most celebrated : Will's, Button's, and Tom's. Will's, as is well known, was closely connected with Dryden, the *Tatler*, and the *Spectator ;* and its wits' room, on the first-floor, was celebrated throughout the town. So was Button's, with its lion's head letter-box, and the young poets in the back room. Tom's, No. 17, on the north side of Russell Street, and of a somewhat later date, was taken down in 1865. The premises remained, with but little alteration, long after they ceased to be a coffee-house. It was named after its original pro-prietor, Thomas West, who, November 26, 1722, threw himself, in a delirium, from the second-floor window into the street, and died immediately. The upper portion of the premises was the coffee-house, under which lived T. Lewis, the bookseller, Pope's publisher.

Will's Coffee-house, known as the Wits', which was very celebrated in its day, was at No. 23, Russell Street, Bow Street. Dryden first made it a resort of wits. The poet used to sit in a room on the first-floor, and his customary seat was by the fireside in the winter, and at the corner of the balcony, looking over the street, in fine weather; he called the two places his winter and his summer seat. In the eighteenth century this room became the dining-room. In Dryden's day people did not sit in boxes, as subsequently, but at various tables which were dispersed through the room. Smoking was permitted in the public room, and was then much in vogue; indeed, it does not seem to have been considered a nuisance, as it was some years later. Here, as in other similar places of meeting, the visitors divided themselves into parties; the young beaux and wits, who seldom approached the principal table, thought it a great honour to have a pinch out of Dryden's snuff-box.

In later years Will's Coffee-house became an open market for libels and lampoons.

Swift thought little of the frequenters of Will's; he used to say the worst conversation he ever heard in his life was to be heard there. The wits (as they were called), said he disparagingly, used formerly to assemble at this house; that is to say, five or six men who had written plays or at least prologues, or had a share in a miscellany, came thither, and entertained one another with their trifling compositions, assuming as grand an air as if they had been the noblest efforts of human nature, or as if the fate of kingdoms depended on them.

It was Swift who framed the rules of the Brothers' Club, which met every Thursday. "The end of our club," said he, "is to advance conversation and friendship, and to reward learning without interest or recommendation. We take in none but men of wit or men of interest; and if we go on as we began, no other club in this town will be worth talking of."

The Brothers', which was really a political club, broke up in 1713, and the next year Swift formed the celebrated Scriblerus Club, an association rather of a literary than a political character. Oxford and St. John, Swift, Arbuthnot, Pope, and Gay were members. Satire upon the abuse of human learning was their leading object. The name originated as follows: Oxford used playfully to call Swift *Martin*, and from this sprang Martinus Scriblerus. Swift, as is well known, is the name of one species of swallow (the largest and most powerful flier of the tribe), and martin is the name of another species, the wall-swallow, which constructs its nest in buildings.

The Scriblerus Club broke up owing to quarrels between Oxford and Bolingbroke. Swift tried the force of humorous expostulation in his fable of the "Fagot," where the Ministers are called upon to contribute their various badges of office to make the bundle strong and secure, but all was in vain. And at length, tired with this scene of murmuring and discontent, quarrel, misunderstanding, and hatred, the Dean, who was almost the only mutual friend who laboured to compose these differences, made a final effort at reconciliation; but his scheme entirely failed.

Button's Coffee-house was another resort of wits. Here, in the early part of the reign of Queen Anne, Swift first began to come, being known as "the mad parson." He knew no one; no one knew him. He would lay his hat down on a table, and walk up and down at a brisk pace for half an hour without speaking to anyone, or seeming to pay attention to anything that was going forward. Then he would snatch up his hat, pay his money at the bar, and walk off without having opened his lips. At last he went one evening to a country gentleman, and very abruptly asked him: "Pray, sir, do you know any good weather in the world?" After staring a little at the singularity of Swift's manner and the oddity of the question, the gentleman answered: "Yes, sir, I thank God I remember a great deal of good weather in my time." "That is more," replied Swift, "than I can say. I never remember any weather that was not too hot or too cold, too wet or too dry; but, however God Almighty contrives it, at the end of the year 'tis all very well."

At Tom's Coffee-house in 1764 was formed a high-class club of about 700 members, paying each a guinea subscription. A card-room was on the first-floor.

The club flourished, so that in 1768, "having considerably enlarged itself of late," Thomas Haines, the then proprietor, took in the front room of the next house westward as a coffee-room. The front room of No. 17 was then appropriated exclusively as a card-room for the subscription club, each member paying one guinea annually, the adjoining apartment being used as a conversation-room.

Tom Haines—Lord Chesterfield, as he was called, on account of his good manners—was succeeded by his son. The house ceased to be a coffee-house in 1814.

It would be interesting to know what has become of the old snuff-box—a most curious relic. It was a big tortoiseshell box, bearing on the lid, in high relief in silver, the portraits of Charles I and Queen Anne; the Boscobel oak, with Charles II amid its branches; and at the foot of the tree, on a silver plate, was inscribed "Thomas Haines." At Will's the small wits grew conceited if they dipped but into Mr. Dryden's snuff-box, and at Tom's the box probably received similar veneration.

The Bedford Coffee-house, in the north-west corner of the Piazza, was another celebrated Covent Garden resort.

Here in its palmy days, about 1754, Foote reigned supreme, his great rival being Garrick, who, however, usually got the worst of the verbal duels which constantly occurred. Garrick in early life had been in the wine trade, and had supplied the Bedford with wine; he was thus described by Foote as living in Durham Yard, with three quarts of vinegar in the cellar, calling himself a wine-merchant.

Leaving the Bedford one night in company with Garrick, Foote dropped a guinea; and not being

able to find it, exclaimed : " Where on earth can it
be gone to ?"   " Gone to the devil, I think," replied
Garrick, who had assisted in the search.   " Well
said, David !" was Foote's reply.   " Let you alone
for making a guinea go farther than anybody else."

Tom King's Coffee-house—a rough shed just
beneath the portico of St. Paul's Church—was a
regular Covent Garden night-house.   This haunt
of night-birds is shown in the background of
Hogarth's print of " Morning," where the prim
maiden lady, walking to church, is confronted
by two fuddled beaux from King's Coffee-house
caressing two frail women.   At the door a drunken
brawl is proceeding, whilst swords and cudgels are
being freely used.

The Piazza (known in the reign of Charles I
as the " Portico walke ") in Covent Garden, the
destruction of a portion of which, in 1858, was,
from an artistic point of view, to be deplored, was
erected between 1634 and 1640 by Inigo Jones,
who also built St. Paul's Church for Francis, Duke
of Bedford.   Though a more ambitious scheme was
originally conceived, only the north and east sides
were, however, built, and half of the latter was
destroyed by fire about the middle of the eighteenth
century.

Several distinguished artists lived in the Piazza,
including Sir Peter Lely and Zoffany.   Sir Godfrey
Kneller came into the Piazza the year after Lely
died, and the house he occupied was near the steps
leading into Covent Garden Theatre.   He had a
garden at the back, reaching as far as Dr. Radcliffe's,
in Bow Street.   Kneller was fond of flowers, and

had a fine collection. As he was intimate with Radcliffe, he permitted him to have a door into his garden; but Radcliffe's servants gathering and destroying the flowers, Kneller sent him word he must shut up the door. Radcliffe replied peevishly: "Tell him he may do anything with it but paint it." "And I," answered Sir Godfrey, "can take anything from him but physic." Sir James Thornhill also lived in the same neighbourhood.

The Piazza Coffee-house, in Covent Garden, was a favourite resort of Sheridan's. Here it was that he sat during the burning of Drury Lane Theatre in 1809, calmly taking some refreshment, which excited the astonishment of a friend. "A man may surely be allowed to take a glass of wine by his own fireside," said Sheridan.

On the site of the Piazza Coffee-house was built the Floral Hall, in the Crystal Palace style of architecture, if the latter word be applicable to such a building. Henrietta Street, close by, was once well known for what seems to have been the first family hotel ever established in London, opened by David Low in 1774.

Gold, silver, and copper medals were struck and distributed by the landlord, as advertisements of his house—the gold to the Princes, silver to the nobility, and copper to the public generally. Mrs. Hudson succeeded him, and advertised her hotel "with stabling for one hundred noblemen and horses." The next proprietors were Richardson and Joy.

For years the hotel was famous for its dinner and coffee room—called the "Star," from the

number of men of rank who frequented it. One
day the Duke of Norfolk entered the dining-room,
and ordered of the waiter two lamb chops, at the
same time inquiring : " John, have you a cucumber ?"
The waiter replied in the negative—it was so early
in the season ; but he would step into the market
and inquire if there were any. The waiter did so,
and returned with—" There are a few, but they
are half a guinea apiece." " Half a guinea apiece !
Are they small or large ?" " Why, rather small."
" Then buy two," was the reply.

Low had purchased the house from the executors
of James West, President of the Royal Society,
and it had originally been the mansion of Sir
Kenelm Digby, who had his laboratory at the back.
In course of time it was practically rebuilt by the
Earl of Orford, better known as Admiral Russell,
who in 1692 defeated Admiral de Tourville. The
façade of the house originally resembled the fore-
castle of a ship, and the fine old staircase was
formed of part of the vessel Admiral Russell com-
manded at La Hogue ; on it were handsomely
carved anchors, ropes, and the coronet and initials
of Lord Orford, who died there in 1727. The
house was afterwards occupied by Thomas, Lord
Archer, who had a well-stocked garden at the back.
Mushrooms and cucumbers were his especial hobby.

In course of time Evans, of Covent Garden
Theatre, removed here from the Cider Cellar in
Maiden Lane, and, using the large dining-room for
a singing-room, prospered until 1844, when he
resigned the property to Mr. John Green, well
known as Paddy Green, under whose rule the

excellence of the entertainment attracted so great an accession of visitors that there was built, in 1855, on the site of the old garden (Sir Kenelm Digby's), a handsome hall, to which the former singing-room formed a sort of vestibule. This was hung with portraits of celebrated actors and actresses collected by the proprietor.

The gallery was said to occupy part of the site of the cottage in which the Kembles occasionally resided during the zenith of their fame at Covent Garden Theatre. Kemble first saw the light there.

In the early seventies Evans's ceased to attract, and, after undergoing various vicissitudes and sheltering several clubs, the house finally became the headquarters of boxing, being now occupied by the National Sporting Club. The original staircase remains, and a number of prints recalling the palmy days of the prize-ring decorate the walls of the club-house.

Ninety years ago, it should be added, the prize-fighting fraternity had a club of their own, called the Daffy Club, which met at the Castle Tavern, Holborn, then kept by the famous boxers, Tom Belcher and Tom Spring. The walls of the long room in which it met were adorned by a number of sporting prints and portraits of famous pugilistic heroes, amongst them Belcher himself, Gentleman Jackson, Dutch Sam, Gregson, Humphreys, Mendoza, Cribb, Molyneux, Gulley, Randall, Turner, Martin, Harmer, Spring, Neat, Hickman, Painter, Scroggins, Tom Owen, and many others.

CHAPTER II

CURIOUS CLUBS OF THE PAST—PRATT'S—
BEEFSTEAK CLUBS, OLD AND NEW

MANY curiously-named clubs existed in the past.
Addison, for instance, speaking of the clubs of his
time, mentions several the names of which were
probably merely humorous exaggerations. Names
such as the Mum Club, the Ugly Club, can hardly
be considered to have been in actual use.

Real clubs were the Lying Club, for which
untruthfulness was supposed to be an indispensable
qualification; the Odd Fellows' Club; the Hum-
bugs (which met at the Blue Posts, in Covent
Garden); the Samsonic Society; the Society of
Bucks; the Purl Drinkers; the Society of Pilgrims,
held at the Woolpack, in the Kingsland Road; the
Thespian Club; the Great Bottle Club; the Aristocratic "Je ne sçai quoi" Club, held at the Star and
Garter, in Pall Mall, of which the Prince of Wales
and the Dukes of York, Clarence, Orleans, Norfolk,
Bedford, and other notabilities, were members; the
Sons of the Thames Society; the Blue Stocking
Club; the "No Pay No Liquor" Club, held at the
Queen and Artichoke, in the Hampstead Road, and
of which the ceremony, on a new member's introduction, was, after his paying a fee on entrance of
one shilling, that he should wear a hat throughout

the first evening of his membership, made in the shape of a quart pot, and drink to the health of his brother members in a gilt goblet of ale. At Camden Town met the "Social Villagers," in a room at the Bedford Arms.

One of the first clubs was the October Club, composed of some hundred and fifty staunch Tories, chiefly country Members of Parliament. They met at the Bell, in King Street, Westminster— that street in which Spenser starved, and Dryden's brother kept a grocer's shop. A portrait of Queen Anne, by Dahl, hung in the club-room.

Another queer eighteenth-century institution was the Golden Fleece Club, the members of which assumed fancy names, such as Sir Timothy Addlepate, Sir Nimmy Sneer, Sir Talkative Do-little, Sir Skinny Fretwell, Sir Rumbus Rattle, Sir Boozy Prate-all, Sir Nicholas Ninny Sip-all, Sir Gregory Growler, Sir Pay-little, and the like. The main object of this club seems to have been a very free conviviality.

Perhaps the most eccentric club of all was "the Everlasting," which, like the modern Brook Club of New York, professed to go on for ever, its doors being kept open night and day throughout the year, whilst the members were divided into watches like sailors at sea.

The craze for queerly-named clubs lasted into the nineteenth century; for instance, the King of Clubs was the fanciful name of a society founded about 1801 by Bobus Smith. At first it consisted of a small knot of lawyers, whose clients were too few, or too civil, to molest their after-dinner recreations ; a few literary characters ; and a small number of visitors, generally introduced by those who took the chief part in conversation, and seemingly selected for the faculty of being good listeners.

The King of Clubs sat on the Saturday of each month in the Strand, at the Crown and Anchor Tavern, which at that time was a nest of boxes, each containing its club, and affording excellent cheer, though afterwards desecrated by indifferent dinners and very questionable wine. The object of the club was conversation. Everyone seemed anxious to bring his contribution of good sense or good humour, and the members discussed books and authors and the prevalent topics of the day, except politics, which were excluded.

Rogers, the banker poet, was a member of the King of Clubs. His funereal appearance gained him the nickname of the Dug-up Dandy, and all sorts of jokes were made concerning him. Once, when Rogers had been at Spa, and was telling Ward (afterwards Lord Dudley) that the place was so full that he could not so much as find a bed to lie in, and that he was obliged on that account to leave it, " Dear me," replied Ward, " was there no room in the churchyard ?" At another time Murray was showing him a portrait of Rogers, observing that " it was done to the life." " To the death, you mean," replied Ward. Amongst other amusing sallies of the same kind was his asking Rogers : " Why don't you keep your hearse, Rogers ? You can well afford it."

A good example of what most of the little old-fashioned clubs of other days were like is furnished by Pratt's, which, though not of very great antiquity, occupies curious old-world premises just off St. James's Street.   This quaint and agreeable little club, still a flourishing institution, appears to have been founded about 1841 ; the old manuscript records of elections still exist.   Though Pratt's has recently been reorganized, its distinctive features have not been impaired, and the house remains much in its original condition—the kitchen downstairs, with its old-fashioned open fire, quaint dresser filled with salmon-fly plates, old-world furniture and prints, forming a delightful relic of the past. A curious niche in this room would seem to have once served as a receptacle for cards or dice, in the days when the house was used for gambling, and raids by the authorities were common.

Next the kitchen is the dining-room, in which is a long table ; the walls here are hung with old prints of the time when the club was founded. Both this room and the kitchen have very curious mantelpieces, the upper portions of which are formed of classical friezes which would seem to have been brought here from some old mansion. Throughout the quaint little building are cases of stuffed birds and fish, and the accessories and general appearance produce a singular effect not lacking in old-world charm.

Pratt's formerly opened only late in the evening, but its hours now admit of members lunching ; indeed, whilst great care has been taken to preserve the original spirit of the club, many modern improvements unobtrusively carried out make it a most comfortable resort, whilst the convenience of members has been studied by the addition of four bedrooms.

By far the most interesting of the old dining clubs was the Sublime Society of Beefsteaks, founded about 1735 by Rich, the famous harlequin and machinist of Covent Garden Theatre. At first it consisted of twenty-four members, but the number was afterwards increased. Hogarth, Wilkes, and many other celebrated men, were members of this society, which had many curious customs.

Its officials consisted of a President of the Day, Vice-President, Bishop, Recorder, and Boots.

The meetings were originally held in a room at Covent Garden Theatre.

The President took his seat after dinner throughout the season, according to the order in which his name appeared on " the rota."

He was invested with the badge of the society by the Boots. His duty was to give the chartered toasts in strict accordance with the list before him ; to propose all resolutions that had been duly made and seconded ; to observe all the ancient forms and customs of the society ; and to enforce them on others. He had no sort of power inherent in his position ; on the contrary, he was closely watched and sharply pulled up if he betrayed either ignorance or forgetfulness on the smallest matter of routine connected with his office. In fact, he was a target for all to shoot at.

A Beefeater's hat and plume hung on the right-hand side of the chair behind him, and a three-cornered hat (erroneously believed to have belonged to Garrick) on the left. When putting a resolution, the President was bound to place the plumed hat on his head and instantly remove it. If he failed in one or the other act, he was equally reminded by being called to order in no silent terms. The most important obligation imposed on him was the necessity of singing, whether he could sing or not, the song of the day.

The Vice was the oldest member of the society present, and had to carry out the President's directions without responsibility.

The Bishop sang the grace and the anthem.

The most important official of all was the Recorder. He had to rebuke everybody for offences, real or imaginary, and with him lay the duty of delivering "the charge" to each newly elected member, which was a burlesque function.

The Boots was the last elected of the members, and there was a grave responsibility attached to his office. He was the fag of the brotherhood, and had to arrive before the dinner-hour, not only to decant the wine, but to fetch it from the cellar. This latter custom was persevered in until the destruction of the old Lyceum by fire, and was only then abandoned by reason of the inaccessibility of the cellar, when the society returned to the new theatre, the rebuilt Lyceum, in 1838. No one was exempted from this ordeal, and woe to him who shirked or neglected it. The greatest enjoyment seemed to be afforded, both to members and guests, by summoning Boots to decant a fresh bottle of port at the moment when a hot plate and a fresh steak were placed before him.

The Duke of Sussex was Boots from the date of

LATER BADGE.

RING.

ORIGINAL BADGE OF THE SUBLIME SOCIETY.

BADGE OF THE AD LIBITUM CLUB.

REVERSE OF AD LIBITUM BADGE.

his election (April, 1808) to April, 1809, when a
vacancy occurred, and Mr. Arnold senior was
elected, releasing His Royal Highness from the
post. Indeed, until the society ceased to exist, the
Duke of Leinster, who had duly served his appren-
ticeship (although he drank nothing stronger than
water himself), constantly usurped the legitimate
duties of the Boots by arriving before him and
performing the accustomed, but not forgotten,
services of the day.

When any Boots showed signs of temper, or
any member was unruly or infringed the rules of
the society, a punishment was in store for him. It
was moved and seconded that such delinquent should
be put in the white sheet and reprimanded by the
Recorder; and if the "Ayes had it" (and they always
did have it), the sentence was carried out.

The offending party was taken from the room by
two members bearing halberds, preceded by a third
carrying the sword, and was brought back again in
the garb of penitence (the tablecloth). Then, after
a lecture from the Recorder, severe or humorous
according to the nature of his offence, he was
allowed to resume his place at the table.

It happened that Brother the Duke of Sussex was
put in the white sheet under the following circumstances: His Royal Highness had come to the
"Steaks" with Brother Hallett, and on the road
the watch-chain belonging to the latter had been
cut and his bunch of seals stolen. The cloth removed, Hallett addressed the President, recounted
the loss he had sustained, and charged the Duke as
the perpetrator of the robbery. The case was tried

on the spot ; and the evidence having clearly established the criminality of the accused (to a Beefsteak jury), it was moved and resolved that His Royal Highness should forthwith be put into the white sheet and reprimanded for an act which might have been considered a fault had the victim been a stranger, but which became a crime when that victim was a Brother. There was no appeal. His Royal Highness reluctantly rose, was taken out in custody, brought before the Recorder (Brother Richards), and received a witty but unsparing admonition for the offence of which he had been unanimously found guilty. For a wonder, His Royal Highness took it ill. He resumed his seat, but remained silent and reserved. No wit could make him smile, no bantering could rouse him, and at an unusually early hour he ordered his carriage and went away.

The next day Mr. Arnold, who had been the mover of the resolution, went to the palace to smooth the ruffled plumes of his royal confrère, and took his son with him. In those days the Duke rode on horseback, and as they turned out of the gate leading from the gardens to the portico his horse was at the door and His Royal Highness in the act of coming out. By the time they neared the entrance his foot was in the stirrup, and he saw them approaching. Without a moment's hesitation he withdrew his foot, released the bridle, and, with both his enormous hands extended, advanced three or four steps to meet Mr. Arnold.

"I know what you've come about," he called loudly out in his accustomed note (probably B flat),

and wringing both Mr. Arnold's hands until he
winced with pain—" I know what you've come
about ! I made a fool of myself last night. You
were quite right, and I quite wrong, so I shall come
next Saturday and do penance again for my bad
temper."

Sometimes a member turned sulky when made to
do penance. On one occasion an individual of a
touchy disposition was put into the white sheet and
brought before the President, who admonished him
as a parent would a child—a Beefsteak sermon without its usual bathos. The recipient listened to the
harangue without moving a muscle of his face. The
lecture done, he resumed his seat, but at the next
meeting sent in his resignation.

Saturday was the day on which the dinners were
held. Each member was allowed to bring one
visitor. If he brought a second, he had to borrow
a name ; in default of obtaining it, the visitor was
doomed to retire.

Visitors, unlike members, were not subjected to
any humorous penalties, but were most ceremoniously treated. They were never unduly urged to
drink more than might be agreeable to them ; one
bumper in the evening was alone imperative, but it
might be drunk in water. They were never pressed,
though always asked, to sing. A " suggestion" to
sing was the adopted word.

The only call to which it was imperative for the
visitor to respond was " a toast." If he hesitated
too long, he was, perhaps abruptly, told he might
give anything the world produced—man, woman, or
child, or any sentiment, social or otherwise. Some-

times it happened that such prompting was in vain, and the confused guest would nine times out of ten propose the only toast he was prohibited from giving—" The prosperity of the Sublime Society of Beefsteaks."

Members were responsible for their guests, who were made to understand that whatever passed within the walls of the S.S.B.S. was sacred. William Jerdan, Editor of the *Literary Gazette*, was a visitor, and at a late hour he was observed to take a note of a brilliant repartee that had been made.

The President, by whose side he sat, pointed to the motto over the chimney-piece:

" Ne fidos inter amicos
Sit qui dicta foras eliminet."*

"Jerdan," he said, " you understand those words?"

" I understand one," said Jerdan, looking sharply round—" sit ; and I mean to do it."

Authors, and dramatic authors in particular, were mercilessly chaffed when they dined with the Sublime Society. Cobb, whose farce " The First-Floor " achieved great popularity, used to accept the satire and raillery of members with great good-humour, generally silencing them one by one. Storace composed some of his finest music for Cobb's comic operas, " The Haunted Tower " and " The Siege of Belgrade," which achieved success. An Indian opera, " Ramah Drûg," did not. Cobb was much chaffed about these operas, especially about the first-named.

" Why ever," one night said Arnold, " did you

* Let none beyond this threshold bear away
What friend to friend in confidence may say.

call your opera by such a name? There was no
spirit in it from beginning to end!" "Anyhow,"
exclaimed another inveterate punster, 'Ramah
Drûg' was the most appropriate title possible, for
it was literally ramming a drug down the public
throat." "True," rejoined Cobb; "but it was a
drug that evinced considerable power, for it operated
on the public twenty nights in succession." "My
good friend," said Arnold triumphantly, "that was
a proof of its weakness, if it took so long in working."
"You are right, Arnold, in that respect," retorted
Cobb. "Your play" (Arnold had brought out a
play, which did not survive the first night) "had
the advantage of mine, for it was so powerful a
drug as to be thrown up as soon as it was taken!"

The first and last Saturdays of the season, and
the Saturday in Easter week, were "private."

On these days no visitors were invited. The
accounts were gone into, and the amount of the
"whip" to regulate the past or accruing expenses
decided, the qualifications of such candidates as
were anxious, on the occasion of a vacancy, to join
the society discussed, and other matters connected
with its well-being debated.

Each member paid 5s. for his dinner, and 10s. 6d.
for his guest. The entrance fee was £26 5s. until
1849, when it was reduced to £10 10s., and there
were generally two annual whips of £5 each.

After the destruction of Covent Garden Theatre,
where it had met for seventy years, the Sublime
Society of Beefsteaks migrated to the Bedford
Coffee-house, where it remained till the building
of the Lyceum Theatre in 1809, in a special room

of which it took up its abode till 1830, when the Lyceum also was burnt down.

After this it adjourned to the Lyceum Tavern, in the Strand, and thence returned to the Bedford Coffee-house, where it remained until 1838, when a suite of rooms was built for it under the new roof of the Lyceum. The original gridiron, dug out of the ruins of Covent Garden and the Lyceum, formed the centre ornament of the dining-room ceiling. The entire room and ceiling were in Gothic architecture, and the walls were hung with paintings and engravings of past and present members, the former the work of Brother Lonsdale. Folding-doors, the entire width of the room, connected it with an anteroom. When the doors were opened on the announcement of dinner, an enormous grating in the form of a gridiron, through which the fire was seen and the steaks handed, afforded members a view of the kitchen.

There was no blackballing, but every would-be member had to be invited at least twice as a guest, in order that his qualifications might be ascertained, and then, if he were put up, he was certain to be elected. As a matter of fact, the formality of a ballot was gone through, though there were no rejections.

When a new member was initiated, he and the visitors were requested after dinner to withdraw to an anteroom, where port and punch were provided for them.

The newly elected member was then brought in blindfolded, accompanied on his right by the Bishop with his mitre on, and holding the volume in which the oath of allegiance to the rules of the society was inscribed, while on his left stood some other member holding the sword of state. Behind were the halberdiers. These were all decked out in the most incongruous and absurd dresses—in all probability originally obtained from Covent Garden Theatre.

" The charge " was then delivered by the Recorder. In it he dwelt on the solemnity of the obligations the new member was about to take on himself. He was made to understand, in tones alternately serious and gay, the true brotherly spirit of the Sublime Society of Beefsteaks ; that while a perfect equality existed among the Brethren, such equality never should be permitted to degenerate into undue familiarity ; that while badinage was encouraged in the freest sense of the word, such badinage must never approach to a personality ; and that good fellowship must be united with good breeding. Above all, attention was drawn to the Horatian motto over the chimney-piece, and the aspirant was warned that ignominious expulsion was the fate of him who carried beyond those walls words uttered there in friendship's confidence.

That done, the following oath, dating from the origin of the society, was administered :

OATH.

YOU SHALL ATTEND DULY,

VOTE IMPARTIALLY,

AND CONFORM TO OUR LAWS AND ORDERS OBEDIENTLY.

YOU SHALL SUPPORT OUR DIGNITY,

PROMOTE OUR WELFARE, AND AT ALL TIMES

BEHAVE AS A WORTHY MEMBER IN THIS SUBLIME SOCIETY.

SO BEEF AND LIBERTY BE YOUR REWARD.

This was read aloud, clause by clause, by the Bishop, and repeated by the candidate; at the end the book was rapidly exchanged by the cook, who was called the Serjeant, for the bone of beef that had served for the day's dinner, carefully protected by a napkin, and after the words

"SO BEEF AND LIBERTY BE MY REWARD"

he was desired to kiss the book. Instead of this he kissed its substitute, and by reason of a friendly downward pressure from behind he generally did so most devoutly.

The bandage was then removed from his eyes; the book on which he had sworn the oath was still before him; and amid the laughter and congratulations of his Brethren he again took his seat as a member of the Sublime Society, and the excluded guests were readmitted.

The Serjeant was a very important figure at the meetings of the Sublime Society, and the office was well filled by Heardson, the cook, whose picture was engraved by J. R. Smith (the print hangs in the modern Beefsteak). So great was his affection for the " Society " that one of his last requests was to be carried into the club-room to take a farewell glance at the familiar scene, and this he was allowed to do.

A great supporter of the Beefsteak Society was the old Duke of Norfolk, and when he dined there he would be ceremoniously ushered to the chair after dinner, and invested with an orange-coloured ribbon, to which a silver medal, in the form of a gridiron, was suspended. In the chair he comported himself with great urbanity and good-humour.

Above all things, this Duke of Norfolk loved long sittings, during which he would consume prodigious quantities of wine, which seemed to affect him but very little. Occasionally, however, towards the close of the evening, the Duke, without exhibiting any symptom of inebriety, became immovable in his chair, as if deprived of all muscular volition. When at his own house he had an especial method of obviating the inconveniences of such a state, and would ask someone to ring the bell three times. This was the signal for bringing in a kind of easy litter, consisting of four equidistant belts, fastened together by a transverse one, which four domestics placed under him, and thus removed his enormous bulk, with a gentle swinging motion, up to his apartment. Upon these occasions the Duke would say nothing, but the whole thing was managed with great system and in perfect silence.

Another prominent member was Charles Morris, who greatly enlivened the dinners by his wit, high spirits, and singing. When he was in town nothing kept him away, even when he was nearly eighty years of age.

"Die when you will, Charles," said Curran, "you'll die in your youth." And his words were verified, for his spirits remained unquenched till within a few days of his death. Morris wrote many songs which he would sing himself. The following is a specimen of his talents in that direction :

" Let them rail who think fit, at my ways or my wit;
   I reply to the foes of good living:
' Heaven bade me be gay—to enjoy's to obey,
   And mirth is my prayer of thanksgiving.'

When the crabbed with spleen would o'ershadow life's scene,
    I light up a spark to dispel it;
And if snarlers exclaim, ' What's this laughing fool's name ?'
    Next verse of my ballad will tell it.

" I'm a brat of old Horace—the song-scribbling Morris,
    More noted for rhyme than for reason ;
One who roars and carouses, makes noise in all houses,
    And takes all good things in their season.
To this classic of joy, I became when a boy
    A pupil most ardent and willing ;
And through life as a man, I've stuck fast to this plan,
    And passed it in flirting and filling."

In his eighty-sixth year Morris bade adieu to the
Sublime Society in verse, but four years later, in
1835, he revisited it, and the members then presented him with a large silver bowl, appropriately
inscribed, as a testimonial of their affectionate
esteem.

As was his habit, Morris did not fail to allude to
the gift in verse :

" When my spirits are low, for relief and delight,
    I still place your splendid Memorial in sight ;
    And call to my Muse, when care strives to pursue,
    ' Bring the Steaks to my Mem'ry, the Bowl to my view.' "

The bowl in question eventually passed into the
hands of the present Beefsteak Club ; most unfortunately, it was some years ago taken away by
thieves, who managed to obtain access to the club
premises, and it has never been recovered.

Charles Morris had very slender means to support
his family, but owing to the generosity of the old
Duke of Norfolk he was able to retire to a charming
rural retreat near Dorking, embosomed amidst the
undulating elevations of Surrey. Here, however,

he seems not to have been entirely at ease, regretting no doubt the sweet, shady side of Pall Mall, of which he had so gracefully sung.

The Duke assisted Morris, owing, it was said, to the kindly suggestion of Kemble, the actor, who one night had been dining at Norfolk House when the Beefsteak bard had also formed one of the party. When the latter had gone, a few guests only remaining with the Duke, who liked late sittings, His Grace began to deplore, somewhat pathetically, the smallness of the stipend upon which poor Charles was obliged to support his family, observing that it was a discredit to the age that a man who had so long gladdened the lives of so many titled and opulent associates should be left to struggle with the difficulties of an inadequate income at a time of life when he had no reasonable hope of augmenting it. Kemble, who had been listening attentively, then broke out in peculiarly emphatic tones : " And does your Grace sincerely lament the destitute condition of your friend, with whom you have passed so many agreeable hours ? Your Grace has described that condition most feelingly. But is it possible that the greatest peer of the realm, luxuriating amidst the prodigalities of fortune, should lament the distress which he does not relieve ? The empty phrase of benevolence, the mere breath and vapour of generous sentiment, become no man ; they certainly are unworthy of your Grace. Providence, my Lord Duke, has placed you in a station where the wish to do good and the doing it are the same thing. An annuity from your overflowing coffers, or a small nook of land clipped from your unbounded domains, would scarcely be felt by your Grace; but you would be repaid with usury, with tears of grateful joy, with prayers warm from a bosom which your bounty will have rendered happy."

The Duke said nothing at the time, except stare with astonishment at so unexpected a lecture; but not a month elapsed before Charles Morris was snugly invested in a beautiful sequestered retreat surrounded by pretty grounds.

Captain Morris lived to the age of ninety-two, dying in July, 1838. He lies in Betchworth Churchyard, near the east end; his grave is simply marked by a head- and foot-stone, with an inscription of three or four lines; he who had sung the praises of so many choice spirits has not here a stanza to his own memory.

As time went on, the old customs and toasts of the Sublime Society became out of date, and, though certain modifications were attempted, it ceased to exist in 1869, when its effects were sold. The following is a list of the most important of them.

An oak dining-table with President's cap, a mitre and a gridiron carved in three separate circular compartments at the top. This relic of past conviviality is now at White's Club, having been purchased by the Hon. Algernon Bourke some years ago.

A carved oak President's chair—now, I believe, at Sandringham—and a number of members' chairs copied in oak from the Glastonbury Chair, the backs carved with the gridiron and the arms and initials of each member. A few of these chairs belong to a firm of brewers.

Forty - seven engraved portraits of members, glazed in oak frames, on which were metal gridirons. One or two of these are in the possession of the present Beefsteak Club.

Other *objets d'art* and curiosities were—

The ribbon and badge of the President in the form of a silver gridiron, dated 1735.

Two brown stoneware jugs, with silver lids and mounts, the thumb-pieces gridirons.

A fine *couteau de chasse*, with engraved and pierced blade, the handle formed of a group of Mars, Venus, and Cupid, in silver, the mounting of the sheath of open-work silver, chased with arabesque figures, scrolls, and flowers. The reputed work of Benvenuto Cellini ; inscribed " Ex Dono Antonio Askew, M.D."

An oval ivory snuff-box, with a cameo of Dante on the lid and inscription inside : " Presented to the S.S.B.S. by B. G. B. [Dr. Babington], an honorary member. The cameo of Dante on the lid of this box was carved by its donor, and its wood formed part of a mummy-case brought by him from Egypt in 1815 ; the surrounding ivory was turned by a friend "—in a leather case.

A circular snuff-box, formed of oak dug from the ruins of the old Lyceum Theatre, after its destruction by fire ; a silver shield engraved with the gridiron on the lid.

A wooden punch-ladle, with open-work handle, and ten doilys.

A cigar-case, formed of a curious piece of oak.

A pair of halberds.

A large Oriental punch-bowl, enamelled with

figures, butterflies, and flowers, inside and out, in a case.   Presented by Lord Saltoun, K.G.

Another enamelled with figures and baskets of flowers in medallions, with red and gold scale borders.   Presented by Baron Heath.

A ditto, enamelled with figures.

A fluted ditto, with flowers.

The President's hat, a hat said to have belonged to Garrick, and a Cardinal's hat.

The mitre of the late Cardinal Gregorio, presented to the Sublime Society of the Beefsteaks by Brother W. Somerville, in silk case.

Facsimile of an agreement between Rich and C. Fleetwood, framed and glazed.

Bust of John Wilkes, in marble.

There was in addition to this a certain amount of plate, including cases of silver forks, engraved with members' names.   One of these cases now belongs to the Beefsteak Club.

At one time the members wore a uniform consisting of a blue coat and buff waistcoat, with brass buttons impressed with the gridiron and motto, ' Beef and Liberty."

They also wore rings bearing the same devices. One of these rings, presented within recent years by a member, is in the Beefsteak Club, which also possesses a number of badges and other relics connected with the Sublime Society and with the Ad Libitum Club, a kindred organization, of which Heardson also appears to have been the cook.

The device of the Ad Libitum was more ornate and graceful than that of the Sublime Society, with which it seems to have been closely connected, though membership of the one did not necessarily imply membership of the other. As far as can be ascertained, no records of the Ad Libitum have been preserved.

The present Beefsteak Club—less convivial in its ways than the Sublime Society—was founded about 1876, and its original dining-place was a room in the building known till its demolition, some years ago, as Toole's Theatre. When this was pulled down, it migrated to premises specially built for it in Green Street, Leicester Square. The membership is small, and consists mostly of men well known in the political, theatrical, and literary worlds. Opening only in the afternoon, it is used chiefly as a place for dining and supping amidst congenial and pleasant conversation.

The club consists of one long room, which has a high-pitched roof in the design of which gridirons are cleverly interposed. Here are hung a quantity of old prints, the majority of them after Hogarth. A number of etchings by Whistler (who was a member) are also to be seen. The Beefsteak owns a good deal of silver, much of which has been presented from time to time by members; the practice of giving plate being a usage of the club. The most valuable possession is a tankard of solid gold, on which are inscribed the names of those members who took part in the Boer War. This was purchased by subscription amongst the members. The example of the Sublime Society is followed in respect of there being one long table in the place of the separate small ones in use at other clubs.

There formerly existed a number of curious dining societies and clubs in the provinces, and some of these still survive, amongst the number of which is the Chelmsford Beefsteak Club, established in 1768. There does not appear to be any book older than 1781, but in the middle of a book which commences in 1829 is written a list of the members from February 5, 1768, to October 18, 1850 ; and as the whole is in the same handwriting, it is clear the earlier lists of members must have been copied from an older book, which has now disappeared.

The oldest book in the possession of the club is one for entering the attendances of members, and commences October 12, 1781. At that time the members appear to have dined together weekly.

At the monthly dinners of the club, the chairman proposes the following toasts :

(a) " Church and Queen."
(b) " The Prince of Wales and the Rest of the Royal Family."
(c) " Our Absent Members."
(d) " Our Visitors, if any."

No one is allowed to stand when proposing or replying to a toast.

Morning dress is worn at dinner.

One of the last of the old school of members of this club was Admiral Johnson, elected 1842, who was the midshipman who supported Nelson's head as he lay dying in the cockpit of the *Victory*. It was no uncommon thing for the Admiral to have three bottles of port put before him at 8 o'clock, which he consumed by about 9.30. He was always called upon for a song, and he used to sing about fourteen verses of " On board the *Arethusa*." His usual hour for retirement was about 10.30, when he would be escorted to his pony, and would ride home to Baddow, three miles away. Admiral Johnson remembered the time when the fine for any member being unfortunate enough to be presented with twins by his wife was the presentation of a pair of buckskin breeches to each member of the club, and he boasted of still possessing a pair that Thomas W. Bramston, whilst member for the county, had to pay him.

At many old county dining clubs penalties of this sort were enforced : members were fined for marrying, for becoming a father, or for moving to another house ; and such fines usually consisted of a certain number of bottles of wine. Other quaint usages included the forfeiture of some small sum for refusing to take the chair at dinner or for leaving it to ring the bell, for allowing a stranger to pay for anything consumed, and similar delinquencies.

Another Beefsteak Club was that at Cambridge, the members of which belonged to the University. This club, now for some years in abeyance, was a quaint survival from the past, and exactly reproduced the dinner of eighteenth-century sportsmen. Twenty-five years ago, when it still flourished, it usually consisted of but four or five members, but guests could be invited. The dining costume was a blue cutaway coat with brass buttons, and buff

waistcoat, the tie being secured with a bull's head.
The dinner was entirely composed of various dishes
of beef, beer only being drunk; some curious old
songs were sung, and the toasts, regulated by in-
flexible precedent, were drunk in port from glasses
of a size regulated by immemorial custom. Amongst
these toasts was the health of the late Mr. Bowes,
who, when he was an undergraduate at Cambridge,
won the Derby with Mundig. This horse, after a
tremendous struggle, beat Ascot, belonging to the
present writer's grandfather, by half a neck.

The dinners used to be held at the Red Lion
Inn, the head-waiter of which hostelry, Dunn by
name, was supposed to be the only individual alive
accurately acquainted with the exact rules and
traditions of the club. The proceedings were enlivened by music played on a fiddle by a well-known
Cambridge character, White-headed Bob.

The Cambridge Beefsteak Club possessed a good
deal of plate, valued at about £1,500. It had also
an income of some £200 a year, arising from sums
of money left to it by former members.

A somewhat similar Cambridge dining club was
the True Blue, which also had few members. They
met several times in a term, wearing eighteenth-
century dress and white wigs; as a matter of fact,
the cost of this costume often deterred men from
joining, as did the rule that a new member should
drink off a bottle of claret at a draught. This
unpleasant custom, which might well have been
modified, seems to have killed the club, for I fancy
that, like the Cambridge Beefsteak, it has not met
for many years.

A remarkable little provincial club which flourished at Norwich at the beginning of the nineteenth century was the Hole-in-the-Wall Club, where a number of clever men used to meet. One of the principal figures here was Dr. Frank Sayers, a poet of no mean inspiration, a sound antiquary, an elegant scholar, and an accomplished gentleman. His accustomed chair was kept for him every Monday, and it would have been a profanation had any other occupant filled it. He was a man of admirable wit, and the characters around him, which no skill of selection could have got together in any other club or in any other town, afforded unfailing objects of his innocent and unwounding pleasantry.

Amongst other eccentric frequenters of the Hole-in-the-Wall was Ozias Lindley, a Minor Canon of the cathedral, and Sheridan's brother-in-law. He was subject, beyond anyone living, to fits of absent-mindedness. He out - Parson - Adamized Parson Adams. One Sunday morning, as he was riding through the Close, on his way to serve his curacy, his horse threw off a shoe. A lady whom he had just passed, having remarked it, called out to him : "Sir, your horse has just cast one of his shoes." "Thank you, madam," returned Ozias ; " will you, then, be kind enough to put it on ?" In preaching, he often turned over two or three pages at once of his sermon ; and when a universal titter and stare convinced him of the transition, he observed coolly, " I find I have omitted a considerable part of my sermon, but it is not worth going back for," and then went on to the end.

Hudson Gurney, at one time M.P. for Newport, Isle of Wight, was also a frequenter of the snug club-room of the Hole-in-the-Wall, and used to bask in the sunshine of Sayers's festive conversation. His own heart, too, at that time beat high with frolic and hilarity. Hudson's was, from his earliest prime, a clear, distinguishing intellect. He was a well-read man, and his poetry, no fragment of which is in print, except his admirable translation of the Cupid and Psyche of Apuleius into English verse, was by no means of a secondary kind.

At this club William Taylor smoked his evening pipe, and lost himself in the cloudier fumes of German metaphysics and German philology. Taylor's translation of Bürger's " Leonore," though apparently now forgotten, was said to be better than the original. While his erudition was unlimited, however, it was principally concerned with books that were not readable by others. His most amusing quality (and it was that which kept an undying grin upon the laughter-loving face of Sayers) was his everlasting love of hypothesis, and it was impossible to withstand the imperturbable gravity with which he put forth his wild German paradoxes. He proved, to the thorough dissatisfaction of those who knew not how to confute him, and to the unspeakable amusement of those who thought it not worth their while—and that, too, by a chemical analysis of colours, and the processes by which animal heat and organic structure affect them —that the first race of mankind was green ! Green, he said, was the primal colour of vegetable existence—the first raiment in which Nature leaped

into existence; the colour on which the eye loved
to repose; and, in the primeval state, the first
quality that attracted man to man, and bound him
up in the circles of those tender charities and
affinities which kept the early societies of the race
together.

At one time Edinburgh was celebrated for its
quaint clubs, one of which was the Soaping Club,
the motto of which was, that "Every man should
soap his own beard"—that is, "indulge his own
humour." The Lawn-market Club was an association of dram-drinking, gossiping citizens, who met
every morning early, and, after proceeding to the
post-office to pick up letters and news, adjourned
to the public-house to talk and drink. The
Edinburgh, a "Viscera" club, flourished till quite a
late date; the members of this were pledged to
dine off food from the entrails of animals, such as
kidneys, liver, and tripe. This club seems to have
rather resembled the more modern Haggis Club.

There were at one time a number of parochial
clubs in London. That of the parish of St.
Margaret's, Westminster, which still exists, and
which consists of "Past Overseers," possesses a
unique heirloom, which is at the same time an
important chronological record of public events.

In 1713 a small fourpenny tobacco-box, bought
at Horn Fair, Charlton, Kent, was presented by
Mr. Monck, a member of the Society of Past
Overseers, to his colleagues.

Seven years later, in 1720, the donor was commemorated by the addition of a silver lid to the
box. In 1726 a silver side case and bottom were

added. In 1740 an embossed border was placed upon the lid, and the under-part enriched with an emblem of Charity. In 1746 Hogarth engraved inside the lid a bust of the Duke of Cumberland, with allegorical figures and scroll commemorating the Battle of Culloden. In 1765 an interwoven scroll was added to the lid, enclosing a plate with the arms of the City of Westminster, and inscribed : " This Box to be delivered to every succeeding set of Overseers, on penalty of five guineas."

The original Horn box being thus ornamented, additional ornamentation in the shape of cases continued to be provided by the senior overseers for the time being. These were embellished with silver plates engraved with emblematical and historical subjects and busts. Among the first are a view of the fireworks in St. James's Park to celebrate the Peace of Aix-la-Chapelle, 1749 ; Admiral Keppel's action off Ushant, and his acquittal after a court-martial; the Battle of the Nile; the repulse of Admiral Linois, 1804 ; the Battle of Trafalgar, 1805 ; the action between the *San Fiorenzo* and *La Piémontaise*, 1808 ; the Battle of Waterloo, 1815 ; the bombardment of Algiers, 1816 ; view of the House of Lords at the trial of Queen Caroline ; the Coronation of George IV ; and his visit to Scotland, 1822.

Features of great interest are : Portraits of John Wilkes, churchwarden in 1759 ; Nelson, Duncan, Howe, Vincent ; Fox and Pitt, 1806 ; George IV as Prince Regent, 1811 ; the Princess Charlotte, 1817 ; and Queen Charlotte, 1818.

In 1813 a large silver plate was added to the outer

case, with a portrait of the Duke of Wellington, commemorating the centenary of the agglomeration of the box. Local occurrences are also commemorated: The interior of Westminster Hall, with the Westminster Volunteers attending Divine service at the drumhead on the Fast Day, 1803; the Old Sessions House; a view of St. Margaret's from the north-east; the west front tower; and the altar-piece. On the outside of the first case is a clever engraving of a cripple. The top of the second case represents the Governors of the Poor in their board-room. It bears this inscription: "The original Box and cases to be given to every succeeding set of Overseers, on penalty of fifty guineas, 1783."

In 1785 Mr. Gilbert exhibited the box to some friends after dinner. That night thieves broke into his house, and carried off all the plate that had been in use; but the box had been removed beforehand to a bedchamber.

In 1793 Mr. Read, a Past Overseer, detained the box because his accounts were not passed. An action was brought for its recovery, which was long delayed, owing to two members of the society giving Read a release, which he successfully pleaded as a bar to the action. This rendered it necessary to take proceedings in equity, and a bill was filed in Chancery against all three, Read being compelled to deposit the box with Master Leeds until the end of the suit. Three years of litigation ensued. Eventually the Chancellor directed the box to be restored to the Overseers' Society, and Mr. Read paid in costs £300. The extra costs amounted to £76 13s. 11d., owing to the illegal proceedings of

Mr. Read. The sum of £91 7s. was at once raised, and the surplus spent upon a third case of octagon shape. The top records the triumph : Justice trampling upon a prostrate man, from whose face a mask falls upon a writhing serpent. A second plate, on the outside of the fly-lid, represents the Lord Chancellor Loughborough pronouncing his decree for the restoration of the box, March 5, 1796.

On the fourth case is shown the anniversary meeting of the Past Overseers' Society, with the churchwardens giving the charge previous to delivering the box to the succeeding overseer. He, on his side, is bound to produce it at certain parochial entertainments, with at least three pipes of tobacco, under the penalty of six bottles of claret, and to return the whole, with some addition, safe and sound, under a penalty of 200 guineas.

In more recent days additions to this box, forming records of various important public events, have from time to time been added. A tobacco-stopper of mother-of-pearl, with a silver chain, is enclosed within the box, and completes this unique memorial.

CHAPTER III

THE original clubland of the West End was St. James's Street, where the first clubs originated from coffee-houses. In this historic thoroughfare— the "dear old Street of Clubs and Cribs," as Frederick Locker called it—most of the sociable institutions founded many decades ago still flourish.

Such are White's, Arthur's, Brooks's, the Cocoa-tree, and Boodle's, the latter of which, after passing through a crisis which came near closing its doors for ever, now once again flourishes as of yore.

This club-house was built about 1765 by John Crunden, from the designs of Adam, but between 1821 and 1824 certain alterations and additions were carried out from the designs of John Papworth, an architect of that day.

From an architectural point of view, Boodle's is an admirable specimen of the work of Robert Adam ; its street façade possesses many fine qualities, whilst the ironwork is of good design.

A year or two ago it was rumoured that, in order to comply with a clause in the lease, an additional story was to be added to the building. Up to the present time, however, to the gratification of all possessing the slightest taste, no alteration has been made; and it is earnestly to be hoped that in these days, when there is so much prating of culture and love of art, such an act of vandalism (which it is understood the club itself would bitterly deplore) will not be committed.

The saloon on the first-floor at Boodle's has a very fine and stately appearance, and opening out of it on each side are two little rooms. One of these, according to tradition, was, in the days of high play, occupied by a cashier who issued counters and occupied himself with details connected with the game; the other was reserved for members wishing to indulge in gaming undisturbed by the noise of the crowd which thronged around the faro tables in the saloon. These tables, it is said, are still in the club. Towards the middle of the last century, though gaming had long ceased to take place in the saloon, there was a great deal of high gambling in the card-room upstairs. As far as can be ascertained, faro was once again played at that period.

Boodle's in old days played a great part in fashionable West End life. One of Gillray's caricatures, entitled "A Standing Dish at Boodle's," represents Sir Frank Standish sitting at a window of this club, which, it may be added, was noted for the large number of Baronets who were members. It was, indeed, said that anyone uttering the words, "Where is Sir John?" in the club-house would immediately find himself surrounded by a crowd of members.

Boodle's, it should be added, has always been closely connected with Shropshire, from which county its membership then, as now, was largely recruited.

The club was originally called the Savoir Vivre, and at its inception was noted for its costly gaieties; in 1774, for instance, its members spent 2,000 guineas upon a ridotto or masquerade.

Gibbon was a member of Boodle's, which, however, in the past, as to-day, principally consisted of county gentlemen.

Up to comparatively recent years, before Boodle's was reorganized, it was managed, not by a committee, but by a species of secret tribunal, the members of which were supposed to be unknown, though their duties corresponded with those of an ordinary club committee. This conclave conducted its proceedings with great secrecy, and its very existence was only inferred from the fact that, at intervals varying from six months to fifteen years, some printed notice appeared in the club rooms. Even so, this generally affected only dogs or strangers, both of whom old-fashioned members regarded with about equal dislike as unpleasant intruders.

Most of these notices, signed " By order of the Managers," quoted the " custom of the house existing from time immemorial," which, though unwritten, was then the only approach to a code of laws for the conduct of the club.

The old elections at Boodle's were peculiar, being presided over by the proprietor. Fifteen years ago or so, when Mr. Gayner, who then occupied that position, was still alive, he would take his seat by the ballot-box near the window in the back room on the ground-floor, whilst in the adjoining front room opening off it were the members. When a candidate was proposed, they walked across, and deposited

5

black or white balls, after which they retired again to the front room. After a short time, Mr. Gayner would shout out " Elected " or " Not elected," as the case might be, the ceremonial being gone through separately for every candidate. Wicked wags used to say that the proprietor never troubled to make a scrutiny as to the number of the balls, no candidate whom he considered suitable for the election ever being rejected, whilst an undesirable one was certain to meet with an evil fate, even should there be no black balls at all.

During Mr. Gayner's reign, Boodle's sustained a severe blow owing to the retirement of the Duke of Beaufort and a number of other old members. On certain evenings, according to a time-honoured custom, there was a house-dinner, and members taking part in this had to put down their names beforehand. The cost of wine, whether a man drank much or little, was pooled, and equally divided between everyone, a usage which, while it well suited some of the older men who belonged to a less temperate age, pressed heavily upon those of a later generation, some of whom scarcely drank anything at all. Resenting the injustice of this exactment, by which they were made to pay for other people's wine, some of the latter remonstrated with Mr. Gayner, and demanded that a more equitable arrangement should be made. The latter, realizing that such a protest was legitimate, then promised that matters should be set right, and to that end spoke to the Duke of Beaufort. The Duke replied that, whilst such a remonstrance might be just, he could not assent to any change without the concurrence of the older members of the club who were in the habit of dining. The majority of these, not unnaturally perhaps, energetically protested against any alteration in an old custom, which, as they quite truthfully declared, had always suited them very well. The Duke then informed Mr. Gayner that if any change were made he and these members would leave the club. Mr. Gayner, however, stood firm, saying he had given his promise and must keep it, in consequence of which the Duke, and the " old guard " with him, carried out their threat, and left Boodle's for ever.

Mr. Gayner carried on the club on very liberal lines, and members were allowed extraordinary credit. They could cash cheques for any amount, for Gayner made a practice of keeping a very large sum of money in his safe. This, it is said, often contained as much as two or three thousand pounds, always in new notes.

At the time of Mr. Gayner's death, he was supposed to have been owed over £10,000 by certain members of the club. He appears to have regarded this as a sort of friendly charge, for a special clause in his will stated that no member of Boodle's was to be asked for money. The best-natured of men, Mr. Gayner frequently assisted members who were in financial difficulties. One of these, a young fellow who had recently joined the club, asked him whether he could indicate any means of raising £500, as he had debts to that amount which demanded immediate payment. " I can't think of allowing you to go to the Jews," said Mr. Gayner; " come with me to my room, and I'll put that all

right." Arrived in his sanctum, he produced notes
for the required amount, and handed them to the
young man, telling him he might settle the debt
any time he liked.

After the death of Mr. Gayner, and of his sister,
who succeeded him, it seemed at one time as if
Boodle's might cease to exist. At a critical moment
in the club's history, however, certain members
stepped forward, and a complete reorganization was
the result. The list of members was thoroughly
sifted, and a most capable secretary, who still presides over the club's fortunes, assumed control.

Some alterations were made in the interior of the
building, but care was taken to leave unimpaired
the old-world charm of the house, which, from an
architectural point of view, possesses much merit.

The fine saloon, which, as has been said, was
originally a gambling-room, was thoroughly restored
and made into a comfortable lounge ; it is a spacious
and well-proportioned room, and contains a finely-
designed mantelpiece and a very ornamental chan-
delier, the latter purchased after the reorganization.
Except for some handsome inkstands and a few
accessories which are of good design and execution,
there are few works of art in this club, the hunting
pictures on the staircase being of no particular value.
Boodle's appears once to have possessed portraits of
Charles James Fox and the Duke of Devonshire,
but these have now disappeared.

The furniture and general appearance of the club
is essentially English, and it is pleasant to observe
that the air of old-world comfort for which Boodle's
has always been noted remains unimpaired.

A curious feature of Boodle's is that the billiard-room is upstairs, a somewhat inconvenient arrangement not infrequent in clubs founded in past days.

It should be added that a rule enforcing the wearing of evening dress by members dining in the coffee-room still remains in force; but a smaller apartment is set aside for those who for any reason do not find it convenient to change their day clothes.

Arthur's Club, in St. James's Street, was the original abode of White's, which occupied it from 1698 to 1755, since which date the house has, of course, undergone a good deal of change. In the eighteenth century, owing to the association of a Mr. Arthur with the management of White's, the latter club was frequently spoken of as Arthur's; this naturally originated an idea that the two clubs were at one time connected, but such in reality was never the case, the presumed parent of Arthur's having been a coffee-house of that name.

The records of Arthur's Club as at present constituted are, unfortunately, somewhat scanty. It would appear, however, that after the migration of White's in 1755 another club was formed at 69 St. James's Street, and that it took the name of Arthur's, which it still retains.

In its present form the club-house was built by Mr. Hopper in 1825, though probably a certain portion of the original coffee-house, erected in 1736, was incorporated in the new building. A room on the ground-floor (at the back of the house) is said to have been the gaming-room of White's Club during its tenure of the premises up to 1755; but if this is the case the decorative frieze and ceiling must have been added later, as in style they belong to the nineteenth century. During the rebuilding of 1825 everything seems to have been sacrificed to the staircase, which now occupies the very large hall, crowned by an elaborately-designed dome. There are, however, some handsome rooms, notably the library, in which is an eighteenth-century English sideboard of admirable design. In this and other rooms there is a good deal of the heavy, solid mahogany furniture so popular about seventy or eighty years ago. The examples in Arthur's Club are certainly the best of their kind, and are well in keeping with the design of the house. There are very few pictures or engravings here—a print or two of Arthur's as it was in old days, a few portraits of members, and an oil-painting of the late Sir John Astley (known as " the Mate ") are about all.

Arthur's possesses a quantity of very fine silver plate, some of which dates from the eighteenth century.

This club still maintains some of the restrictions as regards smoking which were so general in the clubs of other days, no smoking being allowed in the library or morning-room. There are, however, ample facilities for indulgence in tobacco in other parts of the house—notably in the hall, where a very pleasant lounge has recently been contrived.

Only recently has the regulation which prohibited visitors from being admitted to dinner here been repealed. A room on the ground-floor (the one reputed to have been the old gambling-room of White's) is now set aside as a dining-room for those privileged to be the guests of a member of

this very charming club. There is no tradition at
Arthur's of high play at hazard, but whist was once
very popular. "Sheep points and bullocks" on the
rubber were, it is said, quite common in the days
when so many country gentlemen were members.

Arthur's, it should be added, has always been a
very popular club with Wiltshire men, and its close
connection with that county is still maintained.

As has been said, the chocolate-house in St.
James's Street, started by Francis White in 1697,
seems to have stood on the site of part of what is
now Arthur's Club. John Arthur at this time was
White's assistant. Here White carried on business
till he died in 1711. His widow continued to prosper
as proprietress of the house, which became the centre
of the fashionable life of the day, and the place from
which its amusements were directed. Advertisements in the papers show that "Mrs. White's
Chocolate House, in St. James's Street," was the
place of distribution of tickets for all the fashionable
amusements of the early years of the eighteenth
century. Opera was being produced at the Hay-
market, and the announcement of the performance
of each new piece is accompanied by the notice that
tickets are to be obtained at Mrs. White's. A little
later, Heidegger was taking the town by storm
with his masquerades, ridottos, and balls. He was
quick to see that Mrs. White's was an advantageous
ground from which to reach his patrons of the
aristocracy. He accordingly issued his admissions
for these entertainments from White's, and requested
those who were not using them to return them
there, in order to prevent their falling into bad

hands, and so spoiling the select character of his assemblies.

John James Heidegger was a clever Swiss who, after leading a Bohemian life all over Europe, had come to London, where he had for a time co-operated with Handel in producing opera. His celebrity was chiefly due to a remarkable ability for organizing masquerades.

He was a very ugly man, and knew it. Consequently he would not have his portrait painted. The Duke of Montagu, however, determined to obtain a likeness, in order to play a trick at a masquerade.

The Duke induced the Swiss Count, as he was called, to make one of a select party, which (very appropriately) met to dine at the Devil Tavern. The rest of the company, all chosen for their powers of hard drinking, were in the plot, and a few hours after dinner Heidegger was carried out of the room dead drunk. A daughter of Mrs. Salmon, the waxwork-maker, was sent for, and took a mould from the unconscious man's face, from which she was ordered to make a cast in wax, and colour it to nature. The King, who was a party to the joke, was to be present, with the Countess of Yarmouth, at the next of Heidegger's masquerades, The Duke in the mean time bribed his valet to get all the information as to the clothes the Swiss was to wear on the occasion, procured a man of Heidegger's figure, and, with the help of the mask, made him up into a duplicate master of the revels.

When the King arrived with the Countess and

was seated, Heidegger, as was usual, gave the signal to the musicians in the gallery to play the National Anthem. As soon, however, as his back was turned, the sham Heidegger appeared, and ordered them to play "Over the Water to Charlie," the Jacobite song, and the most insulting and treasonable piece that could have been chosen to perform in the presence of royalty.

The whole room was at once thrown into confusion. Heidegger rushed into the gallery, raved, stamped, and swore, and accused the band of conspiring to ruin him. The bewildered musicians at once altered the tune to "God Save the King." Heidegger then left the gallery to make some arrangements in one of the smaller rooms.

As soon as he disappeared, the sham Heidegger again came forward, this time in the middle of the main room, in front of the gallery, and, imitating Heidegger's voice, damned the leader of the band for a blockhead, and asked if he had not told him to play "Over the Water" a minute before. The bandmaster, thinking Heidegger mad or drunk, lost his head, and ordered his men to strike up the Jacobite air a second time.

This was the signal for a confusion worse than before. There was great excitement and fainting of women, and the officers of the Guards who were present were only prevented from kicking Heidegger out of the house by the Duke of Cumberland, who was in the secret. Heidegger rushed back to the theatre, and was met by the Duke of Montagu, who told him that he had deeply offended the King, and that the best thing he could do was to go at once to His Majesty and ask pardon for the behaviour of his men.

Heidegger accordingly approached the King, who, with the Countess, could barely keep his countenance, and made an abject apology. He was in the act of bowing to retire, when he heard his own voice behind him say: "Indeed, Sire, it was not my fault, but that devil's in my likeness!" He turned round, and for the first time saw his double, staggered, and was speechless. The Duke now saw that the joke had gone far enough, and whispered an explanation of the whole affair. Heidegger recovered himself and the masquerade went on, but he swore he would never attend another until "that witch the wax-woman was made to break the mould and melt down the mask" before his face.

Hogarth's plate, "Heidegger in a Rage," was suggested by this story.

Heidegger, it may be added, remained popular with the fashionable world up to his death. He lived at Barn Elms, where the King honoured him with a visit. He bore the reputation of great charity, and died in 1749, "immensely lamented," aged near ninety.

That White's Club was a great success from the very first is shown from the old rate-books, where the prosperity of Mrs. White, the proprietress, is reflected. The entries give us three degrees of comparison: At White's death, positive, "Widow White"; later, comparative, "Mrs. White"; later still, superlative, "Madam White." The Bumble of the period was evidently impressed by her prosperity, and by the fine company which met at her house.

Madam White's, indeed, was never an ordinary coffee-house, a proof of which is that the usual charge of a penny made for entrance into such places appears to have been increased. In earlier days, when it was a chocolate-house, Steele (though he never became a member of the club) was a constant frequenter, for in 1716 he lived opposite. In the first number of the *Tatler*, published in 1709, he informs his readers that "all accounts of gallantry, pleasure, and entertainment shall be under the article of White's Chocolate House," while Will's was to supply the poetry, and the Grecian the learning. We find, accordingly, many of the early numbers of the *Tatler* dated from White's.

Madam White continued at the chocolate-house until some time between 1725 and 1729 (the exact year is uncertain, as the rate-books for those years are missing), and she probably left the place with a fortune.

At Mrs. White's demise, Arthur became proprietor, and largely added to the premises. These were burnt down in 1733, when he removed to Gaunt's Coffee-house till White's had been rebuilt. His son, Robert Arthur, appears as proprietor of the new house in 1736.

During Robert Arthur's life the most fashionable frequenters of his chocolate-house became more and more exclusive, and the proprietor soon found that catering for its members, all men of means and leisure, was the chief part of his business, and more lucrative than the custom of the general public.

His interests, of course, lay in the direction of meeting the wishes of his patrons, and in consequence of this members of the public were eventually excluded. White's Chocolate-house was thus transformed into the private and exclusive society since known as " White's."

Though White's was at this time reputed to be very exclusive, and although certain qualifications were indispensable, some of the members were drawn from a quite unaristocratic class.

In Davies's " Life of Garrick " is the following curious reference to Colley Cibber as a member of White's : " Colley, we are told, had the honour to be a member of the great club at White's ; and so I suppose might any other man who wore good clothes, and paid his money when he lost it. But on what terms did Cibber live with this society ? Why, he feasted most sumptuously, as I have heard his friend Victor say, with an air of triumphant exultation, with Mr. Arthur and his wife, and gave a trifle for his dinner. After he had dined, when the club-room door was opened, and the Laureate was introduced, he was saluted with loud and joyous acclamation of 'O King Coll ! Come in, King Coll !' and ' Welcome, welcome, King Colley !' and this kind of gratulation, Mr. Victor thought, was very gracious and very honourable."

The present White's Club dates from 1755, in which year Robert Arthur removed with the Young and Old Clubs which had met at his house—350 members in all—to the " Great House " in St. James's Street, which, though much altered, is still White's. He had purchased this building from Sir

Whistler Webster. One of its earlier occupants had been the Countess of Northumberland, whom Walpole mentions as one of the last to practise the unmaimed rites of the old peerage. "When she went out," says he, "a footman, bareheaded, walked on each side of her coach, and a second coach with her women attended her. I think, too, that Lady Suffolk told me that her granddaughter-in-law, the Duchess of Somerset, never sat down before her without her leave to do so."

In course of time the management of the club came into the hands of Martindale, a man whose name was connected with high play, of which he frequently figured as an organizer.

The house now began to have something of the organization which prevails in modern clubs.

About 1780, for instance, there was a regular club dinner at White's, when Parliament was sitting, at 12s. a head. In 1797 the charge for this had fallen to 10s. 6d. Hot suppers were provided at 8s., and lighter refreshments, with malt liquors, at 4s. At that time one of the rules decreed "that Every Member who plays at Chess, Draughts, or Backgammon do pay One Shilling each time of playing by daylight, and half-a-crown each by candlelight."

George Raggett, who succeeded Martindale as manager of White's, was quite a character in his way. He understood how to get on with gambling members, and owned the Roxburgh Club in St. James's Square, where whist was played for high stakes. Here, on one occasion, Hervey Combe, Tippoo Smith, Ward, and Sir John Malcolm sat down on a Monday evening, played through the night, through the following Tuesday and Tuesday night, and finally separated at eleven on Wednesday morning. It is interesting to notice that the separation took place then only because Mr. Combe had to attend a funeral. That gentleman rose a winner of £30,000 from Sir John Malcolm.

Before leaving the club, Combe pulled out of his pocket a handful of counters, amounting to several hundred pounds, over and above the thirty thousand he had won from the Baronet, and gave them to Raggett, saying : " I give them to you for sitting so long with us, and providing us with all we required." It was the practice of the astute Raggett to attend his patrons personally whenever there was high play going on. " I make it a rule never to allow any of my servants to be present when gentlemen play at my clubs," said he ; " for it is my invariable custom to sweep the carpet after the gambling is over, and I generally find on the floor a few counters, which pays me for my trouble of sitting up." This practice made his fortune.

As time went on, the club-house of White's underwent considerable alteration. In 1811, for instance, it was resolved to remove the entrance by converting the second window from the bottom of the house into a door, and to enlarge the morning-room by taking in the old entrance hall. This gave room for an additional window. The old doorway was utilized for this purpose, and the famous " Bow-Window at White's " was built out over the entrance steps, which may still be seen supporting it.

Directly this window was made, Brummell, then in the heyday of his fashionable prosperity, took

WHITE'S CLUB PREVIOUS TO 1811.

possession of it, and, together with his followers, made it a very shrine of fashion and an institution of West End club life. At that time only a select few dared to sit in it; an ordinary member of the club would as soon have thought of taking his seat on the throne in the House of Lords as of appropriating one of the chairs in the bow-window. Nice questions of etiquette arose in connection with the bow-window, and were duly discussed and settled. Its occupants were so much in evidence to the outside world in St. James's Street that ladies of their acquaintance could not fail to recognize them in passing. It was decided, after anxious discussion, that no greeting should pass from the bow-window or from any window in the club. As a consequence, the hats of the dandies were doffed to no passers-by.

Not a few of the old school resented monopoly of the famous window by Brummell and Lord Alvanley. "Damn the fellows!" said old Colonel Sebright; "they are upstarts, and fit only for the society of tailors." Brummell made amusing use of his connection with the club. He was reproached by an angry father whose son had gone astray in the Beau's company. "Really, I did all I could for the young fellow," said he; "I once gave him my arm all the way from White's to Watier's." Later, when he was coming to the end of his means and of his career in England, some of his friends who had assisted him with loans became importunate. One of these pressed him for the repayment of £500. "I paid you," said the Beau. "Paid me! When, pray?" "Why, when I was standing at the window at White's, and said as you passed, 'How d'you do !' "

About 1814 Brummell played much and unsuccessfully at White's. One night—the fifth of a most relentless run of ill-luck—his friend Pemberton Mills heard him exclaim that he had lost every shilling, and only wished someone would bind him never to play again. "I will," said Mills, and, taking out a ten-pound note, he offered it to Brummell on condition that he should forfeit a thousand if he played at White's within a month from that evening. The Beau took it, and for a few days discontinued coming to the club; but about a fortnight after, Mills, happening to go in, found him gambling again. Of course the thousand pounds were forfeited; but his friend, instead of claiming them merely went up to him, and, touching him gently on the shoulder, said : " Well, Brummell, you might at least give me back the ten pounds you had the other evening."

After Brummell's day was over, Lord Alvanley (a coloured print of whom as " The Man from White's " still hangs in the club) became the chief of the bow - window party. Most of this nobleman's time seems to have been spent in endeavouring to get rid of a large fortune, the inheritance of which had caused him to leave the Coldstream Guards, in which he had served with distinction in the Peninsular War. Lord Alvanley was the most noted bon-vivant of his day, and was utterly regardless of what his dinners cost. One of his fancies was to have a cold apricot tart on his sideboard every day throughout the year. Another instance of his prodigality was the payment of 200 guineas to Gunter for a luncheon-basket, which by an oversight had been forgotten in arranging a day's boating on the Thames—a costly picnic indeed!

On one occasion Lord Alvanley organized a dinner at White's, at which it was agreed that whoever could produce the most expensive dish should dine for nothing. The winner was the organizer, whose dish was a fricassée composed entirely of the *noix*, or small pieces at each side of the back, taken from thirteen kinds of birds, among them being one hundred snipe, forty woodcocks, twenty pheasants, and so on, the total amounting to about three hundred birds. The cost of the ridiculous dish amounted to £108 5s.

This extravagant and eccentric peer, who, it was said, never paid cash for anything, was once asked by the sarcastic Colonel Armstrong, who knew of this failing, what he had given for a fine horse he was riding. " Nothing," said his lordship ; " I owe Milton 200 guineas for him." Another failing of Lord Alvanley's caused his friends at country-houses some anxiety. He always read in bed, and would never blow out his candle, his method of extinguishing that light being usually to fling it into the middle of the room ; if this was ineffectual, he would throw a pillow at it. Sometimes he would vary the proceedings by putting the burning candle bodily under his bolster.

Another frequenter of the bow - window was Lord Allen, who became such a confirmed lover of London that, during the latter part of his life, it was said his only walk was from White's to Crockford's, over the way and back again. It was also said that he was so accustomed to the roar of the London traffic, that to get him to sleep at Dover, where he was visiting Lord Alvanley, that nobleman hired a hackney coach to drive in front of his window at the inn all night, and sent out the boots at proper intervals to call the time and the weather, like the London watchmen.

Lord Allen was a man of very moderate means, and eked out his income by dining out as much as possible. An incivil remark at dinner to an old lady caused her to say : "My lord, your title must be as good as board wages to you !"

Lord Allen was generally known as "King Allen." In course of time, as a result of his lounging life about town, he lost most of his not very abundant money, when he withdrew to Dublin, where, in Merrion Square, he slept behind a large brass plate with "Viscount Allen" upon it, which verified the old lady's remark ; for it was as good to him as a regular income, and brought endless invitations from people eager to feed a Viscount at any hour of the day or night.

Many distinguished men have belonged to White's, and many more have tried to do so. Louis Napoleon, during his exile in London, is said much to have desired to be a member of White's, but his wish was never gratified.

Count d'Orsay, who drew the portraits of many of his contemporaries, some of whom were members of this club (lithographs of which portraits hang in the morning-room), made several attempts to secure election, but without success. As he was very

popular amongst the men of his day, it was probably merely the fact of his being a foreigner which
kept him out.

Though the shell of Sir Whistler Webster's
" Great House " still exists at White's, many structural alterations have been made from time to time.
The most notable of these was undertaken in 1850,
when Raggett, the then proprietor, entrusted to
Mr. Lockyer the work of remodelling the façade of
the old club-house. Four bas-reliefs, designed by
Mr. George Scharf, jun., representing the four
seasons, were, under Lockyer's direction, inserted in
the place of four sash-windows. At this period the
old balcony rails would seem to have been moved,
and the present elaborate cast-iron work substituted
—a very doubtful improvement. The interior of
the club-house was also then redecorated by the firm
of Morant, and Victorian mantelpieces were introduced into some of the rooms. In all probability
these alterations, carried out at a period when taste
was at a low ebb, robbed White's of much which
the more enlightened taste of to-day would have
wished preserved.

The management of White's by Henry Raggett
only ended at his death in 1859. He was the last
of the proprietors of the club who were also the
owners of the freehold of the club building.

Raggett was succeeded as manager by Percival,
who continued in this position till his death in 1882.
The Misses Raggett, sisters of the late proprietor,
still owned the club-house, and consequently a
certain feeling of insecurity prevailed as to the future
of the club. In 1868 a proposal was made that the

building should be purchased from the Misses Raggett by the members ; but it was found that the property was in Chancery, and that nothing could be done. The club, still feeling unsettled, decided to form a fund to provide against eventualities connected with the tenure of the house. This they accomplished by raising the entrance fee to nineteen guineas, ten of which were devoted to the purpose, and placed in the hands of trustees.

Lord Hartington reported, in 1870, that he had at last induced the trustees of the Raggetts to name a price for the sale of the club building. This was fixed at £60,000. He reported at the same time that Percival held an unexpired lease of ten years at a rental of £2,100. The club very naturally refused to entertain the idea of purchase at any such figure. A reduced offer of £50,000, made a month later, they also refused.

A year afterwards the place was sold by auction. With a view to purchase, members of White's had subscribed for debentures to the amount of £16,000. At the auction, the representative of the club bid £38,000 for the property, but it was bought by Mr. Eaton, M.P., afterwards Lord Cheylesmore, for £46,000.

After some fruitless negotiations in 1877, when the number of members had been increased to 600, Percival, negotiating on his own account with Mr. Eaton, announced that he had obtained a new lease of thirty years, from 1881, at a rent of £3,000 a year. In 1882 Mr. Percival died. The management of White's then passed to his son, as representative of Mrs. Percival, the widow.

In 1888 matters arrived at a crisis.   Mrs. Percival
announced her intention of terminating her lease
with Lord Cheylesmore, and it was proposed by the
committee to grant her a sum of £1,200 in consideration of her carrying on the club business until the end
of the year.   There were various meetings at which
the proposal was discussed, and much was said on
both sides.   Eventually it was carried, and negotiations were entered into with two members of the
club who had expressed themselves willing to
take over the management.   In July of 1888 the
management of the Percivals came to an end by the
signing of an agreement for the future conduct of
White's by a member of the club, Mr. Algernon
Bourke.

Under his management White's resumed its
youth, and was again invested with an air of
sprightly insouciance, which in latter years had been
conspicuous by its absence.   Drastic structural
alterations, carried out under the direction of Mr
Bourke, much improved the convenience of the
building.   The courtyard, where was an old Well
from which, up to quite recent years, the water used
in the club was drawn, was roofed over and converted
into a spacious billiard-room, and the large front
room was converted into a dining-room, certain
alterations being made in the apartment behind
previously used for that purpose.

Within the last two years some further alterations
of a very judicious nature have been carried out in
the club-house.   An upper story containing servants'
bedrooms has been added, but this has scarcely
altered the appearance of the house, and the façade

remains practically the same as it has been for the last fifty-seven years.

Portfolios seem formerly to have been preserved at White's, which contained engravings of well-known members. Many of these were framed by Mr. Bourke, who, adding to the number, formed the present valuable and interesting collection. On each of these prints the date at which its subject belonged to White's is inscribed in pencil. As a club record of past membership the series is unique.

In the dining-room of the club are several paintings, and among them is a portrait of the first Duke of Wellington, by Count d'Orsay. This, I believe, is one of two portraits painted by the Count. The Iron Duke, it is said, was much pleased with them, and declared that D'Orsay was the only artist who had ever painted him as a gentleman.

Other oil-paintings here represent George II and George III—a modern portrait shows the late Duke of Cambridge in undress uniform. There are also a few other pictures, including two of horses by John Wooton. All the pictures in this room, with the exception of the portrait of George II, originally in the house dining-room (now the committee-room next door), were acquired after the reconstitution of the club by Mr. Bourke in 1888. On the other hand, some Italian pictures and a curious portrait of a woman, supposed to have been in White's since its foundation, have disappeared. The same fate, unfortunately, has befallen the fine old silver plate which belonged to the club up to comparatively recent years; and most of the original furniture is in other hands.

The whimsical coat of arms which, carved in wood, hangs over the fireplace in the entrance hall is, of course, a modern copy of the design invented by Horace Walpole and his friends at Strawberry Hill.

The worth of some of the old furniture in White's was great, as may be realized when it is stated that the present possessor of two small sideboards formerly in the dining-room was a short time ago offered £600 apiece for them by a well-known expert. The original eighteenth-century dining-room chairs (the place of which is now supplied by copies) were also of great interest and value.

A curious old oak table, now in the committee-room at White's, is in no way connected with the history of that club. It was originally the dining-table of the Sublime Society of Beefsteaks, and has on it three carvings. Two of these represent the mitre and Beefeater's cap which figured in the ceremonial of that institution, and the centre one a gridiron, which was its crest. As has already been mentioned, this table was purchased by Mr. Bourke.

A richly decorated piano which formerly stood in what is now the card-room has gone, as have also a very ornamental French weather-glass and some other *objets d'art*.

Of late years great efforts have been made to recover anything connected with the past history of White's, and already, owing to the efforts of certain members, several have been discovered and obtained. These include the quaint original ballot-box and a complete set of the old gaming counters, which, like those at Brooks's, are inscribed with the sums they represented.

A feature of the downstairs lounge at White's is the belt presented to Heenan after his celebrated fight with Tom Sayers. This interesting trophy, which is lent by a member (Mr. Gilbert Elliot), now hangs over the mantelpiece beneath a not very successful bas-relief of the late King, which was placed there during the alterations in 1888. It is said that an unsophisticated visitor to the club-house being taken into the lounge, after glancing at the silver belt and the bas-relief above, eagerly inquired, "Did the King win it?" which remark naturally occasioned much amusement.

In the lease of White's Club-house is a clause, dating from the middle of the eighteenth century, which lays down that copies of the *Times* and of the *Racing Calendar* should always be preserved, in consequence of which, up to a few years ago, the cellars were filled with an enormous mass of paper, much of which had been almost reduced to pulp, owing to inflows of water during floods. The collection is now stored elsewhere.

White's Club is just a year older than the Bank of England. It was established before the last of the Stuarts had left the throne, and a number of its members have fought England's battles on land and sea. One of these was Lord St. Vincent, the great sailor, who brought the West Indies to the British Crown and won the naval battle of St. Vincent. Rodney was a member, and his wife, when her husband had been greatly impoverished by gaming debts and election expenses, sent the hat round for him at White's. Very inappropriately, however, the money was provided by a Frenchman, the Marshal de Biron. George Keppel, third Earl of Albemarle, who captured Havana in 1762, was another naval member, as was Charles Saunders, who co-operated with General Wolfe in the assault of the Heights of Abraham ; so too was Boscawen, who went by the name of "Old Dreadnought."

Besides having had a great number of gallant soldiers and sailors on its list, this club can also boast that for many years the destinies of Great Britain were practically in the hands of certain of its members.

Sir Robert Walpole and his able rival, William Pulteney, afterwards Earl of Bath, were members of the old club at White's in 1756. In the debate on the motion for the impeachment of Sir Robert in 1741, the latter, in the course of a speech, quoted a verse from Horace. Pulteney rose and remarked that the right honourable gentleman's Latin and logic were alike inaccurate. Walpole denied it, and a bet of a guinea was made across the floor of the House. The matter was then referred to the Clerk at the table, a noted scholar, and decided against the Minister.

The guinea was handed to Pulteney, and is now in the British Museum, with the following inscription in his handwriting :

"This guinea, I desire, may be kept as an heirloom. It was won of Sir Robert Walpole in the House of Commons ; he asserting the verse in Horace to be 'Nulli pallescere culpæ,' whereas I laid the wager of a guinea that it was ' Nulla pallescere culpa.' I told him that I could take the money without blush on my side, but believed it was the only money he ever gave in the House where the giver and receiver ought not equally to blush. This guinea, I hope, will prove to my posterity the use of knowing Latin, and encourage them in their learning."

The betting-book at White's, which is still in existence, bears witness to the love of a past age for speculating about every manner of thing, grave or gay. At one period of the eighteenth century chess was in high favour at White's. Several matches are recorded in the betting book. Lord Howe, for instance, engages "to play twelve games at chess with Lord Egmont, and bets Lord Egmont twelve guineas to six guineas of each game." It is also recorded that M. de Mirepoix, the French Ambassador, sent an invitation to all chess-players of both clubs* to meet him for a game. He spells the word " clubs " " clamps."

Lord Montfort, who eventually met with a tragic death at his own hands, in consequence, it would appear, of the impecuniosity which followed on his wild gaming, made a curious bet as to his powers as a horseman :

July ye 17*th*, 1752.

Ld. Montfort to ride six days running.

1st. Ld. Montfort gives Ld. Downe one guinea to receive 10 gs. when he rides 35 miles within the first day.

* White's was formed from the old and new clubs into which it was originally divided.

2nd. Ld. Montfort gives Ld. Ashburnham 1 guinea to receive 10 gs. when he rides 25 miles within the second day. *pd.*

3rd. Ld. Montfort gives Ld. Waldegrave one guinea, to receive 10 gs. when he rides 20 miles within the third day. *paid.*

4th. Ld. Montfort gives Mr. Watson 1 guinea, to receive 10 gs. when he rides 15 miles within the fourth day. *pd.*

5th. Ld. Montfort gives Ld. Downe 1 guinea, to receive 10 gs. when he rides 10 miles within the fifth day.

6th. Ld. Montfort gives Ld. Howe 1 guinea to receive 10 guineas when he rides 5 miles within the Sixth day. *Paid.*

Another wager of this nobleman dealt with the matrimonial intentions of the proprietor of White's :

Ld. Montfort wagers Ld. Ravensworth one hundred guineas, Duke of Devonshire Fifty guineas, and Ld. Hartington fifty guineas, that Mr. Arthur is not married in three year from ye date hereof, March 11th, 1754.

N.B. Bob goes Twenty guineas with Ld. Montfort in this bet.*   (Now Sir Robt. Mackreth.)

The following are a few of the very numerous bets of which account is given in this curious record :

November 7th, 1758.

Mr. Cadogan engages to pay Mr. Willis twenty guineas, in consideration of one guinea received from him, whenever he has in his possession, either by purchase or gift, a Post Chaise with a crane neck.

* A note added : "' Bob,' the waiter, married the daughter of Mr. Arthur, the proprietor of the club, became prosperous, and was afterwards knighted. He was subsequently Member for Castle Rising."

The following bet, recorded in 1813, would appear to refer to some incident in the life of Mr. Creevy which has escaped notice :

Col. Osborn bets Sir J. Copley 5 gs. that Mr. Creevy is imprisoned before the announcement of the capture of Dantzic is received.

J. COPLEY.

J. OSBORN. *pd.*

April 2nd.

Mr. Methuen bets Col. Stanhope ten guineas to 1, that a certain worthy Baronet understood between them does not of necessity part with his gold ice-pails, before this day twelvemonth ; the ice-pails being found at a pawnbroker's, will not entitle Col. Stanhope to receive his ten guineas.

H. F. R. STANHOPE.

PAUL METHUEN.

White's, April 10th, 1813.

Mr. Raikes bets Sir Joseph Copley ten guineas that he does not play at cards or dice at any Club in London in a year from this date.

settled.

May 22nd, 1818.

Lord Binning bets Lord Falmouth five guineas that a Roman Catholic Bishop upon formally abjuring his Catholic faith, may be made a Protestant Bishop without any new ordination in the Protestant Church.

BINNING.

FALMOUTH. *pd.*

April 17th, 1825.

Lord George Bentinck bets Col. Walpole a Rouleau that the Duke of St. Albans marries

Mrs. Coutts within six months of this day. Ld. Elliott stands half the bet with Ld. G. Bentinck.

G. BENTINCK.

January 8, 1826.

July 8, paid a pony to the waiter for Col. Walpole.—G. BENTINCK.

1 June pd. a pony Elliott.

Lord Maidstone bets Ld. Kelburne six bets of £50 each that he has six horses now in his own stable which he will ride over and shall clear a 5 feet wall in the Leath country in Lincolnshire.

SIR RICHARD SUTTON, BART. } *to be umpires:*
....

Lord Adolphus FitzClarence bets Mr. George Bentinck £10 that there is not a shot fired in anger in London during the year 1851.

Mr. F. Cavendish bets Mr. H. Brownrigg 2/1 that he does not kill the bluebottle fly before he goes to bed.

W. FREDERICK CAVENDISH.
HENRY M. BROWNRIGG. *recd.* H.B.

July 17, 1856.

At one time very large sums changed hands over the whist-table at White's. One of the most distinguished gamblers was Lord Rivers, known in Paris as Le Wellington des Joueurs. This nobleman, it is said, once lost £3,400 at whist by not remembering that the seven of hearts was in! He played at hazard for the highest stakes that anyone could be got to play, and at one time was supposed to have won nearly £100,000 ; but all, together with a great deal more, went at Crockford's.

In earlier days White's appears to have been an occasional resort of very queer characters indeed. In Hogarth's gambling scene at White's we see the highwayman, with the pistols peeping out of his pocket, waiting by the fireside till the heaviest winner takes his departure, in order to recoup himself of his losings. And in the "Beaux' Stratagem," Aimwell asks of Gibbet : " Ha'n't I seen your face at White's ?"

M'Clean, the fashionable highwayman, had a lodging in St. James's Street, over against White's ; and he was as well known about St. James's as any gentlemen who lived in that quarter, and who, perhaps, went upon the road, too. When M'Clean was taken, in 1750, Horace Walpole tells us that Lord Mountfort, at the head of half White's, went the first day ; his aunt was crying over him. As soon as they were withdrawn, she said to him, knowing they were of White's : " My dear, what did the Lords say to you ? Have you ever been concerned with any of them ?"

Mr. Pelham, the Prime Minister, who had originally been an officer, was a well-known frequenter of the gaming-table at White's, to which he resorted even when in high office—a habit alluded to in the following lines :

" Or chair'd at White's, amidst the doctors sit,
    Teach oaths to gamesters, and to nobles wit."

General Scott, the father-in-law of George Canning and the Duke of Portland, was known to have won at White's £200,000, thanks to his notorious sobriety and knowledge of this game. The General possessed a great advantage over his companions by avoiding the excesses which used not unfrequently to muddle their brains. He confined himself to dining off something very light, such as a boiled chicken with toast and water, and in consequence always came to the whist-table with a clear head. Possessing a remarkable memory, with great coolness of judgment, he was able honestly to win the enormous sum of £200,000.

At Almack's, a rival institution to White's, there was also much high play. According to the rule of the house, every player had to keep not less than twenty to fifty guineas on the table in front of him, and often there was as much as £10,000 in gold on the table. The players, before sitting down at the gaming-table, removed their embroidered clothes and substituted frieze greatcoats, or turned their coats inside out for luck. They also put on short leather sleeves to save their lace ruffles, and in order to guard their eyes from the light and keep their hair in order they wore high-crowned straw hats, with broad brims adorned with flowers and ribbons; whilst to conceal their emotions they also wore shades or masks.

George Selwyn, one evening at White's, saw a member connected with the postal service, Sir Everard Fawkener (the present writer's great-grandfather, and an indifferent card-player), losing a large sum of money at piquet. Selwyn, pointing to the successful player, remarked: "See now, he is robbing the mail!"

On another occasion, in 1756, observing Mr. Ponsonby, the Speaker of the Irish House of Commons, tossing about bank-bills at a hazard-table at Newmarket, "Look," he said, "how easily the Speaker passes the money-bills!"

Of the gambling at White's in former days so much has been written that it would be superfluous to dwell upon this phase in the history of the club when George Selwyn played night after night. Selwyn, however, was something more than a mere gambler, and possessed in a conspicuous degree the power of scourging folly and self-pretension. The following is an instance of his powers in this direction:

One morning, when Selwyn was at the home of the Duke of Queensberry, a newly-appointed Commissioner of Taxes made his appearance. This man was in a tumult of joy at his preferment; but, though it was to the Duke he had primarily been indebted for his good fortune, he hardly thanked him; for he was possessed with the notion that it was from his own merit that he had acquired the promotion. Entering the room, he assumed several consequential airs, thinking that he was now as great a man as the Duke himself.

"So, Mr. Commissioner," said Selwyn—"you will excuse me, sir, I forget your name—you are at length installed, I find." The word "installed" conveyed an awkward idea; for the new Commissioner's grandfather had been a stable-boy.

"Why, sir," replied the other, "if you mean to say that I am at length appointed, I have the pleasure to inform you that the business is settled.

Yes, I am appointed; and though our noble friend, the Duke here, did oblige me with letters to the Minister, yet these letters were of no use; and I was positively promoted to the office without knowing a syllable about the matter, or even taking a single step in it."

" What! not a single step?" cried George.

" No, not one, upon my honour," replied the new-fledged placeman. " Egad, sir! I did not walk a foot out of my way for it."

" And egad, sir!" retorted Selwyn, " you never before uttered half so much truth in so few words. Reptiles, sir, can neither walk nor take steps— nature ordained they should creep."

Like many men of his day, Selwyn did and said many things which a later age would call very snobbish. Happening to be at Bath when it was nearly empty, he was induced, for the mere purpose of killing time, to cultivate the acquaintance of an elderly gentleman he was in the habit of meeting in the Rooms. In the height of the following season Selwyn encountered his old associate in St. James's Street. He endeavoured to pass unnoticed, but in vain. " What! do you not recollect me?" exclaimed the indignant provincial. " I recollect you perfectly," replied Selwyn, " and when I next go to Bath I shall be most happy to become acquainted with you again."

Though Selwyn appears to have preferred White's, he did not entirely confine his attention to it. It was in his day the fashion to belong to as many clubs as possible—Wilberforce, indeed, mentions no fewer than five to which he himself belonged :

Brooks's, Boodle's, White's, Miles and Evans's in New Palace Yard, and Goosetree's, on the site of which stands the Marlborough. As their names imply, all these clubs were originally mere coffee-houses, kept by men of the above names, the most celebrated of whom, next to the proprietors of White's, was Brookes, or Brooks, who founded the present club in St. James's Street.

CHAPTER IV

AT one time considerable rivalry existed between White's and Brooks's. Great festivities took place all over the country in the spring of 1789, and both White's and Brooks's gave balls, which seem to have occasioned much unpleasant feeling between the party of the Prince of Wales and that of the Court.

Pitt was a member of both clubs (having been elected to Brooks's in 1781, on the proposal of Fox), but he had a decided partiality for White's.

The Prince detested White's as the chosen club of Pitt, who had opposed him during the King's illness, and, as soon as the entertainment was announced, forbade his friends to attend it, and it is said, together with the Duke of York, sent their tickets to be sold at a public library.

Three weeks later, on April 21, Brooks's followed with a grand ball at the Opera House, one of the tickets for which is framed in the " strangers' room " on the ground-floor of the club. As a matter of fact, the Prince's conduct towards the ball at White's gave a party character to that at Brooks's, with the result that all the ladies of the Court refused to attend.

Brooks's was originally in Pall Mall, on or near the site of the present Marlborough Club, and the precise date of its removal into St. James's Street cannot be positively fixed; but certain it is that the existing house was built by Brooks, from designs by Holland, the architect, in 1778, and in a letter to G. Selwyn, dated in October of that year, T. Townshend—afterwards first Viscount Sydney—says: "As a proof of our increasing opulence, I need only show the New Opera House, which is now fitting up at a monstrous expense . . . and Brooks's new house, fitted up with great magnificence, which is to be opened in a week or ten days." It was in consequence of these great expenses that the annual subscription was doubled.

The originator of Brooks's seems to have been the Scotsman Almack, whose real name was Macall, and in its early days the club consisted of 150 members at an annual subscription of four guineas, with the proviso that, " in case that proportion falls short of 400 guineas on the whole, such deficiency shall be made good to Mr. Almack." But this small number of members soon expanded, and by 1776 had been doubled, by successive additions of twenty, thirty, fifty, and fifty. Fifteen years passed, and in 1791 another 150 were added, and 100 more in 1816, bringing the numbers up to 550. Twenty-five more were added in 1823, and a like number in 1857, bringing the total up to 600, at which it remained till 1901, when it was raised to 650, the present number.

At the end of 1778 the club moved into its present premises, the new house being owned by Brooks or Brookes, and after that date his name was assumed as a title.

The subscription, fixed at four guineas in 1764,

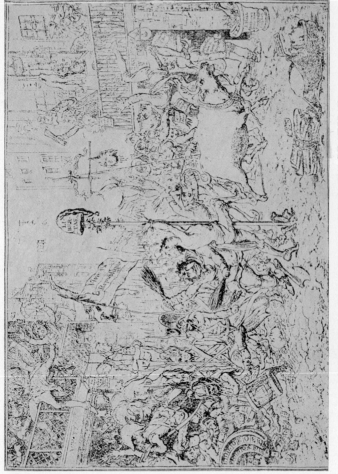

PROMISED HORRORS OF THE FRENCH INVASION, BY GILLRAY.

Showing both White's and Brooks's Clubs.

was before 1779 raised to eight, and on May 25 in that year the committee, or whatever was the governing body, granted Brooks an extra two guineas for two years only, "in consideration of the great expense he hath been at in erecting and fitting up his house"—viz., the present house. Brooks compounded with those that were willing, for sixteen guineas paid down in advance.

On April 17, 1791, the subscription was again raised to ten guineas, and in addition an entrance fee of five guineas was imposed; and it was further resolved that every member should pay one guinea in addition to the subscription for that year, "in order that the new Regulations about Dinner, Forfeits, etc., may take place immediately."

So matters continued until 1815, when the subscription was increased to eleven guineas, "in consideration of the great expense the Masters of the Club had been put to by various alterations of the Club-house."

On March 18, 1817, an additional guinea was imposed—to be paid on January 1, 1818—for the express purpose of increasing the size of the coffee-room.

In 1828 it was resolved that the extra guinea added to the annual subscription in 1815 should be reserved to form a fund, to be invested in the names of the trustees, to be employed as the club should thereafter direct. The present subscription is eleven guineas.

The original rules are very strict on the subject of arrears, Rule XX providing that all subscriptions shall be paid between March 1 and June 25; otherwise the defaulter is to be *ipso facto* excluded and his name erased. This excellent provision, however, seems to have been more honoured in the breach than in the observance, for on June 8, 1800, Griffin, who was the Master, was "authorized to inform members that, being in arrears, they are no longer members of the Club, and the Managers have directed him to recover the arrears due to him." Yet, notwithstanding the resolution of the managers, on May 3, 1806, Griffin reported the arrears to amount to £6,000, which large sum had in 1809 increased to £10,000.

This generous confidence of the Masters in the ultimate solvency of members endured until the death of Banderet, in spite of a periodical protest against the large amount of house accounts outstanding for dinners and other disbursements; and on one occasion it is said that he represented to the managers that a certain member was £800 in his debt, and, although he was quite ready to trust the gentleman to any amount, he did think that, under the circumstances, he need not insist upon having ortolans for his dinner every night.

There is a very general impression that the eleventh guinea of the subscription, still paid, was first imposed to pay the debts of C. J. Fox, but of this there is no evidence whatever. That Fox's debts were paid by his friends is certain, and that he had many friends in Brooks's is equally so, and they doubtless were the chief contributors, but as individuals only; the idea that Brooks's ever contributed in its corporate capacity is absolutely without foundation.

The regulations passed in 1828 laid down that dinner at 10s. 6d. per head shall be ready at a quarter before six every day from November 1 to the Prince of Wales's birthday (August 12th). " If the number at dinner shall not exceed four, they shall have no reckoning to pay but for wine, fruits, etc. If the number exceeds four, the 2 guineas shall be deducted from the whole reckoning."

Dinner was served at half-past four ; and the bill was brought in at seven.   Supper began at eleven, and ended at half an hour after midnight.   The cost of the dinner was 8s. a head, and of the supper 6s. ; and anyone who had been present during any part of the meal hours paid his share of the wine, in accordance with the old law of British conviviality.

No gaming was allowed in the " eating room " except " tossing up for reckonings," under the penalty of paying the whole bill of the members present.

The ballot took place between eleven at night and one in the morning, which custom continued until 1844, when the hours were altered to between three and five in the afternoon.   A single black ball excluded, and a member who joined any other club, except White's, was at once struck off the books.

As manager of the club, Brooks appears to have been a most accommodating individual.   He is described by Tickell, in a copy of verses addressed to Sheridan, as

> " Liberal Brookes, whose speculative skill
>   Is hasty credit and a distant bill ;
>   Who, nursed in clubs, disdains a vulgar trade,
>   Exults to trust, and blushes to be paid."

It may be added that, as a consequence of the above-mentioned diffidence, Brooks died a poor man in 1782. Indeed, according to tradition, his creditors were so rapacious that, in order to defeat them, his body was interred in a small vault, still existing, under the pavement of St. James's Street. For this, however, there is no sort of evidence in the records of the club, and the legend may have been suggested by the smallness of the vault, which would just contain a coffin.

Brooks was succeeded in the management by a Mr. Griffin, whose name can be traced down to 1815, though for the six years preceding this date the management figures as "Griffin and Co." In 1815, however, he disappears, and at some subsequent time the mastership devolved upon Wheelwright, who in 1824 took Halse into partnership, and in 1831 retired; whereupon Halse took Henry Banderet into partnership, himself retiring in 1846, and receiving a grant from the club of £500 on account of his interest in the unexpired lease of the house, and 50 guineas for the surrender of his lodging therein. From that time until his death in 1880, Banderet continued Master; and to him is to be attributed the credit of having established in Brooks's that refined if somewhat solemn comfort which resembles rather the luxury of a first-class private house than a club, and which has led to its being humorously described as "like dining in a Duke's house with the Duke lying dead upstairs." His attention to his duties as Master was unremitting, and it was said that, during the thirty-four years in which he filled that post, he had never been known to be absent, except on one occasion when he was persuaded to take a holiday; but he found himself so miserable that by noon he was back at Brooks's, which he never afterwards left until his death, when the entire management was taken over by the club.

As a building, Brooks's is a handsome and suitable club-house, which from time to time has sustained a number of alterations, most of them of a judicious kind. The balcony on the first-floor, formerly such a feature of the façade, has long been removed.

About twenty years ago considerable changes were made in the club-house, and No. 2 Park Place was incorporated as part of it. Up to that time the coffee-room had been what is now the strangers' smoking-room on the first-floor, the only smoking-room being the round room at the back of the house, now divided into dressing-rooms. There was practically no library, the only apology for one being a small room beyond the coffee-room, containing little except Parliamentary reports, back volumes of the *Edinburgh* and *Quarterly Reviews*, and novels from a circulating library. Opening out of this library was another small room into which hardly anyone ever went, and through that, again, a very small dressing-room which hardly anyone ever used. During the alterations these uncomfortable little rooms, together with the rest of No. 2 Park Place, were swept away, and the present coffee-rooms, with library above, erected in their place, the old drawing-rooms and coffee-rooms being given up to smokers and their guests. At the same time the hall and staircase were entirely reconstructed.

Amongst the important reforms introduced after Banderet's death was the institution of club bedrooms, and also the privilege of inviting guests to dinner, and—in May 1896—to luncheon.

There are some interesting relics of old days at Brooks's, including a complete set of the gaming counters used when the club was the scene of much high play. These are well displayed in a case at the bottom of the staircase. In the room upstairs, once the scene of so many late sittings, the old gambling-table still remains. A semicircular cut in this is said to have been made in order to accommodate the portly form of Charles James Fox, a pastel portrait of whom, by Russell, is one of the treasures of the club.

Some old prints of Brooks's in former days (and a water-colour drawing of the gaming-room by Rowlandson in particular) convey an excellent idea of the past life of the club, while a few portraits of celebrated members decorate its walls.

The fine room upstairs which was once devoted to high play would appear to retain much of its ancient appearance, and the decorative scheme employed on the walls seems to have been little changed.

A treasured possession of this club is the old betting-book, in which are many curious entries, one of which tells that Mr. Thynne, having, according to a note written opposite his name in the club books, "won only £12,000 during the last two months, retired in disgust, March 21, 1772; and that he may never return is the ardent wish of members."

The entries in this volume deal with all sorts of subjects, and range from a bet of five hundred guineas to ten that none of the Cabinet were beheaded by that day three years, to one of fifty that Mlle. Heinel does not dance at the Opera House next winter.

Brooks's possesses a good deal of silver-plate, which taken in the aggregate is valued at some £4,000. The oldest piece is a marrow-spoon of 1793, whilst perhaps the most interesting part of the collection is a number of candlesticks, all Georgian.

There are in Brooks's two snuff-boxes—an antique one of mother-of-pearl, and another of early Victorian date and design.

The tranquillity for which this club is noted has rarely been disturbed in recent times, but in 1886, when Mr. Gladstone introduced his Home Rule Bill, Brooks's became much perturbed and troubled by discord quite out of keeping with the traditions of its sacred precincts. A member who had been in Mr. Gladstone's Cabinet, and who, it was said, had many years before been himself " blackballed " when a candidate, was declared to have spoken contemptuously of the Liberal Unionists as he descended the stairs of the club, where he had been dining as a guest. The irate Liberal Unionists immediately discovered an easy way of revenge. As luck would have it, the son of the ex-Minister came up for election almost immediately after his father's ill-timed outburst of eloquence, and was swiftly made to experience the same fate which had befallen his parent many years before. As a consequence of this the supporters of Mr. Gladstone, at the next opportunity, revenged themselves by treating the eldest son of a Whig Unionist peer in the same way.

Feeling began to run high, and at each successive election the circle of carnage widened and widened, until it began to be whispered that it would soon be impossible for anybody to be elected to Brooks's at all. Matters began to look very serious—one member even declared that the shade of Fox had been observed flitting about the passages ; and though another member surmised that it was only the solid figure of an ancient servitor of the club with a bottle of port in his hand, which had been mistaken for the shade of the statesman, both agreed in acknowledging that the situation was becoming extremely grave. Happily, at this juncture Lord Granville came to the rescue, and at the next election made a speech which caused a general reconciliation. In a few well-chosen words he alluded to the antiquity of the club, and the previous divisions in the party which it had survived, and expressed a hope—using almost the words which Burke had employed in a slightly different connection—which he believed all present in their hearts really shared, that there should at least be one place left in London where a truce might be allowed to the divisions and animosities of mankind, and friends might still be allowed to meet one another on the same terms as of old.

Lord Granville's speech produced a great effect, as the taking of the ballot proved ; for all the candidates, irrespective of their shades of political opinion, were elected. Lord Granville afterwards declared that he had never felt so nervous in his life.

In the earlier days of its existence, Brooks's, like

so many other West End resorts, was the scene of much high gambling, and large sums often changed hands.

Samuel Wilberforce, when he first joined the club, took part (he afterwards declared) from mere shyness in a game of faro, George Selwyn in the bank. A friend, astonished, called out, "What, Wilberforce, is that you?" Selwyn quite resented the interference, and, turning to him, said in his most expressive tone: "Oh, sir, don't interrupt Mr. Wilberforce; he could not be better employed."

As a matter of fact, this was not the sole occasion upon which Wilberforce played, for he once kept the bank at Goosetree's, which Pitt also frequented. Another member, Mr. Bankes, in the absence of a banker, playfully offered the philanthropist a guinea to do so.

Wilberforce, as it happened, was very lucky, and rose the winner of £600. He afterwards declared that the pain he felt at winning so much money from young men who could not afford to lose without inconvenience cured him of all partiality for play.

Goosetree's consisted almost exclusively of budding orators and statesmen, but there was a good deal of gambling there.

One of the largest winners at Brooks's in the days of high play was Alderman Combe, the brewer. One evening, whilst he was Lord Mayor, he chanced to be engaged at a hazard-table there, Beau Brummell being one of the party. " Come, Mash-tub," said Brummell, who was the caster, " what do you set?" " Twenty-five guineas," answered the Alderman. " Well, then," returned the Beau, " have at the '*mare's*' pony." He continued to throw until he drove home the brewer's twelve ponies running ; and then, getting up and making him a low bow, whilst pocketing the cash, he said: " Thank you, Alderman ; for the future I shall never drink any porter but yours." " I wish, sir," replied the brewer, " that every other blackguard in London would tell me the same."

A very successful whist-player at Brooks's was Sir Philip Francis, by some supposed to have written the " Letters of Junius." He had held an appointment in Calcutta, where play flourished, and, devoting his attention to the game, became extraordinarily successful. It was said that his winnings amounted to £30,000, and eventually he was able to return to England a rich man. As a clubman he was noted for his vitriolic utterances.

Sir Philip had been the convivial companion of Fox, and during the short administration of that statesman was made a Knight of the Bath. One evening Roger Wilbraham came up to a whist-table at the club where Sir Philip, who for the first time wore the ribbon of the Order, was engaged in a rubber, and thus accosted him. Laying hold of the ribbon and examining it for some time, he said: " So this is the way they have rewarded you at last; they have given you a little bit of red ribbon for your services, Sir Philip, have they ? A pretty bit of red ribbon to hang about your neck. And that satisfies you, does it ? Now, I wonder what I shall have ? What do you think they will give me, Sir Philip ?"

The newly-made Knight, who had twenty-five guineas depending on the rubber, and who was not very well pleased at the interruption, suddenly turned round, and, looking at him fiercely, exclaimed: "A halter, and be d——d to you!"

Other great whist-players were the two Smiths, father and son, the first a retired Major-General of the Indian Army, who brought home £150,000, and was known as Hyder Ali in the West End. The son was called Tippoo, and, like his father, was a fine whist-player. Indeed, at one time Tippoo Smith was considered the best of his day. Another whist-playing member, an old gentleman nicknamed Neptune, was not so successful; indeed, he once flung himself into the sea in a fit of despair, as it was said, "not being able to keep his head above water." He was, however, fished out in time, and, finding he was still solvent, played on during the remainder of his life.

Even in the days when considerable laxity prevailed as to club elections, Brooks's was very strict in such matters. As a matter of fact, George IV, when Prince of Wales, was the only member of Brooks's who entered the club without being elected by ballot. He was anxious to belong to it in order to have more frequent intercourse with Fox, and on his first appearance every member got up and welcomed him by acclamation.

Fox, soon after he had got to know Sheridan, was so delighted with his company and brilliant conversation that he became exceedingly anxious to get him admitted as a member of this club, which he himself was in the habit of frequenting every night. Sheridan was accordingly proposed, and though on several occasions every gentleman was earnestly canvassed to vote for him, yet he was always found to have one black ball whenever he was balloted for, which was, of course, sufficient to prevent his election.

When Sheridan entered the House of Commons in September, 1780, the members of Fox's party were particularly anxious to get him into the club, which was no easy task, as they well knew. George Selwyn and the Earl of Bessborough, who both hated Sheridan, agreed not to absent themselves during the time allotted by the regulations of the club for ballots; and as one black ball sufficed to exclude a candidate, they twice prevented his election (once in 1778, when proposed by Fox).

This exclusion of Sheridan from Brooks's was the subject of much comment, and, according to one story, some of his friends resolved to find out who the person was that so inveterately opposed the admission of the orator. Accordingly the balls were marked, and old George Selwyn (whose aristocratic prejudices would have induced him to black-ball His Majesty himself, if he could not produce proofs of noble descent for three generations at least) was discovered to be the hostile party. This was told the same evening to Sheridan, who desired that his name might be put up again as usual, and the matter be left entirely in his hands.

The next evening when there happened to be another election, Sheridan arrived at Brooks's, arm in arm with the Prince of Wales, just ten minutes before the balloting began. Being shown into the candidates' waiting-room, the waiter was ordered to tell Mr. Selwyn that the Prince desired to speak with him in the room below-stairs immediately. Selwyn obeyed the summons without delay, and Sheridan entertained him for half an hour with a political story, which interested him very much, but which, of course, was a pure invention.

During this time the ballot proceeded, Sheridan being duly elected. The satisfactory result was announced to the Prince and the successful candidate by the entrance of the waiter, who made the preconcerted signal by stroking his chin with his hand. Sheridan immediately got up, and, apologizing for an absence of a few minutes, told Selwyn "that the Prince would finish the narrative, the end of which he would find very remarkable."

Sheridan then went upstairs, and was formally introduced to the members by Fox, being welcomed in the most flattering manner.

The Prince, however, was left in a very awkward position, for, not having paid much attention to the nonsensical story told by Sheridan to Selwyn, he found himself all at sea. After floundering about for some time, he at last burst out with: "To tell you the truth, I know as little about this infernal story which Sherry has left me to finish as an unborn child; but never mind, Selwyn, let's go upstairs, and I dare say Fox, or some of them, will be able to tell you all about it."

Accordingly the couple proceeded to the club-room, where the puzzled Selwyn soon had his eyes completely opened to the whole manœuvre, when,

8

on his entrance, Sheridan, rising, made him a low bow, and thus addressed him :

" 'Pon my honour, Mr. Selwyn, I beg pardon for being absent so long; but the fact is, I happened to drop into devilish good company. They have just been making me a member without even one black ball, and here I am."

" The devil they have !" exclaimed Selwyn.

" Facts speak for themselves," replied Sheridan ; " and as I know you are very glad of my election, accept my grateful thanks" (pressing his hand on his breast and bowing very low) " for your friendly suffrage. And now, if you will sit down by me, I'll finish my story, for I dare say His Royal Highness has found considerable difficulty in doing so."

At first Selwyn was extremely wroth at the trick which had been played upon him, but before the evening was out he shook hands with Sheridan and welcomed him to the club.

Unfortunately for the reliability of this story, the records of Brooks's show conclusively that, so far as the Prince and Lord Bessborough are concerned, it is without foundation. Sheridan was returned for Stafford, September 12, 1780. Mr. Fitzpatrick proposed him at Brooks's on October 12 in the same year, and he was elected on November 2 ; but Lord Bessborough did not become a member till 1782, nor was the Prince of Wales one till 1783.

Many of Sheridan's *bons mots* were recounted in the club years after his death. During a conversation one day about Lord Henry Petty's projected tax upon iron, one member said that, as there was so much opposition to it, it would be better to raise the proposed sum upon coals. "Hold, my dear fellow!" said Sheridan; "that would be out of the frying-pan into the fire with a vengeance."

On another occasion, Sheridan, having been told that Mr. Gifford, the Editor of the *Quarterly Review*, had boasted of the power of conferring and distributing literary reputation, said: "Yes, and in the present instance I think he has done it so profusely as to have left none for himself."

Another wit at Brooks's was Dunning, Lord Ashburton, a somewhat eccentric member. Though he only lived to the age of fifty-two, and although he was very liberal and extravagant, he had made no less than £150,000 during twenty-five years' practice at the Bar.

In spite of the fact that his name does not appear in the club list, the notorious duellist, George Robert Fitzgerald, who was executed for a cold-blooded murder in 1786, must in a sort of way be regarded as having belonged to the club. He was, however, only in it once, though it was his boast that he had been unanimously chosen a member. The history of this is curious.

Owing to Fitzgerald's well-known duelling propensities, no first-class London club would admit him. Nevertheless, he got Admiral Keith Stewart, who knew that he must fight or comply, to propose him for Brooks's. Accordingly, the duellist went with the Admiral on the day of the election to the club-house, and waited downstairs whilst the ballot was in progress.

The result, a foregone conclusion, was unfavourable to the candidate, not even one white ball being among the black, the Admiral having been among the first to deposit his. Nevertheless, to him it was decided should fall the dangerous task of announcing the result to Fitzgerald. He did not, however, care for such a mission at all.

" I proposed the fellow," said he, " because I knew you would not admit him ; but, by Jove ! I have no inclination to risk my life against that of a madman."

" But, Admiral," replied the Duke of Devonshire, " there being no white ball in the box, he must know that you have blackballed him as well as the rest, and he is sure to call you out in any case."

Eventually it was decided that the waiter should tell Fitzgerald that there was one black ball, and that his name must be put up again if he wished it. In the mean time Fitzgerald had frequently rung the bell to inquire " the state of the poll," and had sent several waiters to ascertain, but none daring to return, Mr. Brooks took the message from the waiter who was descending the staircase, and boldly entered the room with a coffee equipage in his hand.

" Did you call for coffee, sir ?" said Mr. Brooks smartly.

" D—— n your coffee, sir, and you too !" answered Mr. Fitzgerald, in a voice which made the host's blood run cold. " I want to know, sir—and that without one moment's delay, sir—if I am chose yet ?"

" Oh, sir," replied Mr. Brooks, attempting to smile away the appearance of fear, " I beg your pardon, sir, but I was just coming to announce to you, sir, with Admiral Stewart's compliments, sir, that, unfortunately, there was one black ball in the box, sir, and consequently, by the rules of the club, sir, no candidate can be admitted without a new election, sir, which cannot take place, by the standing regulations of the club, sir, until one month from this time, sir."

Thrusting aside Brooks, who protested that non-members might not enter the club rooms, Fitzgerald flew upstairs, and entered the room without any further ceremony than a bow, saying to the members, who indignantly rose at the intrusion: "Your servant, gentlemen; I beg ye will be sated."

Walking up to the fireplace, he thus addressed Admiral Stewart: "So, my dear Admiral, Mr. Brooks informs me that I have been elected three times."

" You have been balloted for, Mr. Fitzgerald, but I am sorry to say you have not been chosen," said Stewart.

" Well, then," replied the duellist, "did you black-ball me ?"

"My good sir," answered the Admiral, "how could you suppose such a thing ?"

"Oh, I supposed no such thing, my dear fellow; I only want to know who it was that dropped the black balls in by accident, as it were."

Fitzgerald now went up to each individual member, and put the same question to all in turn, "Did you blackball me, sir?" until he made the round of the whole club, and in each case he received a reply similar to that of the Admiral. When he had finished his investigations, he thus addressed the whole body: "You see, gentlemen, that, as none of ye have blackballed me, I must be elected—it is Mr. Brooks that has made the mistake. I was convinced it would end in this way, and am only sorry that so much time has been lost as to prevent honourable gentlemen from enjoying each other's company sooner." He then desired the waiter to bring him a bottle of champagne, that he might drink long life to the club and wish them joy of their unanimous election of a "raal gentleman by father and mother, and who never missed his man."

After this nothing more was said by the members, who determined to ignore the presence of their dangerous visitor, who drank three bottles of champagne in enforced silence, for no one would answer him when he spoke. With cool effrontery the latter sat drinking toasts and healths, to the terror of the waiter. At length everyone was much relieved to see him rise and prepare to depart. Before going, however, he took leave with a low bow, at the same time promising to "come earlier next night and have a little more of it." It was then agreed that half a dozen stout constables should be in waiting the next evening to bear him off to the watch-house if he attempted again to intrude, but Mr. Fitzgerald, aware probably of the reception he might get, never did.

The eccentricities of Fighting Fitzgerald bordered closely upon madness, and there is, indeed, reason to think that he was insane. According to the custom of his day, he had in early life been obliged to fight a duel with a man called Swords, who at the first discharge of his pistol had shot off a part of Fitzgerald's skull, materially injuring the fore part of his brain. The consequence was delirium for a considerable time; but those who knew him intimately were of opinion that he was affected by a certain aberration of intellect until the day of his death, for from the period of this wound he became hot-headed, insolent, quarrelsome, cunning, and ferocious.

In the more turbulent days of the past, incidents occurred in clubland which would now be impossible.

On one occasion, about three o'clock in the morning, the Duke of York, Colonel St. Leger, Tom Stepney, and others, came up St. James's Street in very rollicking mood, and, reaching Brooks's, knocked in vain for admission, everyone being asleep. They were determined, however, to get in, and, when the door was at length cautiously held open, rushed into the inner hall. They commenced the destruction of chairs, tables, and chandeliers, and kicked up such a horrible din as might have awakened the dead. Every male and female servant in the establishment now came running towards the hall from all quarters, in a state of semi-nudity, anxious to assist in protecting the house or to escape from the supposed housebreakers. During this riot there was no light, and the uproar made by the maid-servants, who in the confusion rushed into the arms of the intruders, and expected nothing short of immediate violence and murder, was most tremendous.

At length one of the waiters ran for a loaded blunderbuss, which, having been cocked, and poised on an angle of the banisters, he would have discharged amongst the intruders. From doing this, however, he was most providentially deterred by the housekeeper, who, with no other covering than her chemise and flannel petticoat, was fast approaching with a light, which no sooner flashed upon the faces of these midnight disturbers than she exclaimed: " For Heaven's sake, Tom, don't fire ! It is only the Duke of York !" The terror of the servants having vanished by this timely address, the intruding party soon became more peaceable, and were sent home in sedan-chairs to their respective homes.

At that time many a challenge was given and accepted within the club walls. One evening Fox, in the course of conversation, spoke disparagingly of the gunpowder issued by the Government. Adams, who was in some measure responsible for the supply, considered it a reflection, and sent Fox a challenge. Fox went out, and took his station, giving a full front. Adams said : " You must stand sideways." Fox said : " Why, I am as thick one way as the other." " Fire " was given. Adams fired, Fox did not ; and when they said he must, he said : " I'll be d——d if I do ! I have no quarrel." They then advanced to shake hands. Fox said : " Adams, you'd have killed me if it had not been Government powder."

Dandy Raikes, though a member of Brooks's, had never been known to enter the club, till one day in March 1827 he saw Lord Brougham go in, upon which he followed, and grossly insulted him during luncheon, with the result that a challenge became inevitable. Lord Brougham applied to General Ferguson, who had heard part at least of the insulting expressions, to convey a challenge for him to Raikes. This, however, the General peremptorily declined to do, upon the grounds of having been mixed up in so many similar affairs. Brougham eventually got General Sir Robert Wilson to deliver the challenge; but in the mean time he had been taken into custody, carried to Bow Street, and bound over to keep the peace. "This was owing to Jack the Painter, alias Spring Rice, who had been present at the row, and had immediately hastened to Bow Street to inform; his object, no doubt, being not to lose Brougham's vote that night upon that most vital of all subjects, the Catholic question."

The Hon. Frederick Byng, known as "the Poodle," from his curly hair, was a very well-known member of Brooks's. He was one of the hundred additional members selected in 1816 by the special committee, was a prominent figure in London society, and had had many interesting experiences. As a very small boy he had acted as a page of honour to Prince George of Wales at his ill-starred marriage with the Princess Caroline in 1795, and used to relate the curious incident of his being taken to Carlton House to be looked at by the Prince before appointment. He was in Paris in December 1815, and was present at the execution of Marshal Ney.

As an old man, the Poodle was very autocratic in his ways, and something of a bully. He once severely reprimanded a younger member for lighting his cigar beneath the balcony outside the club, which no longer exists. On one occasion Mr. Byng was much disturbed to find seated before the fire in the drawing-room a gentleman who, having pulled off his boots, had rung the bell and asked the waiter for slippers ! It turned out that the perpetrator of this outrage was a new member, an M.P. for some manufacturing constituency, who, of strangely unconventional habits quite unknown to the committee, had been elected without any-one troubling or caring much about him, and who presumably would have been more at home in a commercial room than in the sacred precincts of the club.

Brooks's is connected with an unsolved historical mystery, through one of its members—Mr. Benjamin Bathurst (elected in May 1808)—a diplomatist who disappeared in an unaccountable fashion, whilst on a mission from Vienna to England in 1809, and was never heard of again.

Mr. Bathurst had been sent to Vienna by his relative, Lord Bathurst, at that time Secretary of State for Foreign Affairs. It is believed that the latter sent his kinsman to the Court of Vienna in order to induce Austria to go to war with Napoleon, a mission which was completely successful.

Mr. Bathurst on this account entertained a strong belief that the great Emperor bore him special enmity, and therefore, when the war was over, apprehending, it is said, danger on the road, he resolved to return to London by way of Berlin and North Germany. For this journey he assumed the name of Koch, whilst his private secretary acted as courier, under the name of Fisher.

About midday on November 25, 1809, the two

travellers with a valet arrived at Perleberg, on the route from Berlin to Hamburg, halted at the post-house for refreshments, and ordered fresh horses for the journey to Lenzen, which was the next station. Near the post-house was an inn—the White Swan —to which Bathurst went and ordered an early dinner, the horses not to be put in until he had dined. The White Swan was not far from the gate of the town, through which the road to Hamburg lay, and outside of it was a poor suburb of cottages and artisans' houses. After lunch Bathurst inquired who was in command of the soldiers quartered in the town; and having been directed to his address, he called upon Captain Klitzing, the officer named, and requested that he might be given a guard in the inn, saying that he was a traveller on his way to Hamburg, and that he had strong and well-grounded suspicions that his person was endangered. During this visit it is significant that he showed great signs of agitation and fear. Captain Klitzing, though he laughed at Mr. Bathurst's apprehensions, nevertheless gave him a guard of a couple of soldiers.

When the latter reached the White Swan he countermanded the horses, saying he would not start till night, considering that it would be safer to travel along the dangerous portion of the route by night, when Napoleon's spies would be less likely to be on the alert, and remained in the inn writing and burning papers. At seven o'clock he dismissed his guard, and ordered the horses to be ready at nine. He stood outside the inn, watching his portmanteau being replaced in the carriage, stepped round to the heads of the horses, and disappeared for ever.

After Bathurst's disappearance had been realized—which was not for some time—every effort was made to discover what had become of him. The next morning the river was dragged, outhouses, woods, marshes, ditches were examined, but not a trace could be found ; nor was any trace ever found, except that nearly three weeks later—December 16—two poor women, gathering sticks in a wood, found a pair of breeches which were unquestionably Bathurst's. In the pocket was a paper with writing on it. Two bullet-holes were in the breeches, but no traces of blood about them, which could hardly have been the case had the bullets struck a man wearing them. The paper was a half-finished letter to Mrs. Bathurst, scratched in pencil, stating that he was afraid he would never reach England, and that his ruin would be the work of Count d'Entraigues. Large rewards were offered—£1,000 by the English Government, another £1,000 by the family, and an additional 100 Friedrichs d'or by Prince Frederick of Prussia ; but all was in vain, and from that day to this the fate of Mr. Bathurst remains a mystery.*

No account of Brooks's and its history would be complete without some mention of the Fox Club—a club within a club which holds its meetings in the club-house three or four times in the course of the Parliamentary session, and whose object is to keep alive the memory of probably the most distinguished,

* In December 1910, some woodcutters in the forest of Quitznow, near the spot where the breeches were found, discovered a skeleton which may have been that of Bathurst.

and certainly the most popular, member who has ever belonged to Brooks's—Charles James Fox.

Owing to Fox's love of play, some of his best friends, who would appear to have been inspired by extraordinary affection, were half - ruined in annuities, given by them as securities for him to the Jews. Annuities of Fox and his society to the value of £500,000 a year were at one time advertised to be sold. Walpole wondered what Fox would do when he had sold the estates of all his friends.

He once sat at hazard at Almack's from Tuesday evening, the 4th, till five in the afternoon of Wednesday, the 5th. An hour before he had recovered £12,000 that he had lost, and by dinner, which was at five o'clock, he had ended by losing £11,000. On the Thursday (February 6, 1772) he made a speech on the Thirty-nine Articles, in which one is hardly surprised to hear that he did not shine. That evening he dined at half-past eleven at night, and went to White's, where he drank till seven the next morning; thence to Almack's, where he won £6,000; and between three and four in the afternoon he set out for Newmarket. Well for him that there was no Nonconformist conscience in those days!

Fox during a late club-sitting once sketched out an idea for a kind of new profession, "which was going from horse-race to horse-race, and so by knowing the value and speed of all the horses in England to acquire a certain fortune."

As a youth Fox had received a very lax training from his father, who gave him a large allowance and condoned his extravagances. "Let nothing be done," said his lordship, "to break his spirit; the world will do that for him." At his death, in 1774, he left him £154,000 to pay his debts; it was all hypothecated, and Fox soon became as deeply involved as before.

The chronicle of Fox's financial vicissitudes makes sorry reading—at one time with thousands in his pocket, at another without a shilling to pay his chairmen.

After a run of good luck, Fox would generally make some attempt to liquidate the more pressing of his many liabilities; and on one occasion, when Fortune had been propitious, remembering a long-standing gambling debt which he owed to Sir John Lade, he sent a complimentary card to the latter expressing his desire to discharge the claim. Sir John no sooner saw the money than he called for pen and ink, and began to make some calculations. " What now?" cried Fox. " Only calculating the interest," replied the other. " Are you so?" coolly rejoined Charles James, and pocketed the cash, adding: " I thought it was a debt of honour. As you seem to consider it a trading debt, and as I make it an invariable rule to pay my Jew creditors last, you must wait a little longer for your money."

Fox once played cards with Fitzpatrick at Brooks's from ten o'clock at night till near six o'clock the next morning, a waiter standing by to tell them " whose deal it was," they being too sleepy to know.

The precise circumstances which led to the foundation of the Fox Club are rather obscure, the first recorded dinner having taken place in February 1829, when twenty-three members were present, though "Fox Dinners" seem to have been held previous to that date.

Until 1843 the Fox Club met at the Clarendon, but in that year, on an application signed by sixteen members of the Fox Club, a rule was passed granting permission to that body to use the great room at Brooks's for their meetings. Of these, the first always takes place on the Thursday following the meeting of Parliament, the second and third as may be fixed by the club in the course of the session, and the fourth at Greenwich in July.

No speeches are allowed, and only the four following toasts are given, without "note or comment":

1. " In the memory of Charles James Fox."
2. " Earl Grey and the Reform Bill."
3. " The memory of Lord Holland."

This third toast was added by unanimous resolution on April 24, 1841, and on June 5 following, on motion previously given by Sir Robert Adair and Mr. Clive, £200 were voted from the funds of the club towards the monument proposed to be erected to his memory, now just inside the railings of Holland House, on the Hammersmith Road.

On the pedestal of the monument in question are inscribed the following lines :

> " Nephew of Fox, and friend of Grey,
>   Be this my highest fame :
>   That those who know me best will say,
>   ' He tarnished neither name.'"

4. " To the memory of Lord John Russell "—

added on June 22, 1878, on the motion of Mr. Grenville Berkeley. As originally proposed, the toast was to the memory of "Earl Russell," but at the next meeting it was unanimously carried that the style by which he had been best known should be adopted. This was done with the full approval of Lady Russell, whose wishes in the matter had been consulted.

Before leaving the clubs of St. James's Street, two quaintly-named institutions—the Thatched House and the Cocoa-tree—claim some attention. The latter club-house is remarkable for the golden tree which, spreading through two floors, is visible from the street.

The Cocoa-tree Club originated from the Tory chocolate-house of the same name which flourished in the days of Queen Anne. This was converted into a club, probably before 1746, when the house was the headquarters of the Jacobite party in Parliament. It is thus referred to in the above year by Horace Walpole, in a letter to George Montagu: "The Duke has given Brigadier Mordaunt the Pretender's coach, on condition he rode up to London in it. 'That I will, sir,' said he, 'and drive till it stops of its own accord at the Cocoa-tree.'"

About 1780 very high play prevailed there. Writing to Mann in February of that year, Horace Walpole says: "Within this week there has been a cast at hazard at the Cocoa-tree (in St. James's Street), the difference of which amounted to one hundred and fourscore thousand pounds. Mr. O'Birne, an Irish gamester, had won one hundred thousand pounds of a young Mr. Harvey of Chigwell, just started into an estate by his elder brother's death. O'Birne said: 'You can never pay me.'

' I can,' said the youth ; ' my estate will sell for the debt.' ' No,' was the reply ; ' I will win ten thousand —you shall throw for the odd ninety.' They did, and Harvey won."

Though never as fashionable a resort as White's or Brooks's, the Cocoa-tree was frequented by many aristocratic sportsmen. Here it was that Sir Harry Vane came after the victory of his famous horse Hambletonian in the great match with Mr. Cookson's Diamond in 1799.

" At the Cocoa-tree," wrote Horace Walpole in 1770, " Lord Stavordale, not one-and-twenty, lost eleven thousand last Tuesday, but recovered it by one great hand at hazard. He swore a great oath : ' Now, if I had been playing deep, I might have won millions.' "

Sir Robert Macraith had for several years been head-waiter at the Cocoa-tree, where he was known by the appellation of Bob, and at length rose from that humble situation to the rank of Baronet. He was a clever, good-natured, civil fellow, and greatly liked. When he himself succeeded to the business, he was rather puzzled as to what would be the most appropriate name for his house. George Selwyn calling in one morning, he stated the difficulty to him, saying that he was afraid "Bob's Coffee-house" would sound rather queerly. "Oh no," said George, "just the thing; for then it will be Bob without, and robbing [Robin] within."

Councillor Dunning and Dr. Brocklesby one evening at the Cocoa-tree were conversing on the superfluities of life, and the needless wants which men in society created for their own discomfort.

Selwyn, whose aristocratic notions were such as to look with contempt on occupations of all sorts—on that of a medical man as well as that of a tailor—exclaimed: "Very true, gentlemen; I am myself an example of the justice of your remarks, for I have lived nearly all my life without wanting either a lawyer or a physician."

George Selwyn was an occasional visitor here, and on one occasion happened to be present when a general officer in the American War was describing to the company the phenomena of certain hot and cold springs, which he said he had frequently found quite close to each other, during his campaign in the south-western territory. Just as Selwyn entered the room, he was saying that fish of various sorts abounded in the latter, and that all that those of the army who were fond of fish had to do, after the fatigue of a day's march, in order to provide a dinner, was to angle for a few moments with a string and hook in the cold spring, and, as soon as the bait took, to pull out the fish and pop it in the hot one, where it was boiled in the twinkling of an eye!

This marvellous account operated differently on the several gentlemen present; some were incredulous, others amazed, whilst all agreed that it was exceedingly curious.

"There is nothing at all surprising in the General's narrative, gentlemen," said Selwyn, "and, indeed, I myself can vouch for the truth of it; for when I was in France I was witness to similar phenomena. In Auvergne there are springs similar to those in America, but with this remarkable addition, that there is generally a third, containing hot parsley and butter. Accordingly, the peasants and others who go a-fishing usually carry with them large wooden bowls or ladles, so that, after the fish has been cooked according to the General's receipt, they have a most delicious sauce provided for it at the same moment! You seem to doubt my veracity, gentlemen ; therefore I only beg that those who are incredulous may set out for France as soon as they please, and see the thing with their own eyes."

" But, Mr. Selwyn," said the General, " consider the improbability of parsley and butter."

" I beg your pardon, my good sir," interrupted George ; " I gave you full credit for your story, and you are surely too polite not to believe mine."

A constant frequenter of the Cocoa-tree was the eleventh Duke of Norfolk, who, it may be added, was the first member of the House of Lords to abandon pigtail and hair-powder. Discarding the traditions of his family, he became a nominal Protestant, in order to avoid the political disabilities under which the Roman Catholics of his day suffered. He sat in Parliament, first as Earl of Surrey in the Commons, and afterwards in the Upper House as Duke. A coarse-looking man who looked rather like a butcher, his life was mainly passed in clubs and coffee-houses ; he is, indeed, said to have never been so happy as when dining at the Beefsteak or the Thatched House, or breakfasting or supping at the Cocoa-tree. When under the influence of wine he would say that, "in spite of his having swallowed the Protestant oath, there were, at all events, three good

Catholics in Parliament—Lord Nugent, Gascoyne, and himself," so little store did he set on religion. A very heavy drinker, he could swallow unlimited quantities of wine.

The Duke, in spite of his convivial habits, was very proud of being the head of all the Howards. On one occasion at the Cocoa-tree he declared that it had been his intention to commemorate in 1783 the " tercentenary " anniversary of the creation of his dukedom by giving a dinner at his house in St. James's Square to every person whom he could ascertain to be descended in the male line from the loins of the first Duke. " But having discovered already," he added, " nearly six thousand persons who claimed to be of the family, a great number of whom are in very obscure or indigent circumstances, and believing, as I do, that as many more may be in existence, I have abandoned the design."

The Duke was a constant speaker at public meetings at the Crown and Anchor Tavern, and was deprived of his command of a militia regiment for proposing as a toast, " The People, the Source of Power."

The Thatched House Club probably derives its rural name from an inn which had existed in the days when St. James's was a veritable hospital, and not a palace. When the Court settled at St. James's, it was frequented by persons of fashion, and grew gradually in importance. In 1711 it appears still to have been a very modest hostelry, and even when the Thatched House had grown into a recognized rendezvous of wits, politicians, and men of fashion, Lord Thurlow alluded to it, during one of the debates on the Regency Bill, as the "ale-house." In the days of Pitt and Fox, however, it had become one of the chief taverns at the West End, and had added to its premises a large room for public dinners.

The Thatched House was a favourite resort of Sheridan's. One sharp frosty day, when he was sitting here writing a letter, the Prince of Wales came in and ordered a rump-steak. The day happened to be an excessively cold one, and the Prince ordered a bumper of brandy and water straight away. Having emptied the glass in a twinkling, he called for a second and a third, which also having swallowed, he said, puffing out his cheeks and shrugging his shoulders: "Now I am warm and comfortable ; bring me my steak." The order was instantly obeyed, but before His Royal Highness had eaten the first mouthful Sheridan presented him with the following lines, which greatly increased his good-humour:

> " The Prince came in, and said 'twas cold,
>   Then put to his head the rummer ;
>   Till swallow after swallow came,
>   When he pronounced it summer."

The original Thatched House Tavern was demolished in 1814. The ground-floor front consisted of a range of low-built shops, including that of Rowland, the fashionable hairdresser of Macassar fame. The newer Thatched House Tavern stood on the site of the present Conservative Club, to build which it was pulled down in 1843, when it was moved to another house a few doors nearer to the gate of the palace.

The Thatched House Club will probably be long remembered by lovers of Art as having been the abode of the great collector, the late Mr. George Salting, whose rooms above the club were filled with priceless pictures and *objets d'art*. The Thatched House was, I believe, the only club to which he belonged.

CHAPTER V

CHANGES IN CLUB LIFE AND WAYS

AMONGST the changes which, during the last thirty years, have transformed the West End of London, one of the most salient has been the great increase in the number of clubs. Palatial buildings, each capable of accommodating hundreds of members, now occupy a very great portion of Pall Mall and Piccadilly. Although in other days the latter was by no means a very clubbable thoroughfare, it now, at one end at least, consists largely of clubs, most of them, however, differing widely from those of an older age.

The original conception of a London club was a retreat to which West End men might betake themselves, certain that the troubles and worries of the outside world would not follow into a building which they regarded as a temple of dignified seclusion and repose. Perhaps the best description of a club as it existed in former days was that given by a witty Bishop, who defined it as a place "where women ceased from troubling and the weary were at rest." Another amusing definition was that once given by George Augustus Sala. "A club," said he, "is a weapon used by savages to keep the white woman at a distance."

A club should certainly form a safe retreat from the cares of the world, but it need not necessarily be a shrine of crystallized selfishness.

The aim of club-life should be a sort of defensive alliance tacitly concluded between a number of individuals, all moving in the same sphere of life, against the troubles and perturbations by which humanity is assailed. The fundamental charter of the perfect club ought to be an unassuming, unobtrusive, and unenvious equality.

Within the last twenty-five years or so the spirit of London club-life has entirely changed ; the old-fashioned club-man, whose whole life was bound up with one or other of these institutions, is now, indeed, practically extinct. In the days when the type in question was a feature of the West End, the great majority of men living in that quarter of London had no occupation, or, if they had one, it was of such an easy and accommodating kind as to allow them plenty of spare time for lounging. According to a modern estimate, however, few of the old club-men were rich. The majority usually possessed from four to eight hundred a year, which in the past was considered a comfortable enough income for a bachelor. Living in rooms—a sitting-room and bedroom of a very unluxurious kind, compared with the bachelor flats of to-day—the life of a confirmed frequenter of clubland was uneventful but easy. As a rule, he got up late and lounged about till lunch-time, when he would betake himself to his favourite resort, and remain there till dinner, perhaps indulging in a leisurely stroll in the afternoon. About seven he would return to his rooms, dress, and then go back to his club to dine, after which, except when he went to a party or theatre, he would sit with congenial spirits, often till the small-hours of the morning, a good deal of brandy and soda being incidentally consumed. It must be remembered that there were fewer amusements in those days—no motors, no golf, no restaurants, few theatres, and no palatial music-halls; also, the City had not yet begun to exercise its fascinating and too often costly spell over the inhabitants of the West End of the town.

Strange-looking customers were some of the club-men of that bygone day—old fogies with buff waist-coats, blue coats, and brass buttons; heavy swells with peg-top trousers and long, drooping whiskers; horsy-looking characters with spurs and bespattered riding-boots. No wonder that in a description of a certain club decorated with trophies of the chase there appeared the statement that "many old beasts of members might be seen in the hall." This, of course, arose through the carelessness of a printer.

To realize what most of the old-fashioned West End club-men were like, one has only to turn to the pages of Captain Gronow's "Reminiscences." Writing in 1866, Captain Gronow says:

"How insufferably odious, with a few brilliant exceptions, were the dandies of forty years ago! They were generally middle-aged, some even elderly men, had large appetites, gambled freely, and had no luck; and why they arrogated to themselves the right of setting up their fancied superiority on a self-raised pedestal, and despising their betters,

Heaven only knows. They hated everybody and abused everybody, and would sit together in White's bow-window or the pit-boxes at the Opera. They swore a good deal, never laughed, had their own particular slang, looked hazy after dinner, and had most of them been patronized at one time or other by Brummell or the Prince Regent."

The old-fashioned club-man had comparatively few interests, and even those were of a comparatively narrow kind. His life, indeed, was centred in his club, which often seemed to him the very centre and pivot of the universe.

As compared with those of to-day, the clubs of the past were very primitive in their arrangements, though not a few had that peculiar atmosphere of old-world comfort which is generally lacking in our more hurried and strenuous existence. The clubs of the past were almost without exception sombre and occasionally dingy resorts, entirely devoid of bright-coloured decorations, whilst very few prints or pictures adorned their walls.

When modern improvements were first suggested in clubs, most of the old-fashioned members fought strenuously against them. The introduction of the electric light, for instance, was bitterly opposed; whilst the telephone seemed to not a few of the older generation an attempt to introduce mercantile outposts into the very heart of clubland. The old club-men at first hated, and afterwards feared, the encroachments of business methods into their kingdom. In the heyday of their sway, indeed, few connected with commerce or the City had much chance of being elected to a West End club, and it was only in the seventies of the last century that a few determined scouts contrived to force an entry into the portals through which the vast army of stockbrokers and the like have since surged. At heart the old club-men probably believed that it was undignified for a gentleman to enter any but certain recognized professions, such as the army, navy, or diplomatic service; and the West End was still permeated by the ideas of another age which had only just passed away.

Gradually, as a new and entirely different generation came to the front, the aristocratic traditions which had dominated West End life were discarded, and another kind of club-man began to make his influence felt.

Members of energetic temperament found the atmosphere of idle lassitude which hung about some West End clubs so stifling that a number of them, filled with a desire for exercise, formed what they called a "walking society." One of their favourite excursions was to St. Albans, which they called their halfway house, and to this town they walked backwards and forwards to dinner every Thursday.

Now that the old-fashioned club-man has disappeared, a glance at his ways may not be out of place. Generally a bachelor of the most confirmed kind, his whole life centred in his club, to which he made it a habit to go every day at the same hour, and when possible occupy the same chair, which in course of time was accorded to him as a sort of right.

Often an old-fashioned beau, he was as a rule rather a hard, selfish man, provided by his club with all that he required. Not a few men of this type declined to dine out, because they said they got a better dinner at the club for some ten or twelve shillings than at the best houses in town. " Why," inquired one of them, " should I bore myself with dull society when I can have the comfortable ease of the smoking-room ? If I want to be amused, I go to the theatre ; if I want to read, I go to the library. What have I to do with society," he would ask, with a sneer—"I who have no money, and not even a pretty wife ?" Such an individual was perfectly content with existence. Quiet, comfort, good living, freedom from responsibility and anxiety, were the great objects of his life, "and, begad, you don't get that by marriage," he would remark.

The confirmed club-man of to-day is, perhaps, a shade less cynical, but a variation of the old type still exists, and in most West End clubs, especially those of an old-fashioned sort, there is to be found some member who is generally recognized as an institution of the place.

Such a man is not infrequently the terror of the club servants, upon whom he is ever ready to pounce when there arises the least cause for complaint. He backs his bill remorselessly if the dish which is down for eight o'clock appears a quarter of an hour late, or if the wine-butler makes a mistake about the vintage that is ordered, or the waiter at his table is not perfect in his duties. He knows to a day when everything is in season, and woe betide the steward if at the earliest moment there is no caviare, sufficient supply of plovers' eggs, asparagus, green peas, or new

potatoes. He can tell the exact price of most
things, and instantly checks any attempt on the
part of the club to overcharge. He is the great
authority on club discipline and club etiquette.
Matters outside the club, however, he views with
more or less indifference. Talk to him of some
awful disaster, of some terrible commercial failure,
provided he be not affected by it, of some great
national loss, of the death of some great man, and
his interest will hardly be excited ; but tell him that
an excellent club cook has given notice, or that there
has been a " row " between certain members on a
difference of opinion in the committee, and you will
at once find him an interested and attentive listener.

His daily life is regulated by habits which have
gradually crystallized into an almost undeviating
monotony.

He likes to read the same newspaper in the same
chair in the same place, to write his letters at the
same table, to lunch at the same time, and to have
his dinner served by the same waiter at the same
hour in the same corner of the coffee-room. In such
matters he is the strictest and most staunch of
Conservatives.   Never was there a man whom it is
more easy to find, for one knows the hour to a
moment when he takes his daily stroll, when he
smokes his first cigar, when he lunches, dines, writes
his letters, reads, and goes through the programme
of his thoroughly selfish but not uncomfortable life.
He cares little for society, and, with the exception
of running down for an occasional visit to some
country-house (where he is certain of the cook), or
going to the Riviera for a fortnight, seldom leaves

town. The club is his home, and at heart he dislikes leaving its walls. Unlike the old-fashioned
club-man, however, he is not unaffable to new
members or strangers, and is fully alive to the increased comfort to be obtained from any modern
improvement.

The confirmed frequenter of clubs knows everything that is going on, and imparts such information as he feels inclined to give with none of the
mystery and importance of semi - ignorance, but
simply and naturally. He knows what young women
are going to the altar, and what young men are
going to the dogs ; what people have been prevented
from going to Court, and what spendthrifts are about
to be forced to go through another. He is well
acquainted with the latest good stories about town,
and explains mysterious floating gossip as to
meditated divorces or hushed-up scandals. As a
matter of fact, his conversation is generally amusing,
and occasionally instructive.

The life of such a man, as has been said, is centred
in his club, and he sees members come and go, hears
of their prosperity or ruin, marriages or deaths, with
imperturbable equanimity ; indeed, it would require
an invasion or an earthquake to make him effect any
change in his habits.

So he lunches and dines, dines and lunches, till
the sands of the hourglass have run out, and the
moment comes for him to enter that great club
of which all humanity must perforce become
members.

A few questions will be asked in the club as to
his end, his fortune or lack of fortune ; his witticisms

will linger for a while, and his good or bad points be discussed; but in a year or so he will become as completely forgotten as if he had never been.

As London clubs began to multiply, their gradual increase drew away most of the sporting men from the old hostelries which at one time it had been the fashion to frequent. Theodore Hook alluded to this in some humorous lines:

" If any man loves comfort, and has little cash to buy it, he
    Should get into a crowded club—a most select society;
  While solitude and mutton cutlets serve *infelix uxor*, he
    May have his club (like Hercules), and revel there in luxury.

" Yes, clubs knock houses on the head; e'en Hatchett's can't demolish them;
    Joy grieves to see their magnitude, and Long longs to abolish them.
  The inns are out; hotels for single men scarce can keep alive on it;
    While none but houses that are in the family way thrive on it."

Since those days clubs have multiplied enormously; indeed, almost every profession, every pastime, and every point of view has its club. Whilst most of these institutions are frankly mundane in their aims, a few are very solemn in tone. At one club, for instance, morning and evening prayers are read every day. The club in question was founded for men of very Evangelical views, some of whom, it was wickedly said, were so devout as to demand that a club rule should be passed prohibiting members from entering the coffee-room unless in a " state of grace." Of late years, however, a less severe tone has prevailed amongst its members, many of whom are distinguished men.

Sixty years ago the fact of club membership implied some social position or distinction on the part of the individual. White's, Brooks's, Boodle's, Arthur's, and a few other establishments, constituted really exclusive clubland, and to be elected to them was a matter of no little difficulty. A man of obscure birth, or one unknown to the committee, would have been sure of being blackballed. Clubs were then filled by those who belonged either to the same political party or the same fashionable coterie, the members of which were all more or less known to each other. The Tory patrician belonged to White's; the Whig politician of old family was a member of Brooks's; the country gentleman put his name down at Boodle's or Arthur's; the distinguished lawyer, divine, or man of letters, became a member of the Athenæum; and the soldier, who was a field officer, of the United Service. The membership of such clubs constituted an exclusive circle.

A club was a place in which men wrote letters and met their friends. Beyond being a comfortable lounge, it was of little service to its members.

Many tacitly recognized conventions prevailed in connection with club-life. For instance, it was not then at all the thing to raise one's hat to a lady whom one knew, should she pass the club window. A great many members lunched in the coffee-room with their hats on, whilst in certain clubs evening dress at dinner was obligatory. Some clubs, including Boodle's, even to-day set aside a small apartment, separate from the regular dining-room, for members who prefer to dine in day clothes.

Formerly, it should be added, hats were far more

generally worn in clubs than is now the case. In some it was the traditional custom to wear them at all times and in all parts of the house. At the old " Rag," the practice was said to have survived from the time when the club-house was so cheerless and the funds so limited that the management economized coals, for which reason the members were at great pains to keep themselves warm.

In his own club a man used to be considered as having entirely cut himself off from communication with the outside world, and acknowledging people from the windows by a bow or nod was then quite contrary to club usage, which prescribed an Olympian stare.

At certain of the older clubs a few customs, dating back to the eighteenth century, were up to quite recently still in vogue.

At Arthur's, Boodle's, White's,* and, I think, Brooks's, for instance, change was given in washed silver. The money was first plunged in hot water and cleaned, after which it was placed in a wash-leather bag; this was whirled round in the air at the end of a short cord till all the coins contained in it were dry.

The custom of giving washed silver lasted latest at Arthur's, where it was only abandoned a few years ago. It seems a pity that such a cleanly and hygienic custom should have fallen into disuse.

Another old custom was the house dinner, where members dined together. At White's and Boodle's this function used to be a great feature—highly

* The water from the old well in the courtyard here was supposed to be particularly excellent and healthy, and many members made a daily practice of drinking a glass of it.

appreciated by some of the older, more stingy, or impecunious members. Immemorial custom prescribed that the first four members who put their names down as diners should have dinner "free of cost," and a certain gang of old gentlemen used to make a regular practice of being in these club-houses in good time to inscribe their names.

Wine, of course, had to be paid for, but the most economical contented themselves with table-beer. There was great consternation amongst the " fraternity of free feeders " when, during the early seventies of the last century, these house dinners were abolished.

Some few clubs still retain the snuff-box which once figured on the mantelpiece of every club. In most, however, it has disappeared. Snuff-taking has become obsolete since the triumph of the cigarette—perhaps a more pernicious habit.

The question of smoking has frequently caused great agitation in London clubs. In 1866, for instance, White's, where cigars had not been allowed at all till 1845, was much perturbed concerning tobacco, some of the younger members wishing to be allowed to smoke in the drawing-room, whilst the older ones bitterly opposed such a proposal. A general meeting was held to decide the question, when a number of old gentlemen who had not been seen in the club for years made their appearance, stoutly determined to resist the proposed desecration. " Where do all these old fossils come from ?" inquired a member. " From Kensal Green," was Mr. Alfred Montgomery's reply. " Their hearses, I understand, are waiting to take them back there."

The non-smoking party triumphed, and as an indirect result was founded the Marlborough Club, where, for the first time in the history of West End Clubland, smoking, except in the dining-room, was everywhere allowed.

As a matter of fact, the restrictions as to smoking which still prevail in a number of old-fashioned clubs are for the most part out of date and absurd. At the present time people smoke in ladies' boudoirs, and almost invariably in dining-rooms after dinner. The great restaurants, a large portion of whose clientèle consists of refined ladies, permit smoking everywhere.

Nevertheless, in a number of club morning-rooms, libraries, and sitting-rooms, the resort for the most part of a number of middle-aged men, often of a somewhat derelict-looking type, tobacco is entirely banned.

The whole thing is merely a perpetuation of an out-of-date prejudice. The regulations against smoking which prevail in different clubs clearly demonstrate the small foundation of reason which underlies such restrictions.

The Carlton allows smoking in its library; the Junior Carlton does not. The Conservative Club, on the other hand, has an excéllent rule which permits members to smoke in the morning-room after a certain hour in the morning.

Regulations against smoking in libraries are particularly senseless, as tobacco smoke can have nothing but a beneficial effect upon books, which it has a tendency to preserve.

In old days clubs did not welcome strangers; indeed, it was said that if anyone not a member should fall down in a fit at the door of one or two of the more exclusive clubs, he would be denied even a glass of water. A few clubs allowed visitors, but took care to extend only a cold welcome to them. As a matter of fact, they were usually treated like the members' dogs—they might be left in the hall under proper restraint, but access to any other part of the house, except, perhaps, some cheerless apartment kept as a strangers' dining-room, was forbidden. Of late years, however, all this has been changed except in a very few clubs, such as the Guards', which positively forbids any strangers to enter its doors. Only very recently has Arthur's admitted strangers to dine. The Carlton allows guests only to pass its threshold, but not to go beyond the great hall, and the Athenæum allots them a small room near the entrance, where members may interview their friends. The latter club also allows a member to give a formal dinner-party in the morning-room, converted for the time being into a house dining-room, and here as many as ten guests may be hospitably welcomed. The Travellers' permits strangers to dine, except during the Parliamentary season, whilst the Oxford and Cambridge Club allows six members to entertain two guests apiece. The Garrick is far more liberal, for here a member may introduce three friends to the strangers' coffee-room for dinner, or two for luncheon or supper. Members of this club may also give luncheon-parties to ladies on one day of the week.

As regards the admission of ladies to clubs, it is very doubtful if, according to the strict letter of the law, ladies can be excluded from any institution of this sort which admits strangers, for there is no mention of sex in any book of club rules. Indeed, a member of a certain military club is said once to have brought his wife to dine, and defied the authorities by asking for the book of the rules, in which he triumphantly pointed out that there was no stipulation as to sex.

Not a few clubs in old days were anything but sociable places for young men, who, when elected, were often shy at frequenting them, on account of the stern looks which certain of the older members, who had their particular corners and chairs, were wont to cast at them. Gloomy abodes of misanthropic selfishness some of these clubs seem to have been, where sociability and conversation were at a considerable discount.

Dr. Johnson was probably the most staunch defender of clubs who ever lived; his reply to someone who was rather inclined to decry such institutions is historic. A gentleman venturing one day to say to the learned Doctor that he sometimes wondered at his condescending to attend a club, the latter replied: " Sir, the great chair of a full and pleasant town club is, perhaps, the throne of human felicity."

His, of course, was the day of literary clubs, more suited to the spirit of the eighteenth century than to that of to-day. In modern times most of the literary clubs founded for conversation have been complete failures. So much talking, and nothing said ! Everyone failing, because everyone is attempting ; in a word, nothing of the club feeling, which demands the postponement of our petty self-loves to the general gratification, and strikes only in unison with the feelings and sentiments of all !

A good deal of wine was generally consumed during the symposiums which the great talkers of the past loved. At one meeting-place where a literary club was wont to meet, the landlord was said to keep a special kind of port expressly for such parties, which those who frequented the house christened " the philosopher's port." A cynic declared that in one respect it certainly merited its name, for a good deal of philosophy was necessary to swallow it.

Thackeray, unlike Dr. Johnson, was rather inclined to disparage clubs. Speaking of the town life of a past age, he said : " All that fuddling and boozing shortened the lives and enlarged the waistcoats of the men of that age. They spent many hours of the four-and-twenty, nearly a fourth part of each day, in clubs and coffee-houses, where they dined, drank, and smoked. Wit and news went by word of mouth ; a journal of 1710 contained the very smallest portion of either the one or the other. The chiefs spoke ; the faithful habitués sat around ; strangers came to wonder and to listen. . . . The male society passed over their punch-bowls and tobacco-pipes almost as much time as ladies of that age spent over spadille and manille."

Tom Hood expressed an equally unfavourable view in 1838 :

" One selfish course the Wretches keep ;
    They come at morning chimes ;
To snatch a few short hours of sleep—
    Rise—breakfast—read the *Times*—

> Then take their hats, and post away,
>   Like Clerks or City scrubs,
> And no one sees them all the day—
>   They live, eat, drink, at Clubs !"

Many women regarded such places as dens of iniquity. " I believe that mine will be the fate of Abel," said a devoted wife to her husband one day. " How so ?" inquired the husband. " Because Abel was killed by a club, and your club will kill me if you continue to go to it every night."

Dr. Johnson defined a club as " an assembly of uncertain fellows meeting amidst comfortable surroundings," and in the earliest days, when the club was developing out of the coffee-house as a social institution, its chief attraction lay in the wit of its members and the similarity of their tastes and opinions. Members then were contented with a comparatively simple standard of comfort, and esteemed congenial companionship the best furniture a club could possess ; but with the lapse of years a different spirit began to prevail. In the luxurious palaces of to-day most of the members are very often unknown to one another; such places are, in reality, rather luxurious restaurants and hotels than clubs.

Many clubs now have bedrooms for the use of members ; in a few instances these are let by the year. Such a convenience is highly appreciated, for to a bachelor the advantages of living in a club are very great. Here he may have all the comforts of a private house without its worries, in addition to which every species of modern convenience is at his command.

Latterly a good deal of attention has been devoted

to the decoration of club-houses generally, most of which now contain prints and pictures.

The present being a more or less luxurious age, modern club-men require more pleasing surroundings than their forbears, who asked little beyond comfortable chairs and blazing fires.

Until comparatively recent years, the interior of the great majority of West End clubs was somewhat bare, such attempts at decoration as existed being for the most part confined to feeble designs in stencil, whilst pictures and prints were either few in number or did not exist at all. The furniture was generally of mid-Victorian date— comfortable, though rather heavy in design.

At a certain number of clubs, wax candles were placed upon the dining-tables, and these were very necessary in the days when oil-lamps and gas were the best illuminants procurable. The light of the lamps was not unpleasant, but in some of the rooms lit by gas the heat was often perfectly intolerable.

As an instance of the persistence of club tradition, it may be added that even at the present time, when electricity floods most of the coffee-rooms with light, some clubs still retain the candles which were so useful in the past.

The growth of the club system undoubtedly effected a great revolution in the domestic life of men generally, and especially in that of the younger ones. Married men, accustomed to the refinement and luxury of a club, gradually imported many amenities into their homes, and endeavoured, so far as their means permitted, to reproduce some of the perfections of management as it is found in clubs.

It was, however, in the life of the bachelor that the introduction of this state of affairs caused the greatest change. The solitary lodgings and the tavern dinners were relegated to the limbo of the past. All he now needed was a bedroom, for the club provided him with the rest of his wants. It began to matter little in what dingy street or squalid quarter a man lodged, for the club was his address, and society inquired no further. He did not need to purchase an envelope or a sheet of note-paper throughout the year, for the club provided him with all the stationery he could possibly require. There was no longer any occasion for him to buy a book, a magazine, or newspaper, for in his club he would find a library such as few private houses could furnish, and in the morning-room every news-paper and weekly review that had a respectable circulation.

Here was to be found economy without privation for the man of modest means and small wants, whilst in some clubs even a confirmed sybarite could satisfy his tastes.

The excessively moderate scale of expenditure for which a man can live comfortably at many a club is highly attractive to the parsimonious.

A certain member, as well known for his eco-nomical way as for his vast wealth, made a study of living at the smallest possible cost in the several clubs to which he belonged. It was, for instance, his habit to take full advantage of the privileges to be obtained in return for table-money, and when he dined the table would be covered with pickle-bottles and other things included in such a charge. One evening a fellow-member, noticing this, inquired of the steward the reason why such an array had been collected. " It's for a member, sir," was the reply, " who likes profusion."

The lover of profusion was especially noticeable on account of his unpolished boots, which stupid servants, as he said, were always wanting to wear out by blacking.

A member of several clubs, he once discovered, amongst the rules of a certain old-established one, an ancient and unrepealed rule which laid down that slices of cold ham were to be provided free for any members at their lunch. In high glee, he determined to profit by this, and before long the attention of the committee was called to the quick disappearance of ham after ham, which for a time had furnished a series of Gargantuan meals. The rule, of course, was at once abolished, and the parsimonious member betook himself elsewhere.

Very different in his habits was a witty old gourmet who was always urging the steward to procure luxuries in and out of season. He was especially fond of pâté de foie gras, and made that official promise to get a fine one from Strasbourg. This, however, was a long time in making its appearance ; and after waiting a week or so, the lover of good things became impatient at the delay. Taking the man to task, he reminded him that delays are dangerous, to which the steward replied that he heard pâtés were not good that year. " Nonsense," was the rejoinder, " we will soon put that right. Depend upon it, it is only a false report that has been circulated by some geese."

The same member once had reason for much comical complaint in connection with a pâté which, in this case, had been sent him as a present by a noted connoisseur. Several members of the committee were invited to partake of the delicacy, and they were all agreed as to its peculiar excellence ; as one of them facetiously said, it made one realize that the problem, " Is life worth living ?" was, after all, merely " a question de foi(e)." A few days later, however, what was the surprise of the giver of the feast to receive a reprimand from the committee, calling his attention to the rule which forbade members to bring food into the club !

" Ah," said he, " if I had only told them I was expecting more pâtés, they would have left me alone ; mine was too small, and probably they were annoyed at not having had a second go at it."

Though good-natured and hospitable, this lover of good living was very touchy upon certain gastronomic matters. He did not speak to a friend of his for years owing to the latter's contention that carrots should always be put in a *navarin*—a statement which, the old gourmet declared, placed anyone making it outside the ranks of civilized man.

CHAPTER VI

THE transformation of the West End of London has entailed the destruction of numbers of the old box-like Georgian houses, and when the demand for new clubs arose, the quaint little shops in Pall Mall and St. James's Street—almost the last survival of which is Lock's hat-shop—were gradually demolished, in order to make way for huge edifices of palatial appearance. New political clubs, new professional clubs, new social clubs, sprang into existence, till what was a luxury for the few became a comparative necessity for the many.

In these days rich men often belong to a great number of clubs, and the present writer was told by a well-known cosmopolitan that his subscriptions of this kind amounted at one time to no less than £200 a year. This, however, included various racing and yachting clubs, as well as two or three on the Continent.

There are now clubs accessory to almost every kind of pursuit and sport, and the number increases every year. At the present time London alone possesses more than two hundred, whereas sixty or seventy years ago only about thirty existed. About one hundred have been founded during the

156

past thirty years, dividing between them no fewer than some 120,000 members. At the beginning of the nineteenth century there were probably not more than 1,200 men who belonged to clubs ; at the present day there are probably considerably more than 200,000 !

The revolution as regards clubs in London only commenced about a quarter of a century ago, and has raged with unabated energy ever since till to-day. People in every rank of life have their club, and the social distinction which was formerly attached to membership of a number of these institutions has in consequence sustained a considerable decline, even fashionable West End clubs having lost much of their old prestige.

In consequence of this there would seem to be a somewhat gloomy future in store for some of these formerly exclusive institutions, not a few of which, like old families of ancient lineage, do their best to conceal the straitened condition of their finances, generally produced by paucity of members.

Clubs into which admission could only be gained, twenty or thirty years ago, by those whose names had been on the candidates' book for nine, ten, or even twelve years, are now obliged to elect members put down only a year or two before. In some cases, indeed, it is to be feared that amalgamation with another club is the only policy which will prevent complete extinction and restore healthy vitality   In certain instances, it must be confessed, an apathetic committee, not alive to the changed and changing conditions of club-life, is responsible for the decadence of the institution over which it presides.

An absolute essential to the prosperity of a club is a good committee ; the best of all is that which consists of three elements. In the first place, it should contain two or three well-known men to act as figureheads, their names being a guarantee for the social standing of the club. In the second, one or two members ought to be thoroughly conversant with business matters, and well fitted to deal with the details of club finance. And, lastly, a certain proportion of its members ought to be men well in touch with the life of the club, and therefore thoroughly acquainted with its needs. They should have a wide knowledge of men and social matters, in order to exercise due discrimination in dealing with candidates for election ; and this is especially important in a club where the ordinary members do not take part in the ballot. In these days there are many with axes to grind, and strange things have been done in some West End clubs of late years in order to secure the election of candidates. At times, indeed, certain individuals have become noted for their lack of discretion in proposing individuals whom, for some reason or other, they desired to conciliate. As a matter of fact, the hold which the City has obtained over West End life is largely responsible for the election of many a member to clubs where, thirty or forty years ago, his admission would have been quite out of the question.

In old days everyone in the West End, more or less, knew everyone else ; for society was then a very limited circle compared with what it is to-day, when people come and go with such startling rapidity that it grows increasingly difficult to discover who and what a candidate may be.

Considerable ingenuity has occasionally been exercised in the direction of concealing the antecedents of an undesirable but wealthy candidate.

The election of rich men to a club merely because they are rich has, on occasion, been defended by the vague plea that it is not a bad thing for a club ; as a matter of fact, it is a very bad thing indeed. Whilst a candidate of this sort is usually exceedingly anxious to be elected, it is not unusual, when his aim is achieved, for him to trouble himself no more, his desire having merely been to figure in the list of members. A man of this sort, who had taken infinite trouble to secure election to a certain club, and been successful in his efforts, had no sooner been notified of his membership than he calmly remarked : " Ah, well, I don't suppose I shall use the place, except to wash my hands on my way to the Park !"

It is, indeed, men of moderate means rather than the very rich who use a club most, and who are therefore its principal support. Millionaires and financiers seldom spend much in their clubs, for, possessed of highly trained chefs and luxurious houses, they have naturally little temptation to spend their spare time elsewhere. The pleasures of social intercourse which can be enjoyed at the club are equally easy to obtain at home.

In old days it was exceedingly difficult for men engaged in business to obtain admission to a fashionable West End club.

The son of a famous financier was once up for

election to a fashionable club, and all his friends in the club attended to support him. In those days the ballot took place at night, and as eleven o'clock approached the club became abnormally full ; indeed, members came into the drawing-room, where the election was held, who had not been seen in the club for years. It was, however, soon evident to the proposer and seconder that the crowd of members present had not come to support their candidate. Realizing the situation, they took their stand by the ballot-box, and as each of the strangers stepped up to record his vote, one said to the other : " Here comes another assassin."

At White's, blackballing was carried to such an extreme about the year 1833 that the rules had to be altered, and one blackball was no longer allowed to exclude.

At that time the system of rejection had been carried to a ludicrous pitch. " We must pill that man," a member would say ; " it will do him good." " We really cannot have that fellow," said another ; " I saw him wearing a black tie in the evening." Sometimes there were personal grudges or family quarrels which kept out candidates for years.

In the early part of the last century, Charles Greville and Lord George Bentinck had some difference about a turf transaction. Greville was anxious for the election of Viscount Brackley, after-wards Earl of Ellesmere ; Lord George was equally determined that Viscount Brackley, as Greville's nominee, should remain outside the club. He never failed to attend the ballot and drop in his black ball.

Lord George was accustomed to take his dinner very late. He usually dined at the club at eleven o'clock, at which hour the ballots also took place. On one occasion, when Lord Brackley was up for election, Greville was delighted to find, as he thought, that Lord George was for once absent. "It's all right this time," said he, as the ballot-box was brought to him; "Bentinck's downstairs at dinner, and I shall get Brackley in at last." "Will you?" said a voice near him. He had not noticed Lord George sitting beside him on the sofa.

People who ought to know better sometimes exhibit the most lax conduct in lending their aid to the candidature of disagreeable individuals, whom for some reason or other it may suit them to please. On one occasion the members of a certain somewhat exclusive club were much disgusted at the conduct of a newly-elected member. It was eventually discovered that the objectionable individual had been proposed by a prominent political personage, whose candidate could not very well have been rejected. The matter created great irritation, and it was eventually hinted to the proposer that the new member was anything but popular.

"He's a disagreeable man, I know; but then, you see, it doesn't matter, for I so seldom use the club," was the grossly egotistical reply. No wonder the political party of which this individual is considered one of the shining lights has of late years had a hard struggle to hold its own!

One of the most original reasons for putting down a candidate was that given by a somewhat

11

unpopular member of a certain club. An acquaintance, looking through the candidates' book, observed that a name recently inscribed was that of an individual whom his proposer had always denounced as a regular club bore.

"Why ever did you put him down?" asked the astonished member. "I thought you particularly disliked him."

"Certainly I do," was the reply; "and as, above all things, I wish to prevent his getting in here, I thought the best way of insuring his being pilled would be to propose him myself, being well aware that anyone whom I may support will have but a very slight chance of escaping a good many black balls."

Committee-men are not infrequently placed in a very uncomfortable position when asked by friends to give their support to doubtful candidates. A man of the world, well known for his ingenuity, used to get out of the difficulty by invariably replying: "My dear fellow, you may rely on me to do the proper thing."

With the vast increase of London clubs, an altogether different state of affairs has arisen as regards the numbers of candidates waiting to come up for election, and which in the majority of instances is far less difficult than was formerly the case; few even of the old-established clubs have been able to maintain their ancient exclusiveness.

The Athenæum, Turf, and Travellers' are still, however, not at all easy about electing members. The latter, founded about 1819, in its early days attracted a good deal of notice from the fact that a candidate for admission was required to have been 500 miles distant from London ; and a considerable sensation was once caused by the discovery that several members, who had originally entered their names, had not travelled the prescribed distance. An investigation was made, and the newspapers of the day published lists of places a visit to which was a sufficient qualification for membership of the Travellers'.

In former days, candidates sometimes had to wait for many years before coming up for election. Owing, however, to various causes—of which the chief was, perhaps, the great increase in the number of West End clubs—this period now rarely exceeds two, or at most three, years. The Bath Club is, I believe, an exception, because the facilities for swimming and other exercises which this institution affords to its members (drawn from both sexes) has caused a very large number of names to be inscribed upon its books. In consequence of this, a candidate must now expect a delay of several years before his name comes up for ballot.

At not a few old-established clubs a paucity of candidates has been produced by past injudicious and indiscriminating pilling. Men thinking of joining the club became aware of the fate which might befall them, and so in time the reputation of more than one club for extreme exclusiveness has led from dire necessity to the other extreme of letting in almost anyone willing to join.

Club committees occasionally contain a member who has an innate tendency to blackball everybody ; in such cases a " pill " is always found in the box,

even when the candidate is perfectly eligible. An
individual of this sort was once considerably re-
buffed. During an election it was found that the
minimum quorum of committee - men was not
present, for they were one short. To rectify
matters, a notorious blackballer was hunted up at
his rooms, and told that an election was in progress.
He rushed back to the club, and at once voted, in
most cases putting in a black ball, according to his
wont ; but as his was the only adverse vote, the
rules having been observed, all candidates were
elected. At the Athenæum as many as ninety-
three black balls were once allotted to an unpopular candidate. But the greatest instance
of blackballing probably ever known took place
some years ago at a ladies' club, where one
candidate received three more black balls than
the number of members present—a case of excessive zeal indeed !

At one West End club, where the election of
members was conducted in a somewhat peculiar
manner, a curious incident once happened.

Here the election was by the members in general,
and not by a committee, and the ballot was held in
a room on the left of the entrance hall. At one
time it used to be a regular custom for the friends
of a candidate to hang about the door of this room
canvassing in his favour, whilst, if possible, detain-
ing anyone likely to insert a black ball, by all possible
means. During a certain election, a visitor, coming
to call upon a friend at his club, found himself, on
passing its portals, almost forcibly bustled into this
room, and eventually, thoroughly confused, made

to vote for an individual who would otherwise not have gained admission to the club.

While, as a rule, the resignation of a member or several members on account of their candidates being rejected, or for some other reason, does not affect the prosperity of a club, there have been instances of serious injury being inflicted upon a club's prestige by the defection of some very influential member. Many years ago the prosperity of White's was seriously affected by the displeasure shown by the late King at the continuance of some old-fashioned and absurd regulations as to smoking; and Boodle's, now in such a flourishing condition, was terribly damaged at one time when the late Duke of Beaufort withdrew his name. The black-balling of candidates submitted for election by prominent members occasionally leads to much acrimonious comment, and sometimes causes a number of resignations.

Election or non-election to a club depends in some cases upon many different causes, and a young man about whom nothing is known at all often stands a better chance than a distinguished individual who during his life has made enemies. Occasionally rejection is a compliment.

The resignation of members disappointed at the failure of their candidate is unreasonable, for a club is in reality a republic, where everyone is equal, and no one has any right to level a pistol at the heads of his fellow-members, or of his committee, whilst saying: " Vote for my candidate, or I will leave the club." Such an act is but a revolutionary protest against the equality of club-life. If an influential or popular member supports some candidate, the latter has the advantage of the influence of his support, but there the preference should end. The question really is not whether a particular candidate deserves or does not deserve to be admitted, but whether the club chooses to elect him, and anything beyond this is a breach of those principles which conduce to the prosperity of clubland.

The best method of filling up vacancies in the membership of a club would really be selection rather than election, and there is no valid reason why such a method of recruiting the membership of clubs should not generally prevail. Were such a reasonable system in vogue, no one would be submitted to the barbarous mortification of being rejected. As things are now, anyone who has obtained a reputation is bound to make enemies, and the more widely he is known, the more enemies he is certain to have. Indeed, a prominent individual has often a very bad chance of being elected under the system generally observed, an absurdity emphasized by the fact that the late Mr. Gladstone was once rejected for the club at Biarritz.

Anyone whose life has been passed amidst publicity must have offended many. Some hate him merely because they happen never to have met him, and others because they have done so. Others hate him because their friends do, and others, again, disapprove of him merely on political grounds. It is, indeed, impossible to enumerate the variety of motives which cause people to hate each other with reason, and even without reason. This being so, one may well doubt the expediency of compelling men to undergo the disgrace of being rejected for a club, according to the system which at present prevails. As matters stand now, a candidate's rejection implies that he is unfit to be a member; but in reality, in a large number of cases, it simply means that he is of sufficient importance to have attracted the ill-will, envy, or dislike of a number of people, many of whom know him only by repute.

Another desirable reform, though one which is unlikely ever to be carried out, would consist in investing committees or members with the power of ejection as well as election. There would be little hardship in a rule conferring the right of exclusion in cases of general unpopularity, and this probably would seldom have to be exercised, as the very fact of its existence would act as a check.

Within recent years a good many club committees have shown a tendency in the direction of the multiplication of rules.

The old aristocratic clubs of the past troubled themselves little with regulations and restrictions. In fact, they were excessively lenient. With the gradual incursion of the commercial class into West End life, however, a very different state of affairs has been brought about.

All over Europe, and especially in England, the *bourgeoisie* adore regulating somebody or something, and the tendency remains long after members of this class have entered what are known as fashionable circles, and managed to obtain a hold upon the committees of exclusive clubs. In such a position, not a few of them have added largely to the number of rules, some of which in certain clubs are multi-plied to the point of absolute absurdity.

Occasionally edicts of this kind possess a certain unconscious humour, as is well exemplified in a by-law, still amongst the rules of a certain club, which sets forth that "Members smoking pipes may not sit or stand in the windows."

Whether legally such an edict can be enforced would seem to be very doubtful. It is certainly within the right of a committee to prohibit pipe-smoking altogether, and such a regulation prevails in several clubs ; in many more it is an unwritten law. In rooms, however, in which pipe-smoking is allowed, it is certainly not within the powers of a committee to define exactly where members shall station themselves whilst "blowing their cloud." As a matter of fact, committee-men not infrequently fall into the error of thinking that a club committee can issue any decrees it likes. Such, however, is very far from being the case, and the reports of various lawsuits between individual members and certain committees will show that in the majority of instances the latter have not proved victorious.

If, for instance, the subscription of a club be raised, members who joined before the alteration cannot be compelled to pay more than their original subscription. The great increase in club rules and regulations has sometimes produced confusion as to what members may or may not do—a state of affairs which was non-existent when the older West End clubs were founded.

The nature of the regulations then in vogue may be realized from an inspection of a number of interesting volumes, dating back to 1737, still preserved at White's, in which are inscribed the names of members of the old and new clubs, together with the few rules in force in the eighteenth century.

The books of rules issued in the middle of the last century contain very much the same provisions. The earlier books are entirely in manuscript, some of them elaborately bound; whilst those issued about 1840, though smaller, are beautifully printed, and they still retain a certain air of old-world luxury. The register of members kept by the proprietor of White's about seventy years ago much resembles one of those huge gilt-edged tomes which were in use for registering various matters connected with the Court of Versailles before the French Revolution. The calligraphy in this volume and in some of the earlier club lists is remarkable for its graceful and ornate character. Looking at them, one realizes what an exclusive coterie frequented the old club-house in the days when the aristocracy of England ruled supreme.

West End club committees of old days were extremely conciliatory regarding any minor breach of club law, in many cases straining a point to overlook delinquencies which were not directly injurious to the best interests of the members generally. Considerable laxity existed as to debts incurred in a club, coffee-room accounts extending into three figures being common; some of these were liquidated only at long intervals. Expelling, or even threatening to expel, a member was considered a step of extreme gravity, and one to be avoided by all possible means.

During the last twenty-five years, however, club-life, like everything else, has become " more strenuous," and anyone who habitually breaks the rules is soon made to realize that he must either alter his ways or go.

Committee-men, it should be added, whether good, bad, or indifferent, generally have a rather difficult task, for they are certain to arouse the opposition of some professional grumbler or other who is ever ready to blame. As a matter of fact, very often the best-meant schemes are the most unpopular, and there is a peculiar type of committee-man who often incurs the hostility of members on account of his merits. This is the individual who, possessed of an especial gift for management, takes the direction of a club into his own hands, and, becoming practically an autocrat, resents interference with his policy, which, it may be added, is not infrequently a sound one, for this type of man has generally made club management his hobby. Nevertheless, let him do as well as possible, sooner or later his rule will become unpopular, members disliking the idea of a one-man domination.

It cannot be said that the majority of house committees are in any way zealous about carrying out their functions. Where club cooking and its material are above all criticism, the credit generally lies with the efficient secretary, who in reality runs most clubs.

Some clubs have numberless sub-committees to deal with different details of management—wine committee, cigar committee, and goodness knows what else. It is, however, doubtful whether the united efforts of all the committee-men and sub-committee-men in the world are as successful as those of one dominating individual, who knows exactly what the needs of a club really are, and gets them satisfied. On the whole, the cooking and food in West End clubs is very fair, and in many cases, if some further degree of attention were devoted to minor details, would be above criticism.

A deplorable tendency, however, is the neglect of that old-fashioned English cookery which in perfection is the delight of true gastronomists.

What is wanted in clubs is the very best material properly served and cooked. Alas ! it is to be feared that, with the exception of a very few clubs, the best of everything now goes to the palatial restaurants, who absolutely will not purchase the indifferent meat, game, and vegetables which are foisted upon more easy-going customers.

The craze for elaborate cooking in clubs would appear to have been originated by George IV when Prince Regent. During dinner one evening at Carlton House, the conversation chancing to turn upon club dinners, Sir Thomas Stepney described them as being intensely dull, owing to their eternal joints, beefsteaks, or boiled fowl with oyster sauce, followed by an apple tart. Upon this the Prince, who was much interested, sent for Watier, his own chef, and invited him then and there to take a house and organize a dinner club. Accordingly a club was started at 81 Piccadilly, by Watier ; Madison, the Prince's page, being manager ; and Labourier, one of the cooks from the royal kitchen, chef. It was soon joined by the principal dandies, including Beau Brummell, and became the scene of much high play, chiefly at macao.

Brummell one day, when he had lost a large sum, called to the waiter: "Bring me a flat candlestick and a pistol"; upon which another member, Mr. Hythe, reputed as mad as a hatter, produced a couple of loaded pistols from his pocket, which he placed on the table, coolly saying: "Mr. Brummell, if you wish to put an end to your existence, I am extremely happy to offer you the means without troubling the waiter." During another evening's play, Raikes began to rally Jack Bouverie, brother of Lord Heytesbury, on his bad luck, and the latter took it in such bad part that he threw his play-bowl full of counters at Raikes's head. A great row ensued. Watier's closed about 1819, many of its leading members being then utterly ruined. After this the club-house was run by a set of blacklegs as a common gaming-house, which eventually was taken over by Crockford, who, in partnership with a man named Taylor, set up a very successful hazard bank.

Though Watier's had but a short existence, it lasted long enough to give men about town a taste for elaborate cooking, and no doubt contributed to send many good old English dishes out of fashion.

Owing to the large staff of servants maintained in most clubs, life is rendered very easy for the members, though a certain number are ever complaining of inattention on the part of the servants. These, as a matter of fact, are kept more or less in perpetual motion. On the whole, they are a most civil class of men, and for this reason thoroughly deserve the

Christmas subscription which serves as a sort of gigantic, but quite justifiable, tip. This is a comparatively new institution. It must be realized that club servants are not overpaid, and when upon duty their work is particularly severe. The electric bells never cease ringing until the club closes ; every member expects his wants to command immediate attention, and not a few are capricious and exacting. In some of the big clubs the total of the contributions is considerable—considerably over £500. This seems large, but, as there are over 1,000 members in several clubs, such a sum is only what might be expected.

Club servants are an especial class apart, and some waiters change constantly from club to club. This, of course, is not the case at certain of these institutions, such as the Junior Carlton, which, having a servants' pension fund, attracts the very best class. In all clubs, however, there are generally two or three old and popular servants who are looked upon as regular features of the place.

In the past, certain old retainers often became privileged characters, and presumed upon their position. A waiter named Samuel Spring, having on one occasion to write to George IV, when the latter was Prince of Wales, commenced his letter as follows : "Sam, the waiter at the Cocoa-tree, presents his compliments to the Prince of Wales," etc. His Royal Highness next day saw Sam, and, after noticing the receiving of his note and the freedom of the style, said : " Sam, this may be very well between you and me, but it will not do with the Norfolks and Arundels."

The most important servant in a club is, of course, the hall-porter.   To fill this post to perfection, very exceptional qualities are required.

A hall-porter, in his capacity as a trusted and confidential club servant, is acquainted with many delicate matters, and for this reason should be a man of tact ; he must, besides, discriminate between those visitors a member may wish to see and those to whom the answer " Out of town " must be given, in tones which admit of no further inquiry.   He must ever be on guard, carefully scanning every stranger who passes the club portals, and, like royalty, should possess an unerring and inexhaustible memory for faces.   He must, of course, know every member by sight, and never be obliged to ask his name, even when long absence abroad may have altered his appearance, and rendered him almost unrecognizable to acquaintances of other days.   A good hall-porter, in short, should know everything and everybody.

A Scotch hall-porter—Shand, of the Turf Club —was a great character in his way.   Somewhat blunt and bluff by nature, he was very outspoken about anything which did not meet with his approval, and at times would hazard caustic remarks as to various phases of the club-life.   Shand was possessed of considerable shrewdness and commonsense, and it was sometimes said that in certain matters his advice was better than that of any two first-class lawyers together.   Shand had his likes and dislikes amongst members.   This he made little attempt to conceal, his manner varying in a marked degree.   He was no respecter of persons, but on

account of his shrewdness and many sterling qualities was allowed much latitude.

On one occasion a member, before leaving for the
country, instructed Shand to forward a packet of
photographs when it should arrive. The gentleman
was away two months, but no photographs were
sent to him. On his return to town he went to
the Turf, where, much to his astonishment, he was
handed a proof photograph which had, he found,
arrived six weeks before. Shand was interrogated
as to his reasons for not obeying instructions. " You
said photographs," replied he. " Seeing there was
only one, and knowing you were away with your
wife, I was not going to be such a fool as to
send it."

Many of the old school of club porters rather
despised confirmed bachelors who yielded to the
allurements of matrimony. " No, sir," said one of
these to an inquirer, " Mr.—— don't come here now
as he used; since his marriage his habits ain't reg'lar."

Club porters are very cognizant of the peculiar
ways of members, and quick to notice anything out
of harmony with the general tenor of club-life.
The porter at a club where most of the members
were so old and infirm that quantities of crutches
were left in the hall was genuinely shocked to see
a new member going quickly upstairs.

Failure to recognize faces—which, in justice to
club porters it should be said, is in their case comparatively rare—has on occasion led to serious
consequences.

The hall-porter of a certain great club, quartered
upon another during the autumnal period of renova-

tion, was one day asked by a member who strode hurriedly into the club, "Are there any letters for Mr. X. ?" giving a name in the club list. The porter looked hard at the gentleman, for he could not positively convince himself for the moment that he knew his face as one of the 1,500 members of the club. His gaze, however, was met unflinchingly, and the new arrival's air and appearance generally giving no cause for suspicion, the porter, having eventually concluded that this must be a member who had been out of England for some time, handed over the letters, with which the gentleman retired into the inner recesses of the club.

Half an hour or so later a jeweller arrived and asked for Mr. X., to whom he handed over a valuable piece of jewellery worth several hundreds of pounds, which, he told the hall-porter on leaving, this gentleman (as to whose social position and solvency there could be no question) had ordered two days ago by letter.

In due course Mr. X., after giving instructions that no letters were to be forwarded, departed, taking the piece of jewellery with him.

What was the hall-porter's horror the next morning to find himself confronted by another, and this time a real, Mr. X., who, on being told the story of his double, at once dashed off to Scotland Yard. The first Mr. X., it appeared, was an adroit swindler, who having by some means discovered that the real Mr. X., an exceedingly wealthy man, had ordered a jeweller to meet him at the club with a recent purchase, sent a telegram from the latter saying that the setting would not be completed till the next day, and had then gone to the club and personated this member, who he knew only used it upon rare occasions.

Another more impudent fraud was the case of a discharged club waiter, who, disguising himself in a pair of blue spectacles, actually walked into the club-house from which he had been dismissed two days before, and, giving a well-known member's name, cashed a cheque. He victimized two other clubs in the same manner, and was eventually detected at a fourth.

One of the smaller West End clubs was formerly renowned for its mechanical hall-porter, an individual who had but an arm and a leg, and moved, it was said, entirely by machinery, the creaking of which, people declared, could be heard when he handed out letters.

A word here as to the porters' boxes which now exist in every club. In former days very few, if any, of these institutions contained such a convenience. The porter used to sit in a chair in the hall, with a rack containing the members' letters behind him. He played much the same part as the head-foot-man who opens the door at a private house. As late as the eighties of the last century there was no porter's box at White's, and the same state of affairs prevailed at Boodle's up to quite recent years. In former days, when life was more simple, there was little necessity for the complicated arrangements of bells, telephones, and speaking-tubes, which are essential to the life of a modern club. Members then did not dash in and out, and clubland was distinguished by its air of grave solemnity and calm.

12

CHAPTER VII

LATE SITTINGS—FINES—CARDS—CHARACTERS—
SUPPER CLUBS

AMONGST the changes in club-life in London, perhaps
the most striking is the almost total cessation of the
late sittings in which members formerly indulged.
Various causes have contributed to make people in
the West End of London keep earlier hours, of
which the most notable is that the number of un-
occupied men, who once formed a large proportion
of those living in what is called the fashionable part
of the town, has shrunk to a very small number, if
it has not altogether ceased to exist. In other days
there were plenty of young bachelors with something under a thousand a year who spent their life
in complete idleness. A club was the pivot of their
existence, and here they would often sit till the
small-hours of the morning.

Another cause of early hours is the great popularity of motoring and golf, the widespread indulgence in which does anything but promote a
love of sitting up late.

At the time when a great number of people had
nothing to do all day, not a few regarded the night
as being the most amusing part of their existence,
when they could forgather with choice spirits and

178

sit talking one against the other, as the old phrase had it, " till all was blue."

As illustrating the lateness of the hours formerly kept by members of some West End clubs, a story used to be told about a staid country member who, arriving at one of these institutions, having travelled by a night train, went up to the coffee-room and began to order breakfast, upon which he was told, by a sleepy waiter, that no suppers were served after 6 a.m.

One of the latest sitters was Theodore Hook, so renowned for spontaneous wit. He was very proud of a peculiar receipt of his own for the prevention of exposure to the evil effects of night air. " I was once very ill," said he, " and my doctor gave me particular orders not to expose myself to it ; so I come up (from Fulham) every day to Crockford's, or some other place, to dinner, ever since which I have made it a rule on no account to go home again till about four or five o'clock in the morning."

Those were the days when the closing hours of a number of West End clubs were much later than is at present the case. Now there are seldom many members to be found in a club-house after one, and fines have become rare. Up to about fifteen or twenty years ago, considerable laxity prevailed as to enforcing these penalties which are exacted for sitting up after a certain hour, but the introduction of more business-like habits into West End life has put an end to such a state of affairs. Late sittings at clubs were, of course, in the vast majority of instances, connected with card-playing; and when this pastime was more prevalent than is now the case, some confirmed lovers of whist, and later of bridge, occasionally sat very late indeed.

Whist is now practically an obsolete game, and it is curious to recall that the introduction of short whist was once considered a great innovation. "Major A.," the author of "Short Whist," a book which was famous in the middle of the last century, gives the following account of its origin: "This revolution was occasioned by a worthy Welsh Baronet preferring his lobster for supper hot. Four first-rate whist-players—consequently four great men—adjourned from the House of Commons to Brooks's, and proposed a rubber while the cook was busy. 'The lobster must be hot,' said the Baronet. 'A rubber may last an hour,' said another, 'and the lobster may be cold again or spoiled before we finish.' 'It is too long,' said a third. 'Let us cut it shorter,' said the fourth. Carried *nem. con.* Down they sat, and found it very lively to win or lose so much quicker. Besides furnishing conversation for supper, the thing was new—they were legislators, and had a fine opportunity to exercise their calling."

Another version was supplied by James Clay, who was one of the principal authorities on whist in his day. His account is as follows:

"Some eighty years back, Lord Peterborough having one night lost a large sum of money, the friends with whom he was playing proposed to make the game five points instead of ten, in order to give the loser a chance, at a quicker game, of recovering his loss. The late Mr. Hoare of Bath, a very good whist-player, and without a superior at piquet, was one of this party, and used frequently to tell this story."

Whatever the origin of short whist may have been, the controversy between the advocates of long whist and those who supported the new game was a bitter struggle. Innovators are always hated, and have their characters blackened by those who have grown too old to care for the new, or those who are too unintelligent to do so. The clergy to a man were for long whist.

The laws of whist were first codified in England at the instance of Mr. Baldwin. The Turf Club in 1863 was called the Arlington. The matter was suggested to the committee of the Arlington, and a number of members were appointed to investigate matters and compile a code. These were: George Bentinck, M.P. for West Norfolk; John Bushe, son of the Chief Justice of "Patronage" fame; J. Clay, M.P., chairman; Charles C. Grenville; Sir Rainald Knightley, M.P.; H. B. Mayne, G. Payne, and Colonel Ripon. When completed, the code was submitted to the Portland Club, and a committee of this the chief whist club of the country considered its contents. This committee consisted of H. D. Jones, chairman, the father of the late "Cavendish," who died in 1899; Charles Adams, W. F. Baring, H. Fitzroy, Samuel Petrie, H. M. Riddell, and R. Wheble. It was on April 30, 1864, that the code was officially sanctioned—a red-letter day in the annals of whist.

The triumph of bridge over whist is a matter

of recent social history which will be dealt with later on.

The greatest breach of regulations ever committed was probably that which occurred in a well-known West End club some thirteen or fourteen years ago, when two members sat through the whole night at cards, and became so absorbed in their game that they were still sitting there at the re-opening at nine the next morning. Notwithstanding the arrival of a number of outraged members, they continued playing till one, when, having reluctantly risen from the card-table, they walked out into the sunlight, handing in their resignations as they left. As a matter of fact, the stakes played for were comparatively moderate, and the differences at the close of the séance were consequently small. Both men, it should be added, were confirmed sitters-up, and the abnormal hours kept by them on several previous occasions had called forth remonstrances from the committee. At the majority of London clubs, fines are inflicted on those sitting up after the hours of one-thirty or two, though in some cases they begin earlier or later. In such club-houses as are not definitely closed at two-thirty or three, the fines gradually rise till the hour of five or six o'clock is reached, when any further sojourn in the club-house is punished by expulsion.

The amount to be paid for remaining in certain clubs till the actual time of closing is considerable ; nevertheless there have been instances of members remaining to the very last minute who were not card-players, and merely sat up through indifference or thoughtlessness.

The present writer remembers one member who actually had to pay a fine of £17 for sitting all alone in a club till the doors were closed. This gentleman had a perfect mania for not going to bed, and his habit of keeping the whole club-house going, long after the other members were in bed, eventually caused a complete readjustment of the scale of fines and the adoption of an earlier hour for closing. As a matter of fact, though he paid the heavy fines with perfect complacency, the sums received were not sufficient to cover the expenses of lighting, servants, and the like, for the whole establishment, of course, had to be kept going till it was his pleasure to depart.

In old days, quite a number of club-men would habitually turn night into day; but this is no longer the case, and the few members who still adhere to the habits of another age are generally regarded with little favour by committees. Several clubs, as a matter of fact, have altered their hours entirely to prevent the club-house from being kept open solely for the benefit of one or two members.

Another complaint against late sitters is that the club servants, in consequence of being obliged to keep later hours, are unfitted for their work; but there is really no particular reason why this should be the case, as a different staff comes on duty towards the evening, the members of which, at several clubs, are allotted a certain proportion of any fines.

The latest club of all used formerly to be the Garrick, where, in the days when the late Sir Henry Irving, Mr. Toole, and others, came to supper in the small dining-room, very late or rather very early hours indeed were kept. Within the last few years, late sittings have ceased to be the order of the day except on certain occasions, and new rules have been made, the general tendency of which is to encourage a comparatively early retirement to bed. An exception, however, is made in favour of Saturday night, the traditional evening for suppers at the Garrick.

One of the latest clubs in London used to be the St. James', founded more than forty years ago by the late Marquis d'Azeglio and others. One of the objects for which this club was formed was to provide a meeting-place for secretaries and attachés after balls and parties, and for this reason no fine at all was inflicted before 4 p.m. It may also be added that in former years such fines as did exist were not very rigorously enforced. Quite a different state of affairs, however, now prevails, the whole scale of fines having been readjusted some years ago, owing to which—and other causes—late sittings are now things of the past.

The Beefsteak Club, like the Garrick, once contained quite a number of members who had a great disinclination to go to bed, and who lingered late over the pleasant talk of the supper-table. Here also the spirit of the age has effected a change, for practically all the old school of Beefsteakers, of which that most delightful of men, the late Joseph Knight, was such a brilliant example, are gone, and the hours kept are now very reasonable.

The Turf Club, which used formerly to be full of people after the theatres were closed, is now somewhat deserted at night, and the same state of affairs prevails at practically all the West End clubs.

The late hours once kept by many club-men were in a great measure the cause of the dislike with which a number of old-fashioned, strait-laced people used to regard London clubs, which, as has already been said, were denounced as pernicious resorts where drinking and gaming were by no means unknown. To-day such accusations can no longer with any justice be sustained.

In France, however, the state of affairs as regards gaming, at least, is very different, for, owing to the heavy tax levied by Government upon club funds, no institution of the nature of a club can be prosperously conducted without some amount of gambling. Indeed, most French clubs of any social standing derive a considerable portion of their income from card-money, and not a few permit baccarat, the profits of which, drawn from the Cagnotte, bring in a large sum of money to the club funds. In England, however, except in a few exceptional cases—Crockford's, for instance—no club has ever existed for the avowed purpose of play. To begin with, public opinion has always viewed this pastime (which so often degenerates into a vice) with extremely unfavourable eyes, and no one of any position has cared to be seen openly risking large sums of money upon the turn of a card. In addition to this, any protracted continuance of high play in a club has always been reprobated by a large majority of members as being likely to produce a scandal—and, as a matter of fact, a scandal has almost invariably followed in the wake of high play.

The French, many of whom set aside a certain amount of money to be used for play—a *bourse du jeu*, as it is called—are well aware of the danger of losing their heads at cards ; but the vast majority of Englishmen are soon made nervous and excited when once they have been caught by the fascination of play. For this reason—or some other—a high game never goes on very long without the occurrence of a catastrophe, for sooner or later someone will lose a far larger sum of money than he can either afford or pay. The generality of club members limit their gambling to a mild game of bridge, and there is very little play at anything else now. Some twenty years ago, however, there was a slight epidemic of the gaming fever in the West End of London, and quite a number of so-called " clubs," the only object of which was high play, were started, mostly by shrewd veterans of the sporting world, some of whom remembered the days when hazard had extracted such vast sums from the pockets of careless Corinthians, and when wily Crockford conducted his great Temple of Chance in St. James's Street. Such clubs were, of course, furnished with a committee and an elaborate set of rules, the most respected of which were those relating to the fines. These, after a certain hour, brought much grist to the proprietors' mills. Such clubs were in reality little but miniature casinos, and the main, if not the sole, qualification for membership lay in being possessed of ample funds and a tendency to part with them easily. The chief of these institutions were situated off Piccadilly and St. James's Street, about which the spirit of that reckless speculation which raged in this neighbourhood so fiercely in the eighteenth century has always had a tendency to linger.

Baccarat was the game played at these haunts, and, though everything was quite fairly conducted, the loss of large sums by well-known young men about town eventually attracted considerable comment, and before very long the Park Club was raided by the police, upon which occasion a high legal luminary, it is said, was with the greatest difficulty smuggled out of the place. A celebrated trial, at the end of which baccarat was finally ruled to be an illegal game, resulted in the closing of this club. A somewhat similar institution, the Field Club, rose on its ashes, but this also was eventually raided and put an end to. Since that time one or two small clubs have been formed by a certain number of people desirous of playing bridge or poker for high stakes, but all of them have had a brief existence. The clubs just mentioned, it should be added, were quite different from the gaming clubs of the past, the members being rich men well able to take care of themselves, and the only reason for their cessation was that, as the membership was in every case very limited, they got tired of playing at the game of dog eat dog.

Sixty years ago, and later, there was a good deal of high play in London clubs. During the action for libel brought by Lord de Ros, when he had been accused of cheating at Graham's, one witness admitted that in the course of fifteen years he had won £35,000, chiefly at whist; another said that his winnings averaged £1,600 a year. He generally played from three to five hours daily before dinner, and did not deny often having played all night.

Graham's, 87 St. James's Street, was at that time the headquarters of whist, and here it was said Lord Henry Bentinck invented the " Blue Peter," or call for trumps.

Here Lieutenant-Colonel Aubrey, who declared that, next to winning, losing was the greatest pleasure in the world, is supposed once to have lost £35,000.

Bridge is said to have been first played in London at the Portland in the autumn of 1894, when it was introduced by Lord Brougham.

He was, it is said, playing whist, and, as he dealt the last card, neglected to turn it face upwards. By way of apology he then said : " I'm sorry, but I thought I was playing bridge ;" and by way of explanation he gave a brief description of the new game, which so attracted his fellow-members that it soon took the place of whist.

Bridge, however, had been played long before this in Eastern Europe, and even in Persia, where the present writer perfectly remembers it as a popular game as far back as 1888.

The members of a colony of Greeks, indeed, are said to have played a sort of bridge in Manchester eighteen years before this, though the value of no trumps and of four aces was rather less than is now the case.

The headquarters of bridge is the Portland Club, now located at the corner of St. James's Square. It moved here from Stratford Place, its old original

home having been in Bloomsbury Square. For
everything connected with bridge, as it was
formerly for whist, the Portland is the acknowledged authority as the arbiter of disputes and for
the promulgation of rules. There are about three
hundred members of this club, which admits guests
to dine, after which they may play in a small card-
room specially reserved for their use.

Another card-playing club, which, however,
admits no strangers, is the Baldwin, in Pall Mall
East, which opens at two o'clock in the afternoon.
The stakes here are very small.

Besides these admirably-conducted institutions,
as Theodore Hook wrote, there are several

" Clubs for men upon the turf (I wonder they aren't under
    it) ;
  Clubs where the winning ways of sharper folks pervert the
    use of clubs,
    Where *knaves* will make subscribers cry,
    ' Egad ! this is the *deuce* of clubs.' "

The latter term certainly applied to Crockford's,
which was flourishing when the lines in question
were written. Here the wily proprietor neglected
nothing to attract men of fashion of that day, most
of whose money eventually drifted into his pockets.

Well knowing the value of a first-class cuisine,
he provided every sort of culinary luxury, and took
care that the suppers should be so excellent as to
make his club the resort of all sorts of men about
town, who flocked in about midnight from White's,
Brooks's, and the Opera, to titillate their palates
and try their luck at the hazard-table afterwards.
Many who began cautiously, and risked but little,

by degrees acquired a taste for the excitement of play, and ended by staking large sums, which they generally lost. Some few only were lucky ; a certain young blood, for instance, who one night won the price of his "troop" in the Life Guards, purchased it, and never touched a dice-box again.

If, however, people were more or less sure to lose their money at Crockford's, they were equally certain of getting admirable food at a quite nominal price, and for this reason many men of small means had little reason to complain of the great gambling institution in St. James's Street.

As was once wittily said, a certain text of Scripture exactly applied to the proprietor. This was : "He hath filled the hungry with good things, and the rich he hath sent empty away."

Benjamin Crockford had begun life as a fishmonger near Temple Bar, but, being of a sporting character, was accustomed to stake a few shillings nightly at a low gaming - house kept by George Smith in King's Place ; later, he was lucky in a turf transaction. His first venture as a gaming-house proprietor was the purchase, for £100, of a fourth share in a hell at No. 5, King Street. His partners here were men named Abbott, Austin, and Holdsworth, and their operations were not above suspicion. Afterwards Crockford, in partnership with two others, opened a French hazard bank at 81 Piccadilly, and here again there was foul-play. The bank cleared £200,000 in a very short time ; false dice were found on the premises and exhibited in a shop window in Bond Street for some days, and Crockford was sued by numbers of his victims, but took care to compromise every action before it had entered upon such an acute stage as to entail publicity.

Crockford's patrons were all men of rank and breeding, the utmost decorum was observed, and society at the club was of the most pleasant and fashionable character. There was no smoking-room, and in the summer evenings the habitués of Crockford's used to stand outside in the porch, with their cigars, drinking champagne and seltzer, and looking at the people going home from parties or the Opera. White's, except in the afternoons, was deserted, members naturally going across the way, where there was a first-rate supper with wine of unexceptionable quality provided free of cost.

Crockford was well repaid for his liberality in these matters. By the profits of the hazard-table he realized in the course of a few years the enormous sum of £1,200,000.

Though the days when a certain number of London clubs were merely gaming-houses in disguise have long gone, there still exist club-men whose principal interest is the turf, and these not infrequently are much interested in the tape, around which they congregate when any important race is being run, the while mysterious murmurings and vague vaticinations prevail. Such members are generally young ; with the increase of years they become, for the most part, profoundly indifferent to the expensive question of first, second, or third. A few ardent enthusiasts, however, retain their taste for this form of speculation, in spite of the long and inevitable series of disappointments which are the lot of the vast majority of starting-price backers. Rushing wildly into the club, they fly at once to the tape, generally dashing off to the telephone to put more money into some bookmaker's pocket.

The cricket enthusiast is another great patron of the tape, by which he is either thoroughly depressed or rendered radiant, according to the comparative failure or success of his favourite county. He is generally a very kindly man, of innocent tastes and habits, which speaks well for the humanizing influence of Lord's and the Oval.

Two clubs which are much frequented by the best class of sporting men are the comparatively old-established Raleigh (founded in 1858), in Regent Street, and the newer Badminton (founded in 1876), in Piccadilly, both of them well-managed institutions.

The Raleigh, which has always enjoyed a reputation for its cooking, in its earlier days was the scene of many an amusing prank played by younger members. All this, however, has long been a thing of the past.

A striking change in club-life is the vastly decreased consumption of alcohol. In former days, quite a number of members used every day to imbibe a considerable quantity of pernicious brandy and soda, the excess of which, without doubt, sent so many of the last generation to a premature grave. I do not by any means wish to imply that such men became intoxicated. Thirty or forty years ago, the drinking habits, so prevalent at the beginning of the last century, had already fallen into great disrepute, but brandy and soda was, for some unknown reason, considered a fairly harmless drink, and many club-men imbibed small quantities of it all the day through without in any way showing the slightest effect. Nevertheless, the continuous stream of alcohol insidiously ruined many a fine constitution. Sensible men of the present age study their health far more carefully, and the amount of what are known as "drinks" served daily in the best West End clubs is now very small indeed. On the other hand, "teas," which forty years ago were little indulged in, are taken by almost everyone.

As late as the early seventies of the past century most clubs contained a few members of decidedly bibulous habits. These were often by courtesy known as the "Captain" or "Major," military titles for which a short term of service in the auxiliary forces had scarcely qualified them. They were, however, often original characters, whose occasional eccentricities deserved the good-humoured toleration with which they were viewed.

To-day, however, a very different state of affairs prevails, and even the slightest tendency to habitual excess is seriously resented; a decided stigma, indeed, attaches to anyone even suspected of intemperance, whilst any open demonstration of inebriety would certainly call forth demands for drastic measures being applied to the member indulging in such a breach of unwritten club law.

The great diminution of drinking amongst the more prosperous classes is nowhere more strikingly shown than by the great decrease of club receipts derived from the sale of wine and spirits. On the other hand, the consumption of mineral waters and other non-alcoholic beverages has largely increased.

Within the last two decades there has been a marked tendency in West End clubland to relax the somewhat harsh restrictions formerly in force on Sunday, which in England is so often a day of dulness and gloom, causing one to wonder how Longfellow could ever have described it as "the golden clasp which binds together the volume of the week." At some clubs it is still a very quiet day, no billiards or cards being played by members; but in others "sabbatarian strictness" has been relaxed. In one or two clubs a sort of compromise exists, and members are permitted to play billiards without the services of a marker.

Club customs have, on the whole, changed but little. Curiously enough, in spite of the increase of democratic ways in most West End clubs, the custom of sitting down to dinner in evening dress has tended to increase rather than to diminish. At the same time it must be acknowledged that the greatest freedom is permitted in matters of costume, whilst the smart frock-coat, once so conspicuous in clubland, has practically disappeared. Straw hats and deerstalkers abound on club hat-pegs, and lounge suits are worn throughout the day till dinner; top-hats and black coats have decreased in number.

Almost unlimited freedom now prevails as to choice of dress, and sometimes, perhaps, this licence is carried too far.

In the autumn most members of London clubs become wanderers, their houses being given over to painters and decorators, whilst they receive the hospitality of other clubs. A few, amongst which are the National Liberal and the Garrick, never close ; and, indeed, the membership of the former is too large for this club to be received by any other. The painting and decorating in clubs which never leave their habitations is done by easy stages, one or two rooms at a time being given over to the workmen engaged upon the renovating process which London smoke renders so necessary.

Whilst club-life, on the whole, has become less formal and ceremonious, a certain number of old-established clubs still maintain a grave solemnity of tone, and such institutions generally contain a considerable number of " permanent officials "—the class which, whatever party may nominally be in control, really runs the country.

These men, whose lives are passed at various Government Offices, in course of time acquire a peculiar look and manner, so entirely different from that of ordinary humanity that the careful observer and student of the "permanent official" is irresistibly prompted to inquire whether he can ever have been young ? The cut of his clothes, his walk, his mannerisms, and the stately slowness of his movements, all betoken a life passed amidst Government forms, schedules, and official papers. Everything he does is prompted by routine, even to the ordering of a generally well-chosen and moderate dinner.

As he is perfectly aware of the fact that he belongs to the real ruling caste of the land, the permanent official not unnaturally exudes the dignity which he feels is necessary to his high posi-

tion. One pictures him in a tornado or an earthquake still speaking in the same measured tones,
and briefly asking (for he is generally a man of few
words) who is responsible ?

The permanent official, when married, generally
has a very presentable wife, chosen no doubt, like
his dinner, with a view to not upsetting the even
tenor of his daily round. It is, however, almost
impossible to believe that he has ever been in love.
If he has, any amorous communications penned by
him must, one is sure, have been carefully copied
and docketed for future reference.

Many permanent officials—but not those of the
Foreign Office, who are generally agreeable men of
the world—develop into mere automata, radiating a
sort of orderly gloom.

The majority live to a good age, in latter years
evolving into an even less vivacious type—the
"retired permanent official"— very solemn and
silent, not infrequently pompous, speaking scarcely
at all.

A foreigner of distinction, owing to his official
position, had been made an honorary member of a
well-known London club. The number of permanent officials included in its membership was
such that the club was a veritable Palace of Silence,
and the foreigner, becoming depressed by the per-
vading atmosphere of gloom, one day ventured to
remark to an acquaintance, a retired official of
high rank : " You seem to have little conversation
here." " Meet me to-morrow afternoon at three
o'clock in the smoking-room, and we will have a
talk," was the solemn reply. On the morrow the

foreigner duly repaired to the appointed place and met his friend, who, settling himself upon a comfortable sofa, took out his watch, looked at it, and said: " I am sorry I can only give you twenty-five minutes." For this space of time they talked, or rather the foreigner did, for the other uttered little but an occasional word. Precisely as the clock marked the appointed hour the latter rose, and, somewhat wearily saying good-bye, walked out of the building. Judge of the foreigner's horror the next morning when, on opening his paper, he read that Sir —— ——, his friend of the day before, had fallen down dead in Pall Mall, stricken by cerebral collapse ! The unwonted effort of the previous day's conversation had been too much for the poor man. For years past he had been used to the almost unbroken silence of the club, which with undeviating regularity he was wont to frequent. The foreigner, who felt that he was practically guilty of homicide, declared he would speak no more in English clubs, and would take good care to warn his foreign friends against any similar murderous tactics should they come to England.

In many clubs there is a mysterious member or two, about whom nothing seems to be known. No one can say who he is, what locality gave him birth, or what his available means of subsistence may be. He is the child of mystery, nor does he ever attempt to raise the veil, except when he vaguely alludes to "his people in the North"; but whether he means the North of England or the North of London no one whom he honours with his acquaintance is ever able to discover. Everything about such a man is a mystery, including the circumstances which led to his election.

Whilst eccentricity, for the most part, takes the innocuous form of avoidance of society, there have been people who have suffered from a disquieting love of sociability. Such a one used to make a practice of speaking to all his fellow-members, whether he knew them or not. One day, however, finding himself seated opposite an old gentleman who was reading a newspaper, this individual entirely failed to obtain any answer at all to an incessant flow of talk, so, becoming angry, he at last kicked up his foot and sent the paper flying into its astonished reader's face, the result being that the aggressor very shortly afterwards retired from the club.

It is said that a little leaven leaveneth the whole lump, and it is surprising how disagreeable one cantankerous man who uses his club can make it to those around him. He is always coming upon the scene when not wanted. If you go up to the library, you find him snoring on the sofa, with the very book you have come in search of in his useless grasp. If you dine accidentally at the club, your table is sure to be placed next to his. Are you having a quiet chat with a friend, most assuredly will this wretched being drop in and spoil the conversation. He is always quarrelling with people, and asking you to support his complaints. Such a man has no friends, and the list of his acquaintances is limited.

In past days old members were sometimes very severe in their comments upon newly-elected young

men of whose ways they did not approve.   One of
the latter, just elected to a club, having somehow
incurred the wrath of a certain irascible character,
to his amazement heard him saying: "What an
insupportable cub that fellow is!   What on earth
were the committee doing to elect him!   Why, I'd
give him a pony not to belong now.'   This perturbed the new member, who left the club-house
thinking what course he ought to take, and, as
luck would have it, met on the staircase a member
who bore the well-deserved reputation of being a
thorough man of the world.   Stopping the latter,
he told him of the insulting remark, and inquired
what he ought to do.   "Do?" was the reply;
"why, nothing at present.   After you've used the
club for another month, you'll probably be offered
a hundred!"

In more or less every club there are one or two
solemn-looking members, who are seldom known to
speak to anyone, but spend their time in what is,
or looks like, deep study.   Votaries of almost perpetual silence, they are easily made to frown at the
sound of conversation.   The favourite haunt of such
as these is generally the library, which they regard
as their own domain, and where on no account must
they be disturbed.

One of this class, who in the more expansive
days of his youth, twenty years before, had had a
great friend who, after leaving the University, went
out to live in the East, was one day, according to his
usual wont, reading in the library of his club, when,
to his horror, he heard the door briskly open.   A
robust figure, whose countenance seemed not

entirely unfamiliar, strode up to him, and, seizing his hand heartily, shook it. " Well, old fellow," said the intruder, "it's many a long day since we met. Now let's hear what you have been doing all these years." Without saying a word, the ruffled student raised a warning finger, and pointed at the placard of " Silence " on the mantelpiece.

" I was glad to see the man again," said he afterwards; "but he had no business to break one of our rules."

Another kind of club-man is the irascible pedant, whose idiosyncrasies make conversation almost impossible. He will address you; he will lecture; he will instruct you; but he will not chat with you— conversation with him is a monologue. He is to preach, you are to listen. If you interrupt him, he will look at you as if sincerely pained by your audacity; if you advance an opinion, he will promptly contradict it; and even if you ask him a question upon a subject of which he knows nothing, he will reply at enormous length.

It was a man of this kind who once described Niagara as a horrid place where you couldn't hear the sound of your own voice.

In former days many clubs included amongst their members a privileged joker or two, to whom very great tolerance was extended. This type of individual used to be particularly fond of exercising his propensities at the expense of the most solemn and pompous of his fellow-members, on whom he would play all sorts of childish tricks.

On one occasion, for instance, having got possession of an old gentleman's spectacles, a joker of this kind took out the glasses. When the old man found them again, he was much concerned at not being able to see, and exclaimed : " Why, I've lost my sight !" Thinking, however, that the impediment to vision might be caused by the dirtiness of the glasses, he then took them off to wipe them, but, not feeling anything, became still more frightened, and cried out: " Why, what's happened now ? I've lost my feeling, too !"

Some irrepressible jokers have paid for their love of fun by having to resign their membership. One of them, whose escapades were notorious in London twenty years ago, sitting half asleep in a certain Bohemian club, became very much annoyed at a very red-headed waiter who kept buzzing about his chair. The sight of the fiery locks was eventually too much for this wild spirit, and, darting up and seizing the man, he emptied an inkstand over his head before he could escape.

The result, of course, was expulsion from the club, besides which very substantial compensation was rightly paid to the poor waiter, who complained that he could not go about his work in a parti-coloured condition, and it would take some time before the effects of the ink disappeared.

Members who have developed undue eccentricity occasionally cause uneasiness to their fellow-club-men, for it is sometimes difficult exactly to define the point where personal idiosyncrasies become disquieting to others.

One individual, whom the writer recollects, used to enter a certain club and call for all the back numbers which could be obtained of some weekly paper, and then sit solemnly writing at a table surrounded by pile upon pile of the periodical in question. After about an hour of this, he would gather his papers together, and, striding up to the porter's box, would say : " Please inform the Prime Minister that, after due consideration, I have decided that the Cabinet must resign. I will call next Monday and leave word as to the composition of the new one."

A very eccentric member of one club had a disquieting craze which caused him to walk perpetually up and down stairs. The moment he came in of a morning he started for the top floor, going upstairs with a preoccupied air, as though he had serious business on hand. Arrived at the topmost landing, he would strike his forehead with the absent-minded despair of a short memory, then turn on his heel and run down again. This operation he would repeat many times a day. The installation of a lift was said to have been a sad blow to him ; at first he regarded it with profound distrust, until, with increasing years, he discovered its value, when he became very objectionable to his fellow-members by his excessive use of it.

Another original character who belonged to a well-known club used to spend a considerable time every day contemplating himself in a huge mirror, and bursting into explosive fits of laughter. During the whole of this man's membership he was supposed only to have once spoken to a fellow-member, who, it should be added, was also rather eccentric.

A less misanthropic though highly unconventional club-man used to remain in bed all day, getting up only about seven, when he would go to his club to have dinner, which was really a breakfast. This habit, it was said, had been considerably strengthened by reason of the fact that, having once broken through it, and got up early in order to witness some sporting event, he had on his return found himself minus his watch—a loss which more than ever convinced him of the dangers of early rising.

Eccentric behaviour in a club once led to an amusing election incident.

A well-known character, who had sat for a certain borough for years, got into considerable trouble at his club—a very exclusive one—owing to having one wet day taken off his boots in the smoking-room, and sat warming his stockinged feet before the fire. Complaints were made to the committee, the members of which, highly indignant, at first proposed to turn the offender out. Eventually he escaped that extreme indignity, though he was severely reprimanded.

Shortly after this the culprit, owing to a General Election, found himself obliged to defend his seat against an exceedingly active Radical opponent possessed of much caustic wit.

At this time hustings still existed, and candidates exchanged raillery, amounting occasionally to abuse.

Both candidates happened to have foreign names, and both entreated the electors to give their votes only to a true-born Englishman.

The sitting member was especially bitter, and indulged in uncompromising abuse of his opponent—an alien against whose exotic ways he cautioned the electors.

" Alien indeed !" retorted the other. " Anyhow, I have never been nearly turned out of a club for indecent exposure, like my traducer !"

" Only my boots !" roared out his opponent.

But all was in vain, and the electors, fully convinced that their old member had appeared naked in his club, declined to re-elect him.

About two years ago West End clubs were, it is said, at their worst as regards membership; but since then the tide seems to have turned, and a few then in a parlous state have once more found the path of prosperity.

As a matter of fact, the competition of restaurants has improved the cooking in clubs, and many committees have sensibly come to recognize that an attitude of indifference to modern improvements and the changed needs of members does not conduce to the well-being of the institutions over which they preside.

Then, too, a number of clubs which had been tottering for years have disappeared, with the result that a number of others have gained members. Of late years also, the craze for founding new clubs seems rather to have died away, whilst the fashionable "restaurant clubs," which for a short time seemed likely to become popular features of West End life, have entirely ceased to exist.

The chief of these was the Amphitryon, established some twenty years ago at 41 Albemarle Street, Piccadilly, and presided over by M. Émile

Aoust, once maître d'hôtel at Bignon's in Paris. The object of the club was to provide the attractions of a first-rate French restaurant, which at the same time should be absolutely exclusive. The subscription was three guineas, and no entrance fee was paid by the first 200 members who joined the club, amongst whom were the then Prince of Wales and the Duke of Connaught.

The small club-house was comfortable enough, and the cuisine left little to grumble at. About 700 members were enrolled, and candidates kept flocking in. Members were only allowed to introduce three guests at a time, for the accommodation in the dining-room was very limited.

An inaugural dinner was given to the Prince of Wales, and a highly successful evening was enjoyed by fourteen selected guests at the cost of £120. " Kirsch glacé," one of the *plats* which figured in the menu, is said to have caused some amusement, the *k* being called a misprint for *h*, the first letter of the name of a prominent foreign financier then in great favour with smart society.

The chief faults of this club were its expense and its limited accommodation. A first-class dinner was absurdly expensive, costing close upon £10 a head. In addition to this, the little tables were, on account of the smallness of the premises, so closely packed that intimate conversation was next to impossible. It must be observed, however, that there were private rooms upstairs which could be reserved for dinner-parties, and many were given.

After a short time the Amphitryon closed its doors, and left behind it nothing but the memory of some excellent dinners and a certain number of heavy unpaid bills.

A somewhat similar institution was the Maison Dorée Club, at No. 38 Dover Street. The committee was an influential one, numbering amongst its members the Dukes of St. Albans and Wellington, Lord Breadalbane, Lord Dungarvan, Lord Castletown, Lord Camoys, Lord Lurgan, Prince Henry of Pless, and Lord Suffield. The entrance fee was two guineas, and the annual subscription the same sum. The cuisine was under the management of the Maison Dorée, which was then in the last days of its existence in Paris.

The club - house was almost too elaborately decorated. Gold, indeed, had spread even to the area railings, and the lock of the area door itself was adorned with heavy dull gold! The pantry-maid, it was said, had a solid gold key to open and shut the latter for the convenience of any favoured policeman! On the whole, the building presented a most imposing, if rather gaudy, appearance. The decorations of the dining-room consisted principally of pastoral scenes painted on tapestry panels in the French style, whilst a large glass tea-house overhung the garden, and was supposed to form a highly attractive feature.

The club, however, met with the same fate as the Amphitryon; indeed, it fared a great deal worse, the latter for a time, at least, having been a success, which the Maison Dorée never was. Lingering on in a moribund state, it soon flickered out, its disappearance being followed some time later by that of the parent restaurant in Paris, which, owing to lack of support, ended its career, to the regret of all lovers of high-class gastronomy.

Later on, one or two other restaurants made an attempt to introduce "supper clubs," where members might remain after 12.30, the closing hour which a ridiculous Act of Parliament fixes for all licensed premises. None of these supper clubs, however, proved successful. Quite naturally, people soon became tired of seeing the same faces ; besides, there is nothing that amuses ladies so much as scanning and criticizing the heterogeneous crowds which nightly flock to restaurants after the theatre. Willis's—for a time much frequented by the smart world—was remodelled and spoilt in order to make room for a club of this sort, with the result that an excellent restaurant lost its popularity, and finally disappeared altogether.

Not very many years ago, before the registration of clubs was made compulsory by law, there were many so-called " clubs " in London which were little but revivals of the old night-houses and gaming-hells, though the latter were always subject to occasional raids. Whether the suppression of markedly Bohemian clubs generally was an entirely wise measure seems somewhat doubtful ; the mere hounding of dissipation from one haunt to another effects no good, and in all probability the best plan would have been to tolerate a certain number of such resorts, provided they were orderly and did not constitute a nuisance to the neighbourhood.

The gambling clubs, often run by very shady characters, undoubtedly did considerable harm to numbers of pigeons, who, however, would in most instances have lost their money even had such resorts not existed. The best known of these so-called "clubs," however, were started solely to pillage some rich young dupes who formed the support of such places and their crowd of most dubious members. Clubs of this kind often provided a very luxurious supper free, it being well worth the while of the proprietor to attract anyone likely to keep the place going. As a rule, the individual in question also laid the odds during the afternoon, and some colossal pieces of roguery were not infrequently perpetrated in connection with turf speculation. As late as the early eighties of the last century, young men about town were exposed to every kind of insidious robbery. The more blatant forms of West End brigandage seem now to have abated ; but human nature does not change, and very likely they have merely altered in form.

CHAPTER VIII

THOUGH, as has before been said, the majority of West End clubs have been obliged by force of circumstances to relax the exclusiveness which was formerly one of their most salient features, a few still manage to retain that social prestige which was the pride of quite a number in the past.

A conspicuous instance is the Travellers', a club which from the days of its foundation has always been somewhat capricious in electing members. The list of public men who have been blackballed here is considerable. The late Mr. Cecil Rhodes was rejected in 1895, and at different times the late Lord Sherbrooke, the late Lord Lytton, Lord Randolph Churchill, and other public men have met with the same ill fate.

The Travellers' Club was founded in the second decade of the nineteenth century by Lord Castlereagh, the present club-house being built by Barry in 1832. Considerable amusement was aroused by the qualification for membership (which still exists). This laid down that candidates must have travelled out of the British Isles to a distance of at least 500 miles from London in a straight line.

The supposed partiality of members for exploration was amusingly set forth by Theodore Hook in the following lines :

" The travellers are in Pall Mall, and smoke cigars so cosily,
    And dream they climb the highest Alps, or rove the plains
       of Moselai.
The world for them has nothing new, they have explored
    all parts of it ;
And now they are club-footed ! and they sit and look at
    charts of it."

The club-house would appear to have been little altered since its erection, with the exception that a recess for smokers has been contrived in the entrance hall. The building, it should be added, narrowly escaped destruction on October 24, 1850, when a fire did great damage to the billiard-rooms. These were, by the way, an afterthought, and an addition to the original building ; but they were by no means an improvement upon the first design, for they greatly impaired the beauty of the garden front.

The library at the Travellers' is a delightful room, most admirably designed, with a fine classical frieze. A relic preserved here is Thackeray's chair ; but as the only connection of the great novelist with this club appears to have been a blackballing, the presence of such a memento seems rather strange.

Except the dining-room and the library, the interior of the Travellers' Club is somewhat cold and bare. No pictures decorate its walls, and the general appearance of the place, whilst highly decorous, is hardly calculated to delight the eye.

The Travellers' still clings to certain rules framed

in a more formal age, and smoking is prohibited except in certain rooms. It is rather curious that, in days when ladies tolerate cigarettes in their very boudoirs, not a few clubs should still treat smokers in the same way as prevailed in the days when tobacco was only tolerated in one or two uncomfortable apartments.

Several distinguished men have belonged to this club, the membership of which includes many high Government officials—heads of Departments, Ambassadors, and Chargés d'Affaires. The general tone here is one of solemn tranquillity; and though in former days there was a regular muster of whist-players, which included Talleyrand, no game of cards seems now to be played.

During the season of autumnal renovation the Travellers' extends its hospitality to one or two other clubs. A dashing young soldier, becoming in this way a visitor, and being desirous of playing bridge, called for a couple of packs of cards and a well-known racing paper. To his intense disgust the astounded waiter who took the order, after making inquiry, reported that the cards would have to be obtained from outside, and the Travellers' did not take in the paper asked for.

Though in a certain way a sociable club—for a large proportion of the members are acquainted with one another—the Travellers' is principally given up to reading, dozing, and meditation. Of conversation there is but little.

Another club which was founded during the same epoch as the Travellers' was the Oriental.

A hundred years ago there were several institu-

tions connected with the East in the West End.
Such were the Calcutta Club, the Madras Club, the
Bombay Club, and the China Club, frequented
chiefly by merchants and bankers. These, however, were in reality associations rather than clubs.

The Bombay Club was located at 13 Albemarle
Street, and consisted of one large news-room and
an anteroom. It opened at ten in the morning
and closed at midnight, light refreshments being
obtainable of the porter, whilst smoking was strictly
prohibited.

The need for a regular club-house where Anglo-
Indians and others might meet in comfort gradually
came to be felt, and in July 1824 the Oriental
Club was started at 16 Lower Grosvenor Street.
The original club-house, it may be added, has now
become business premises, being occupied by Messrs.
Collard and Collard. It is said that when the
owner of this house gave it up to the club he sold
some of its furniture and effects to a certain
Mr. Joseph Sedley, afterwards immortalized by
Thackeray as the pseudo - collector of Boggley
Wallah.

The first steward of the Oriental was a Mr.
Pottanco, who had long been employed by Sir
John Malcolm, probably in the East. Members
presented books and pictures, and one, Sir Charles
Forbes, cheered the hearts of the Anglo-Indians
by sometimes sending a fine turtle to be converted
into soup.

The first chairman of the Oriental Club was Sir
John Malcolm, a very popular figure in society.
Sir John was a great talker, on account of which

he had been nicknamed " Bahawder Jaw," it was said, by Canning. There were ten Malcolm brothers, two of them Admirals. All ten seem to have possessed the same characteristic, for when Lord Wellesley was assured by Sir John that he and three brothers had once met together in India, the Governor-General declared it to be " impossible— quite impossible !" Malcolm reiterated his statement. " I repeat it is impossible ; if four Malcolms had come together, we should have heard the noise all over India."

Some of the members of the Oriental Club in old days, no doubt owing to having resided for prolonged periods in the East, had eccentric ways. One member was dissatisfied with the Gruyère cheese, calling it French, not Swiss, and insisted that the waiter who brought it to him should taste it. The waiter demurred, upon which the member complained of his misconduct to the committee. The latter, however, took the waiter's part, rightly conceiving that it was no part of the waiter's duty to act as cheese-taster. In another case, a member removed his boots before the library fire, and presently walked off in his stockinged feet into another room. The library waiter, finding the ownerless boots, took them away, and the member on his return was so greatly annoyed that he stormed at the waiter, speaking to him, according to the waiter's evidence, " very strong." Here again the committee, to whom it was referred, sided with the waiter.

There was no provision for smoking in the original club-house of the Oriental, and permission to smoke within the walls was not accorded for some forty years, although it was a constant source of dispute between opposing factions.

There are about thirty portraits in the Oriental Club; several of them of a high class have been copied for public buildings and institutions in India, where the individuals portrayed passed most of their careers.

The Iron Duke, Lords Clive, Cornwallis, Wellesley, Lake, Hastings, Gough, Warren Hastings, Major-General Stringer Lawrence, Sir John Malcolm, Sir Henry Pottinger, Sir David Ochterlony, and Sir James Outram are amongst the distinguished men whose portraits adorn this club, which also possesses a painting of considerable historical interest, representing the surrender to Marquis Cornwallis of the sons of Tippoo as hostages for the fulfilment of the treaty of 1792. This was painted by Walter Brown in 1793, and presented to the club in 1883 by O. C. V. Aldis, Esq.

Besides paintings and busts which have been presented, there is here a silver snuff-box, the gift of a member, and a handsome silver candelabrum presented to the club by Mr. John Rutherford on the completion of fifty years of membership in 1880.

In the Strangers' Dining-Room hangs a stag-hunt by Snyders, the figures by Rubens. The busts in this club include Sir Henry Taylor, by D. Brucciani; and Sir Jamsetjee Jejeebhoy, by Baron Marochetti; whilst a curious coloured print after P. Carpenter shows the ground of the Calcutta Cricket Club on January 15, 1861. A number of fine heads and sporting trophies presented by members decorate the interior of the house. It should be added that the library at the Oriental, though not a large one, is of considerable interest, as many of its books have been written and presented by members.

Though the St. James' Club, at 106 Piccadilly, was not, like the Travellers' and the Oriental, founded for those who wander far afield, its membership, owing to the club's connection with diplomacy, generally embraces many with an intimate knowledge of foreign countries, and even the Far East.

The club-house of the St. James' was formerly the abode of the Coventry Club, a somewhat Bohemian institution, where there was a good deal of gambling and a free supper. It seems to have been an amusing place, to which many diplomatists belonged. This club was established at 106 Piccadilly—formerly Coventry House—in the early fifties of the last century, and lasted a very short time, being closed in March 1854. In 1860 the house became the residence of Count Flahaut, the French Ambassador, who added the eagles now to be seen amidst the decorations of the dining-room ceiling of the present St. James' Club.

The fine mansion was originally built for Sir Hugh Hunlock by the architect Kent, on the site of the old Greyhound Inn, and was bought by the Earl of Coventry, in 1764, for £10,000, subject to the ground-rent of £75 per annum. Sir Hugh must have found the expenses of completing the house too much for him, for he does not seem ever to have lived there, and, according to tradition, Lord Coventry bought the building before the roof was on.

Nevertheless a relic of Sir Hugh still remains in the area, and may be seen from Piccadilly ; this is a very fine leaden eighteenth-century cistern, which is embellished with some moulding of good design and the letters " H. H., 1761."

It is said that when the house was built it was the only mansion standing west of Devonshire House.

Up to 1889 there were no pictures or engravings in the St. James' Club, but in that year, when considerable additions were made at the back of the building, a number of prints were presented by the various embassies and legations. The most valuable gift received was a water-colour drawing by Turner of the village of Clunie, near Lausanne, given by the late Sir Julian Goldsmid. Some fine heads, a picture by Herbert Schmaltz, and more prints were presented by other members. A certain number of bedrooms exist for the use of the members, and from the point of view of comfort the club leaves very little to be desired.

The principal artistic feature of interest in the house is the magnificent ceiling in the large dining-room, which is enriched with a number of small paintings by Angelica Kauffmann. The centre painting is surrounded by a number of cartouches set amidst a decorative design of considerable artistic merit, probably the work of the brothers Adam.

Here and in the adjoining smaller dining-room (where, most sensibly, smoking is allowed after lunch and dinner) hang modern chandeliers of admirable design. Both rooms were judiciously restored twelve years ago, at which time some fine mahogany doors were rescued from the rubbish heap.

Special features of Coventry House in old days were two octagon rooms, both of which had fine marble mantelpieces (now covered up) immediately beneath windows. The octagon room on the first-floor—a boudoir—was, as its remains still show, a triumph of eighteenth-century ornamentation. Indeed, the exquisite taste exhibited on the walls, over-door, and ceiling, give great cause for regret that such a perfect example of English art should have been defaced in order to form the serving-room which it now is. The carpet had been worked by Barbara, Countess of Coventry, wife of the original owner of the mansion; and when the house ceased to belong to the Coventry family, they took with them this carpet, which in course of time was divided into two, the separate portions going to different branches. The portion belonging to the present Earl was some years ago once more completed by the addition of a new half worked at the School of Art Needlework, and now forms the centre of the drawing-room carpet at Croome.

Worked in cross-stitch, it is of many colours on a neutral-tinted ground; garlands and wreaths tied up with ribbons form part of the design of this curious heirloom, which has been comparatively uninjured by time.

In connection with the St. James' Club, it should be added that, according to tradition, an underground passage once ran beneath Piccadilly into the Park opposite, where the Lady Coventry who has just been mentioned is supposed to have had a garden. This story was probably suggested by the fact that the Ranger's Lodge was nearly opposite, and it is possible that there was some communication between that structure and Coventry House.

The St. James' is one of the most agreeable and sociable clubs in London, and still maintains much of that spirit of vitality which seems within the last two decades to have deserted so many London clubs.

In the early days of the St. James' it was located in Bennett Street, St. James', and was later moved to No. 4 Grafton Street, now the abode of the New Club. This is a fine old house, which still retains some of the features it possessed when it was the residence of Lord Brougham.

In the same house in Bennett Street first originated the Turf Club, which was evolved from the Arlington.

Of the Turf, which is probably the most exclusive club in London, there is little to be said ; for it is of quite modern foundation, and the club-house, though comfortable in the extreme, has no particular interest from an artistic point of view. Like the Athenæum, the Turf employs a design taken from an antique gem on its notepaper, a centaur having very appropriately been chosen.

The lighting of the Turf was formerly by candles set in the chandeliers. The latter still remain, but, now that electric light is used, the candles are no longer lighted.

Another fashionable club is the Marlborough, opposite Marlborough House in Pall Mall. This was originally founded as a club where members should not be restricted in their indulgence in tobacco at a time when a number of regulations as to this habit existed in other clubs. King Edward VII, then Prince of Wales, interested himself in the foundation of the Marlborough Club, having sympathized, it was understood, with the attempt made in 1866 to modify a rule at White's which forbade smoking in the drawing-room. The motion was defeated by a majority of twenty-three votes, for the old school were bitterly opposed to such an innovation. In consequence, the Prince, though remaining an honorary member, ceased to use the club, the newly-founded Marlborough proving more congenial to his tastes.

At the present day the Marlborough is used chiefly as a lunching club. At night, like many other clubs, it is now generally more or less empty.

The club-house, being quite modern, contains little to call for mention. In a former club, however, which stood on the same site, there was in the days of high play a special room downstairs where money-lenders used to interview such members as necessity had made their clients. The room in question was known as the "Jerusalem Chamber."

The club-house of the Isthmian, at No. 105 Piccadilly, has known many vicissitudes. At one time it was the Pulteney Hotel, and afterwards it became the abode of Lord Hertford. Subsequently the house passed into the hands of the late Sir Julian Goldsmid, who possessed an example of the work of every living Royal Academician, as well as masterpieces by Sir Joshua Reynolds and Romney. His collection of works of art was very fine.

In its early days, when the club-house was in

Grafton Street, the Isthmian was nicknamed the "Crèche." It was originally founded as a club for public-school men, and some of its members were very young—a fact which gave rise to the humorous appellation in question. From Grafton Street this club migrated to Walsingham House, where it remained until that short-lived building was pulled down to make way for the palatial Ritz Hotel.

The Isthmian, it should be added, following the example of two or three other modern clubs, reserves a portion of its club-house for the entertainment of ladies, who are allotted a special entrance of their own in Brick Street.

The nickname of the "Crèche" applied to the Isthmian in its early days was rather exceptional in its wit, for most of the attempts at humorous club names have missed their mark. Another amusing instance, however, was a suggested title for the now long-defunct Lotus, an institution which was founded for the lighter forms of social intercourse between ladies of the then flourishing burlesque stage and men about town. This was the "Frou-Frou"—a delicate allusion alike to the principal founder, Mr. Russell, and the fairer portion of the membership.

A pleasant social club which has recently been structurally improved, bedrooms having been added, is the Windham, No. 11 St. James's Square. This club owes its name to the fact that the mansion was once the residence of William Windham, who was considered a model of the true English gentleman of his day. Though William Windham was a great supporter of old English sports, including

OLD MANSIONS IN PICCADILLY, NOW CLUBS.

From a drawing of 1807.

bull-baiting (which he defended with such success in the House of Commons that only after his death could a Bill against it be passed), he was at the same time an accomplished scholar and mathematician. Dr. Johnson, writing of a visit which Windham paid him, said : " Such conversation I shall not have again till I come back to the regions of literature, and there Windham is 'inter stellas luna minores.'"

In this house also lived the accomplished John, Duke of Roxburghe ; and here the Roxburghe Library was sold in 1812. Lord Chief Justice Ellenborough lived in the mansion in 1814, and subsequently it was occupied by the Earl of Blessington, who possessed a fine collection of pictures. The Windham, it should be added, was founded by Lord Nugent for those connected with each other by a common bond of literary or personal acquaintance.

The club-house, which is very comfortable, contains a number of prints, but, as the vast majority of these are modern, they scarcely call for mention.

The Bachelors', at the corner of Piccadilly and Park Lane, is essentially a young man's club. Only bachelors can be elected, and any member who becomes a Benedict must submit himself to the ballot in order to be permitted to remain a member, being also obliged to pay a fine of £25. Ladies may be introduced as visitors, but, it is almost needless to add, their introducer is responsible for his guests being of a standing eligible for presentation at Court.

The same hospitable usage prevails at the Orleans in King Street, a pleasant little club decorated with sporting engravings, which has always prided itself upon the excellence of its cuisine.

The Wellington, like the Bachelors' and Orleans, is another sociable club which offers its members the privilege of entertaining ladies in a portion of the building specially set aside for their use. In the club-house is a collection of fine heads, trophies of the successful big-game shooting expeditions of sporting members.

A long-established non-political club, essentially English in tone, is the Union, at the south-west angle of Trafalgar Square. The original home of this club was Cumberland House, where it was first started in 1805, the chairman then being the Marquis of Headfort. George Raggett, well known as the manager of White's, became club-master in 1807, and at that time the membership was not to be less than 250. The Dukes of Sussex and York, together with Byron and a number of other well-known men, joined the club in 1812. Nine years later it was decided to reconstitute the club and to build a new club-house, and Sir Robert Peel and four other members of the committee selected the present site. By that time the membership had increased to 800, and it was the first members' club in London. The fine club-house in Trafalgar Square, built by Sir Robert Smirke, R.A., was opened in 1824. A most comfortable club, the Union well maintains its long-established reputation for good English fare and carefully selected wines. In old days its haunch of mutton and apple tart were widely celebrated, and many gourmets belonged to it. Amongst these was Sir James Aylott, a two-bottle man, who was one day shocked to observe James Smith (part author of "The Rejected Addresses") with half a pint of sherry before him. After eyeing the modest bottle with contempt, Aylott at last burst out with: "So I see you have taken to those d——d life-preservers!"

Most of the furniture at the Union is that supplied by Dowbiggin, the celebrated upholsterer, seventy or eighty years ago, and there are some good clocks by the royal clockmaker, Vulliamy. A good deal of the club plate is silver bearing the date 1822, and there is a good library. No pictures hang on the walls. The Union has been, ever since its institution, an abode of solid comfort, and it prides itself upon keeping up the old traditions of a London club-house as these were understood a century ago.

Amongst London's political clubs, the Carlton unquestionably takes the first place. Originally founded by the great Duke of Wellington and a few of his most intimate political friends, it was first established in Charles Street, St. James's, in the year 1831. In the following year it removed to larger premises, Lord Kensington's, in Carlton Gardens. In 1836 an entirely new club-house was built in Pall Mall by Sir Robert Smirke, R.A.; this was small, and soon became inadequate to its wants, though a very large addition was made to it in 1846 by Mr. Sydney Smirke, who in 1854 rebuilt the whole house, copying Sansovino's Library of St. Mark at Venice.

This club contains members of every kind of Conservatism, many of them men of high position in fortune and politics.

The Carlton has been the scene of many important political consultations and combinations.

It was in the hall here that Lord Randolph Churchill learnt of the appointment of Mr. Goschen to the Chancellorship of the Exchequer, which, it is said, he had just resigned under the impression that, being the only possible man for the position, he would be begged to reconsider his decision.

He was in the hall with a friend, when a boy came through to put up a slip of telegraphic news. Lord Randolph stopped him and read the telegram, after which he said : " All great men make mistakes ! Napoleon forgot Blücher—I forgot Goschen."

A well-known figure at the Carlton some years ago was Mr. Andrew Montagu, known to his intimate friends as " the Little Squire," whose death created a considerable sensation ; for, as was well known, he had rendered great financial assistance to his party. He had, indeed, played a more important part in the secret history of his own times than was realized by the outside world. It has been asserted that about two millions of his money was out on mortgage—partly advanced to important politicians, and partly distributed amongst institutions connected with Tory organizations. Mr. Montagu was a most generous and open-handed man, and would always use his interest to assist young aspirants to place and position, though he himself cared nothing for these. He was, it is said, frequently offered a peerage ; but as the particular title which he desired was claimed by someone else, to whom it was eventually given, he died plain

Mr. Montagu, which he had been perfectly content to remain.

The library upstairs contains a large number of volumes, and a most complete collection of books necessary to the politician. Smoking is allowed in the larger room, but not in the small library adjoining.

A number of oil-paintings representing celebrated Conservative statesmen decorate the walls of the Carlton. In the large entrance hall are portraits of Lord North, Lord Chatham, Lord Castlereagh, and the great Sir Robert Peel; on the staircase a portrait of the first Lord Cranbrook; whilst the first floor is adorned by fine full-length pictures of the late Lord Salisbury by Sir Hubert Herkomer, and of Lord Abergavenny by Mr. Mark Milbanke. The dining-room at the Carlton also contains several portraits, amongst them Lord Beaconsfield,* after Millais. Mr. Balfour, by Sargent, subscribed for by members, has been added within recent years. Owing to an entirely new scheme of colour decoration, the interior of this club-house is now very much improved. The conversion of the great central hall into a comfortable carpeted lounge with chairs is also an innovation of a most convenient kind.

The Carlton possesses a quantity of good silver, and in the way of comfort stands in front of almost all clubs in the world. Nowhere, perhaps, are the minor details of everyday life so well looked after ; every kind of notepaper is at the command of members, whilst the facilities for reference are un-

* One of the dining-room chairs bears the inscription : Lord Beaconsfield's chair."

15

equalled. This club has a fine library, which is presided over by a librarian.

Perhaps the most prosperous club in London is the Junior Carlton, which owns its own freehold. The property is said to be worth over £200,000. This palatial club-house is modern in style, but in a small room off the hall is a fine old mantelpiece, which was originally in one of the houses pulled down to make way for the new building.

Statues of Lord Beaconsfield and the fourteenth Earl of Derby decorate the hall, whilst the pictures in the club-house include full-length portraits of the late Queen Victoria by Sir Hubert Herkomer. and of the late King Edward by the Hon. A. Stuart-Wortley. This was painted when the King was Prince of Wales. In the smoking-room hang portraits of Lord Beaconsfield, Lord Derby, Lord Abergavenny, the Iron Duke, and other statesmen. A few pictures also hang on the staircase and elsewhere.

The picture of the Duke of Wellington originally represented him standing in the House of Lords, but for some reason or other the background of benches was painted out by the artist. Within recent years, however, the Upper Chamber has once more asserted itself by bursting through the coat of paint.

The library at the Junior Carlton Club is one of the most delightful rooms in London—an abode of restful peace which was highly appreciated by the late Lord Salisbury, who was often to be observed here reading. It was said that he frequented this room because he was sure of finding undisturbed quiet. Huge placards, on which are printed the word " SILENCE," are on each of the mantelpieces, and the reposeful atmosphere of the place is seldom troubled by any sound louder than footfalls on the soft carpet or the turning over of book-leaves.

A round table in this club, used for private dinner-parties, is said to be the biggest in London ; twenty-five people can sit at it.

The Conservative Club, which occupies a portion of the site of the old Thatched House Tavern (pulled down in 1843), 74 St. James's Street, was designed by Sydney Smirke and George Basevi, 1845. The upper portion is Corinthian, with columns and pilasters, and a frieze sculptured with the imperial crown and oak wreaths ; the lower order is Roman-Doric, and the wings are slightly advanced, with an enriched entrance porch north and a bay - window south. The interior was painted in colour by Mr. Sang, by whom, after long years, it has since been redecorated. This happened a few years ago, when, after considerable discussion, it was decided to restore the original scheme of decoration which some little time before had been discarded in favour of plain white marble.

A bust of the late Queen Victoria is on the landing of the very handsome staircase of the Conservative Club, and on the first-floor are other busts, together with a full-length statue of Lord Beaconsfield. A picture of the Piazza San Marco at Venice, by Canaletto, hangs in the large smoking-room upstairs.

A feature of this club is the excellent library,

which is especially rich in county histories. It is a quiet, restful room, and has everything necessary to render it an ideal resort for lovers of books.

The dining-tables in the Conservative Club date from its foundation, and are of mahogany. The pleasing old custom of removing the tablecloth after dinner still prevails. Unfortunately, about eleven years ago the great majority of these little tables were sent to have their surfaces planed down ! The committee of that day (who must have been totally devoid of any vestige of taste) were of opinion that the surface was becoming too " old-looking." The result is, that it will require a great number of years before these tables regain the beautiful *patine* which still distinguishes those— about eight in number—which happily escaped renovation.

The Devonshire Club, in St. James's Street, though originally a Liberal or rather a Whig Club, now includes many shades of opinion, Liberal Unionists being plentiful. There is a good library here. The club-house, it is interesting to remember, was once a magnificent Temple of Chance, over which presided the celebrated Crockford.

The present building is, with some alterations, the same as the one constructed in 1827—on the site of three houses then demolished—for the famous ex-fishmonger by the brothers Wyatt. The decorations alone, it is said, cost £94,000, and consist of two wings and a centre, with four Corinthian pilasters and entablature, and a balustrade throughout ; the ground - floor has Venetian windows, and the upper story large

CROCKFORD'S IN 1828.
From a drawing by T. H. Shepherd.

French windows. The entrance hall has a screen of Roman-Ionic scagliola columns with gilt capitals, and a cupola of gilding and stained glass. The staircase was panelled with scagliola, and enriched with Corinthian columns. The grand drawing-room was in the style of Louis Quatorze, as it was understood at that day; its ceiling had enrichments of bronze-gilt, with door paintings à la Watteau. Upon the opening of the club-house, it was described as "the New Pandemonium." The gambling-room (now the dining-room of the Devonshire Club) consisted of four chambers: the first an anteroom, opening to a saloon embellished to a high degree; out of it a small curiously-formed cabinet or boudoir, opening to the supper-room. All these rooms were panelled in the most gorgeous manner, spaces being adorned with mirrors, silk or gold enrichments, and the ceilings as gorgeous as the walls. A billiard-room on the upper floor completed the number of apartments professedly dedicated to the use of the members. Whenever any secret manœuvre was to be carried on, there were smaller and more retired places, whose walls might be relied upon to tell no tales.

Crockford, next to the late M. Blanc, of Monte Carlo fame, was probably the most efficient manager of a gambling establishment who ever existed.

He possessed great tact, and thoroughly understood how to humour his clients, most of whose money eventually drifted into his pockets.

A newly-elected member one night, during a lull in play, jokingly said to Crockford: " I will bet a sovereign against the choice of your pictures, of which there are many hanging round the walls, that I throw in six mains." To this he consented. The member took the box, and threw in seven times successively, and then walked round the room to make his selection. There was a St. Cecilia, by Westall, which he had before admired, and that he chose, which of course provoked a good deal of laughter. Other members then followed his example; the result being that they won several of the oil - paintings, which they bore triumphantly away.

The cook, Louis Eustache Ude, was celebrated throughout Europe, as was his successor Francatelli. Crockford's policy was to run his establishment on the most luxurious lines, making no profit except on the gambling; and therefore the dinners, though perfect, were very reasonable in price. In addition, all the dainties of the season, fish, flesh, and fowl, were cooked after the most approved Parisian models, and were tortured into shapes that defied recognition. One of the favourite dishes was Boudin de cerises à la Bentinck—cherry pudding without the stones—which was named after Lord George, a frequent visitor to the club. No one was charged for ale or porter, until one day a hungry member dined off the joint and drank three pints of bottled ale, after which Crockford made a change in the charges, with the remark that "a glass or two was all very well, but three pints were too much of a good thing."

On one occasion, in the list of game on August 10, appeared some grouse. The Marquis of Queensberry, a great sportsman, summoned Ude to Bow Street, and had him fined for infringing the Game Laws. The following day Lord Queensberry looked at the bill of fare, and no grouse appeared in it. He was about to sit down to dinner, when a friend came in, who proposed joining him. Each selected his own dishes. When they were served, there was a slight hesitation in Ude's manner, but they attributed it to the fine he had recently paid. An entrée followed some excellent soup and fish, Ude saying, "This is my lord's," uncovering a dish containing a mutton cutlet à la soubise, "and this Sir John's," placing the latter as far from the noble Marquis as possible. "Have a cutlet," said Lord Queensberry. The Baronet assented. "And you in return can have some of my entrée." At last it came to the moment when Sir John's dish was to be uncovered. "What on earth is this?" asked Ude's prosecutor, as he took up a leg of the salmis; "it cannot be partridge or pheasant; bring the bill of fare." The waiter obeyed. "Why, what does this mean? 'Salmis de fruit défendu!' —grouse, I verily believe." Ude apologized, declaring that the grouse had been in the house before he was summoned. The Marquis chose to believe his statement, and allowed the matter to drop.

Some members were very particular and trying to the patience of the world-famed French cook. At one period of his presidency, the ground of a complaint formally addressed to the committee was that there was an admixture of onion in the soubise. This chef was sensitive as to complaints.

Colonel Damer, happening to enter Crockford's one evening to dine early, found Ude walking up and down in a towering passion, and naturally inquired what was the matter. "No matter, Monsieur le Colonel! Did you see that gentleman who has just gone out? Well, he ordered a red mullet for his dinner. I made him a delicious little sauce with my own hands. The price of the mullet was marked as two shillings, and I asked sixpence for the sauce; this he refuses to pay. The imbecile must think that the red mullets come out of the sea with my sauce in their pockets."

The Devonshire Club possesses some relics of Crockford's in the shape of an etching by R. Seymour, which hangs in the corridor smoking-room, where are also six of the original chairs used in the old gaming-room. The etching of Crockford was presented by Captain Shean; the chairs, in 1902, by another member—Mr. T. J. Barratt.

The Reform Club, in Pall Mall, took its name from the great Reform movement, which it was founded to promote, in opposition to the Carlton. Its virtual founder and first chairman was Edward Ellice, who drew his wealth from the Hudson Bay Company, and his political influence from his long representation of Coventry and from his energy in supporting Reform. It was said that he had more to do with the passing of the Reform Bill of 1832 than any other man. The club was established in 1836, to be a nursery of the great political idea which that Bill represented. For a few years it was domiciled in Gwydyr House, Whitehall. At the house in Pall Mall, some years previously, the

INTERIOR OF THE REFORM CLUB.
From a drawing of 1841.

temporary National Gallery had remained in the house of Mr. Angerstein, whose pictures were the nucleus of the national collection. While, therefore, the Reform Club was rising to accommodate its members, the National Gallery was being built in Trafalgar Square to receive the pictures.

The architect of the new building was instructed to do his best to produce a club-house finer than any yet built. The Reform is mostly Italian in style, copied by Barry in some respects from the Farnese Palace at Rome, designed by Michael Angelo. The chief feature of the interior is a hall running up to the top of the building, an Italian cortile surrounded by a colonnade, half Ionic and half Corinthian. The Reform is about the only one of the older clubs which provides bedrooms for its members—a convenience much appreciated by members.

Let into the walls of this hall are a number of portraits of Liberal politicians of the past. Amongst them are Bright and Palmerston. There are also some busts of former great lights of the party, such as Mr. Gladstone. A graceful statue of Elektra is another conspicuous ornament of this well-proportioned hall.

Like the Carlton, the Reform Club possesses a quantity of silver plate, dating from the time of its foundation.

The kitchen of the Reform was long presided over by Alexis Soyer, one of the great cooks of history. He came to England on a visit to his brother, who was chef to the old Duke of Cambridge, son of George III, and afterwards was cook to

several noblemen, till eventually appointed chef of
the club. Soyer created a great sensation in
culinary circles by introducing steam and gas. He
cooked some famous political banquets for the club,
among them a dinner to O'Connell, another to
Ibrahim Pasha, and a third to Lord Palmerston.
Soyer, indeed, became quite a public character,
being sent to Ireland during the great famine, to
teach the starving people how to dine on little or
nothing; and at the worst period of the Crimean
winter it was hoped he might make amends for a
defective commissariat.

Madame Soyer was as clever as her husband in
another line: a woman of considerable artistic
attainments, she painted quite prettily in water-
colours.

Both she and the great chef sleep their last sleep
in Kensal Green Cemetery, where a sort of mauso-
leum bears the appropriate inscription: "Soyer
tranquil."

One of the Reform Club's triumphs was the
breakfast given there on the occasion of the
Queen's Coronation, which won high commenda-
tion. The excellent cooking imparted celebrity to
the great political banquets given at the Reform.

Soyer was a man of discrimination, taste, and
genius. He was led to conceive the idea of his
great book on cookery—"Gastronomic Regenera-
tion"—he declared, by observing in the elegant
library of an accomplished nobleman the works of
Shakespeare, Milton, and Johnson, in gorgeous
bindings, but wholly dust-clad and overlooked,
while a book on cookery bore every indication of

being daily consulted and revered. "This is fame," exclaimed Soyer, seizing the happy inference, and forthwith seized his pen.

John Bright was often at the Reform, where it was said he passed his time indulging in billiards and abstaining from wine. Other well-known men who were members were Douglas Jerrold, Sala, William Black, James Payn, and Thackeray, who became a member in 1840. He used to stand in the smoking-room, his back to the fire, his legs rather wide apart, his hands thrust into his trousers pockets, and his head stiffly thrown backward, while he joined in the talk of the men occupying the semicircle of chairs in front of him. It is said that on one occasion, observing beans and bacon on the evening dinner list, he cancelled without hesitation a dinner engagement elsewhere, on the ground that "he had met an old friend he had not seen for many a long day."

At one time a small group of men, which Bernal Osborne nicknamed "the press gang," met daily for lunch at a table in one of the windows looking out upon the gardens in front of Carlton Terrace. This group was originally composed of James Payn and William Black, J. R. Robinson of the *Daily News*, J. C. Parkinson, and Sir T. Wemyss Reid, but as time went on others joined. At these luncheons there was always a great deal of pleasant and harmless chaff, with some more serious talk, although by mutual agreement politics were generally tabooed. James Payn was the life and soul of the party, and dedicated one of the best of his novels—"By Proxy"—to the group which he had so often enlivened. Another lively spirit here was William Black, who, though not as brilliant a talker as Payn, could cap his jests with an epigram or quaint joke of much flavour.

Bernal Osborne occasionally attended these lunches, where, however, he curbed that mordant wit which was known to all and feared by most. At the Reform lunches he was always harmless, though unable to resist referring to Black's habit of drinking a pint of champagne at luncheon. He would point to the bottle, and say: " Young man, in ten years' time you will not be doing that." Ten years later, however, Black recalled Bernal Osborne's warnings, and dwelt with pride upon the fact that he had survived his censor.

The very large political clubs, such as the Constitutional, the Junior Constitutional, and the National Liberal, hardly come within the scope of this book. It may, however, be mentioned that, whilst the National Liberal has an ingeniously contrived system (the idea of which was originally conceived by Mr. Arthur Williams, sometime M.P. for Glamorgan) whereby very young men are attracted to join the club, nothing of the sort seems to have been attempted by any similar institution purporting to further the spread of Conservative principles.

CHAPTER IX

THE NATIONAL — OXFORD AND CAMBRIDGE —
UNITED UNIVERSITY—NEW UNIVERSITY—NEW
OXFORD AND CAMBRIDGE—UNITED SERVICE—
ARMY AND NAVY—NAVAL AND MILITARY—
GUARDS—ROYAL NAVAL CLUB—CALEDONIAN
—JUNIOR ATHENÆUM

ABOUT the most valuable artistic possession owned
by any London club is the fine set of Flemish
tapestries in the drawing-room of the National Club,
1 Whitehall Gardens. These were acquired with the
club-house in 1845 from Lord Ailsa, who had bought
them in Belgium shortly after Waterloo. The
price paid was very moderate—£200—and at the
present time the tapestries in question are in all
probability worth over ten times as much.

A curious and interesting feature at the National
is the building which now serves as a billiard-room;
careful inspection reveals that in the days before
the construction of the Thames Embankment this
was a boat-house, up to which water flowed. An
old member of the club perfectly remembers barges
coming up the river and unloading the bricks with
which an additional story was built.

The National Club was originally founded for
those holding strongly Evangelical views; the late

Lord Shaftesbury, of philanthropic fame, was a member, and to it some staunch pillars of Protestantism still belong. Of recent years a number of Government officials and literary men have somewhat relieved the austerity of tone which formerly prevailed, but the National yet adheres to most of the practices instituted at its foundation, and remains the only club where morning and evening prayers are regularly read.

The tone of the National is rather more intellectual than that of the majority of West End clubs. It somewhat resembles that of the grave institutions frequented by Deans and Bishops, where the membership is limited to those who have been at one of the great Universities.

Of such clubs, the best known is the Oxford and Cambridge, which was originally started, in 1830, at a meeting presided over by Lord Palmerston at the British Coffee-house, in Cockspur Street. The club's first home was a house in St. James's Square, where it remained till suitable premises were built, in 1836-37, on the Crown property in Pall Mall. These premises it still occupies. The architects were Sir Robert Smirke and his brother Sydney, who produced an imposing façade on Pall Mall, with very rich ornamental details. In panels over the upper windows, seven in number, are arranged several bas-reliefs, executed by Mr. Nicholl, who was also employed on those of the Fitzwilliam Museum at Cambridge. The subject of that at the east end of the building is Homer; then follow Bacon and Shakespeare. The centre panel contains a group of Apollo and the Muses, with Minerva on his right hand, and a female, personifying the fountain Hippocrene, on his left.   The three remaining panels represent Milton, Newton, and Virgil.

In addition to many ordinary amenities of club-life, two chief attractions here are the fine library and the excellent cellar, which enjoys a well-deserved reputation for fine claret.

The United University Club, the entrance of which is in Suffolk Street, Pall Mall, was originally housed in a building constructed by W. Wilkins, R.A., and J. P. Gandy, in 1826.   An upper floor, with a smoking-room, was added in 1852.   A few years ago, however, the club-house was entirely rebuilt from designs by Blomfield, the new club-house being a sort of compromise between the Adam and Louis Seize styles.   A feature of this club is the very interesting collection of Oxford University Calendars, with ornately engraved views and scenes, many of them highly picturesque and quaint.   The smoking-room also contains a number of views of colleges, whilst in the dining-room hang portraits in oil of the first Duke of Wellington, Lord Melbourne, and Mr. Gladstone.   Membership of this club is limited to 1,000—500 of the University of Oxford, and 500 of the University of Cambridge.

This was Mr. Gladstone's favourite club, where he might sometimes have been seen partaking of a simple dinner, his attention divided between a chop and some learned work.

Members of this club must have taken a degree at one of the two great Universities, and many distinguished men have belonged to it—the Church and the Bar being generally well represented.

The New University Club, in St. James's Street, built by Alfred Waterhouse, R.A., in 1868, and the New Oxford and Cambridge, in Pall Mall, are also flourishing institutions, which, however, do not appear to contain any pictures or *objets d'art* of conspicuous interest.

Amongst the most important clubs of London are those used by the military. In old days most officers spent a good deal of time in London, many leading a life of luxurious ease. A curious incident illustrating this occurred in 1858.

In that year, on the occasion of one of the regiments of the Life Guards being ordered to take part in a course of instruction at Aldershot, a wealthy Captain tendered his resignation. The Commander-in-Chief, however, declined to accept it, and eventually the gallant Captain was persuaded by his Colonel to remain in the regiment, and undergo for a short period the vicissitudes of camp life. At that time it was with some difficulty that officers could be obtained for the Household Cavalry, for to be a military man was often much the same thing as being a man of pleasure. Clubs were thronged with officers at certain times of the year. Though this state of affairs has passed away, the service clubs still retain their popularity. Excellent management distinguishes these institutions, of which the first to be established was the United Service. This was founded in May 1831, as the General Military Club for naval and military officers, by Sir Thomas Graham (afterwards Lord Lynedoch), Lord Hill, and some other officers. Naval men, however, were admitted in the following year,

when the name was changed.   At first it was only
open to officers of field rank, beginning with a
Major in the army, and the corresponding rank of
Commander in the navy.   The club's original abode
was in Charles Street, St. James's ; the site of the
present premises in Pall Mall was obtained ten
years later on a ninety years' lease from the Crown.
The old club-house was then sold to the new Junior
United Service Club for £17,442, which considerable sum went to defray the cost of the new building in Pall Mall.   This, with furniture, amounted
to £49,743.   Nash was the architect, and it was
finished in November 1828.   An addition was made
about 1858 by the acquisition of the lease of the
adjoining site, the sum of £34,000 being spent in
connecting it with the older house and adapting it
for the purposes of a club.

The club-house is a fine building with a classical
portico in the front facing Pall Mall.   The interior
is well planned, and is a good specimen of the
style popular in Nash's day.   The Senior and
Junior United Service, with the Army and Navy,
or "Rag," once received the three nicknames
of "Cripplegate," "Billingsgate," and "Hell-
gate"—the first from the prevailing advanced
years and infirmity of its members ; the second on
account of the supposed tendencies of certain officers
who followed the traditions of the army which
"swore in Flanders"; and the last from its love of
high play.

The United Service contains many interesting
pictures and some statuary, the most striking
example of which, in the entrance hall, is a colossal

16

bust of the Duke of Wellington, by Pistrucci. Six other busts represent Lord Seaton, by G. G. Adam; King William IV, by Joseph; Nelson, by Flaxman; Sir Henry Keppel, by H.S.H. Prince Victor of Hohenlohe - Langenburg; and Lieutenant-General Lord Cardigan, by Marochetti (the gift of his widow). The sculptor of the sixth bust, representing Admiral Sir Thomas M. Hardy, Bart., is unknown.

The pictures in the morning-, coffee-, and smoking-rooms include the following portraits: Admiral Viscount Exmouth (a copy by S. Lane, after Lawrence); General Sir John Moore (a copy by W. Robinson, after Lawrence); Major-General Charles G. Gordon, by Dickinson, from a photograph; Field-Marshal Lord Raglan, by F. Grant; Field-Marshal Lord Clyde (a copy by Graves, after F. Grant); Admiral Lord Rodney (a copy by Bullock, after Reynolds); Field-Marshal H.R.H. the Duke of Cambridge, by A. S. Cope, A.R.A.; Field-Marshal Sir John F. Burgoyne, by Graves, from a photograph; Field-Marshal Viscount Combermere, by W. Ross; Charles, fifth Duke of Richmond, K.G., by A. Baccani; John, first Duke of Marlborough, by Sir G. Kneller; Field-Marshal the Marquis of Anglesey (a copy by W. Ross, after Lawrence); General Lord Lynedoch, by Sir T. Lawrence; Admiral Lord de Saumarez, by S. Lane; General Sir James Macdonell (a copy by Say); Admiral Earl St. Vincent, by Sir W. Beechey; Admiral Sir Thomas Troubridge, Bart., by S. Drummond; Earl de Grey, by H. W. Pickersgill; Field-Marshal Viscount Gough, by Sir F. Grant,

R.A.; Lieutenant-General Lord Saltoun, by Sir T. Lawrence; Vice-Admiral Sir Francis Drake (a copy by Lane from an original in the possession of the donor, Sir T. T. Drake); General Sir Ralph Abercrombie, by Colvin Smith; Admiral of the Fleet Sir George Cockburn, by T. Mackay; Field-Marshal Sir Edward Blakeney, by Catterson Smith, R.H.A.; General Viscount Beresford, by Reuben Sayers; Field-Marshal Lord Seaton, by W. Fisher; General Hon. Sir G. Lowry Cole (a copy by Harrison after Lawrence); Admiral Sir Pulteney Malcolm (a copy by Dickinson, after Lane); General Sir J. Frederick Love, by A. Baccani; Field-Marshal Lord Strathnairn, by Bassano, from a photograph; Admiral Viscount Keith (a copy by Hayes, after Saunders); Admiral Sir Charles Napier, by J. M. Joy; General George Augustus Elliott, Lord Heathfield (a copy by S. Lane, after Sir T. Reynolds); Admiral Earl Howe (a copy by J. Harrison); the Emperor Napoleon I, by an unknown artist (the gift of Colonel Bivar); Allied Generals before Sevastopol; Major-General Sir R. Dick, by W. Salter; General Sir George Brown, by Werner; Field-Marshal Lord Napier of Magdala (a replica by S. Dickenson); Admiral of the Fleet Sir Thomas Byam Martin, by T. Mackay.

The grand staircase is embellished by a statue of H.R.H. the Duke of York, by T. Campbell, and the following pictures: The Battle of Trafalgar, by C. Stanfield; Admiral Lord Nelson, the head by Jackson, finished by W. Robinson; Field-Marshal the Duke of Wellington, by W. Robinson; General Lord Hill, a replica by H. W. Pickersgill; and

Admiral Lord Collingwood, a copy by Colvin Smith, after Owen. There is also a picture of The Battle of Waterloo, by G. Jones.

In the upper billiard-room is a picture of the Battle of Trafalgar, the frame of which is wood from the timbers of the *Victory*.

The Junior United Service Club, amongst other valuable pictures, possesses two from the brush of Sir Thomas Lawrence. Here are also a number of military relics, including the sword which Lord Hill carried at Waterloo. A more grim souvenir is some locks of hair from the heads of women and children massacred during the Indian Mutiny at Cawnpore.

Lord Kitchener and Sir John French are old members of this club.

The Army and Navy Club, in Pall Mall, known as the "Rag," possesses one of the finest club-houses in the world. It was originally established as the Army Club, but owing to a desire expressed by the Iron Duke, naval officers were admitted, and the name altered in consequence. The club-house in Pall Mall was only opened some ten years later, having been built as a copy of the Palazzo Rezzonico at Venice. The original model for the building is still in the club. Captain William Duff, of the 23rd Royal Welsh Fusiliers, first invented the nickname of the "Rag." He was a celebrated man about town at a time when knocker-wrenching and other similar pranks were in favour; Billy Duff's exploits in such a line were notorious. Coming in to supper late one night, the refreshment obtainable appeared so meagre that he nicknamed the club the "Rag and Famish." This tickled the fancy of

THE ARMY AND NAVY CLUB.
From an early drawing.

the members, and a club button, bearing the nick-name and a starving man gnawing a bone, was designed, and for a time worn by many members in evening dress. Such buttons are still made.

The original premises occupied by the Army and Navy Club, when it was opened in 1838, were at the corner of King Street and St. James's Square, in a house, then numbered 16, which in 1814 had been Lord Castlereagh's. Two doors down was the house occupied by Mrs. Boehm in 1815. This lady, who " gave fashionable balls and masquerades," was entertaining the Prince Regent at dinner when the news of the victory of Waterloo arrived. The post-chaise, containing Major Henry Percy, with the despatches, stopped first at Lord Castlereagh's, and then went on to Mrs. Boehm's. The carriage, out of the windows of which three French eagles projected, was followed by a great crowd. The site of Mrs. Boehm's house now forms part of the East India United Service Club.

Before the Army and Navy Club, another club, the Oxford and Cambridge New University, occu-pied No. 16. The Army and Navy remained here until the purchase of its present freehold site ; but while the new house was being built it moved into No. 13, then known as Lichfield House, and the next but one to the north west corner of the square. It was so called after the Earl of Lichfield, who was Postmaster-General in Lord Melbourne's Adminis-tration, and it was the home of the club until February 25, 1851.

The new club-house has a frontage of 80 feet in Pall Mall and 100 feet in St. James's Square. The price of the site, together with the excavations, concreting, and so forth, amounted to £52,000 ; the building cost £54,000, and furnishing £10,000 more ; so that the total outlay on the club-house was £116,000. The architects were Messrs. Parnell and Smith, who adopted as their model the well-known Palazzo Rezzonico, which occupies a prominent position on the Grand Canal in Venice. Representations of this palace hang in various rooms of the club. The builders of the house were Messrs. Trego, Smith, and Appleford, and the first stone of the new building was laid on May 13, 1848, by Colonel Daniell, of the Coldstream Guards.

The freeholds purchased by the club included a house owned by the trustees of the Baroness de Mauley, which had formerly been in the possession of Spencer, Earl of Wilmington, and afterwards of John, Earl of Buckinghamshire. This was No. 20, St. James's Square, which had at more recent dates been occupied by the Hon. W. Ponsonby and by the Parthenon and Colonial Clubs. Other properties purchased were the freehold of Mr. Martineau, No. 3 George Street ; Nos. 36 and 37, the freehold of Mr. Malton ; Mrs. Justice's freehold, No. 38 Pall Mall ; and that of Mr. Tegart, No. 39 Pall Mall.

This club contains some interesting relics ; amongst them, in the smoking-room, is a mantel-piece from the Malmaison, carved by Canova. One of the figures supporting this, however, is modern, and the difference from the other carved by the great sculptor can be clearly discerned.

Another treasured possession of the Army and

Navy Club is the Nell Gwynn mirror, which is over the fireplace in the members' smoking-room. This was in Lord de Mauley's house, and is probably a genuine relic. A silver fruit-knife which is said to have belonged to the celebrated beauty, bearing the date 1680, has its place in the smoking-room, just below the mirror. The portrait of her by Sir Peter Lely which hangs in the same room was presented by a member, and took the place of another for years said to be Louise de Querouaille. In reality, this represents Mary of Modena.

As late as the eighteenth century the back room on the ground-floor of the old house on this site was covered with looking-glass, as was said to have been the ceiling also. Over the chimney-piece was a picture of Nell Gwynn, whilst a portrait of her sister hung in another room. The house then belonged to Thomas Brand, Esq., of the Hoo, in Hertfordshire.

The tradition that Nell Gwynn lived in the house standing on the ground now occupied by the Army and Navy Club, whilst now generally accepted, has been questioned by some. According to another tradition it was the house opposite— up to recent years used as part of the War Office —which really belonged to the Merry Monarch's favourite. This, it is said, communicated by an underground passage with the house pulled down when the present club was built. The passage was stopped up within the last fifty years.

Whether or not Nell Gwynn resided in a house on the site of which the Army and Navy Club now stands, it is at any rate certain that part of it was connected with the grant made by Charles II to her; for among the title-deeds of the club property is a deed, dated 1725, which recites that King Charles II, by letters patent dated April 1 in the seventeenth year of his reign, gave and granted unto certain persons several pieces or parcels of ground which formed part of a field or close called Pell Mell Field, otherwise St. James's Field. This grant was made on the nomination of Henry Jermyn, Earl of St. Albans, to Baptist May and Abraham Cowley, in trust for the second Earl of St. Albans, his heirs and assigns, for ever. Evelyn records in his Diary that he saw and heard the King (Charles II) in familiar discourse with " an impudent comedian, Mrs. Nellie, as they called her," who was looking over the garden wall of a house standing on the north side of Pall Mall. The " Mall " was not then the same as the present street, but an avenue shaded by trees lying north of it, and following the line of the present south side of St. James's Square, so that a house on the north side of Pall Mall might very well occupy the position of the corner house incorporated with the club.

A constant frequenter of the Army and Navy Club in old days was Prince Louis Napoleon, afterwards the Emperor Napoleon III, who always took great interest in everything connected with it. He had known it as a young man when—an obscure and impoverished exile—he lived in a modest lodging in King Street, St. James's, in the immediate neighbourhood of the club, which he practically made his home. Soon after his accession to power in France, he presented the club with the fine piece of tapestry which hangs on the grand staircase. This is dated 1849, the year after he became Prince President of the French Republic. It represents " The Worship of Pales," and is of Gobelins manufacture in 1784.

The Emperor ever cherished a kindly feeling for the club. When he returned to England after his downfall, he gladly resumed his honorary membership, and on his visits to town from Chislehurst he was frequently seen in the club, lunching constantly in the coffee-room, with his equerry seated opposite to him. He never failed to express a great liking for the club, because, as he said, he was always treated in it as a private person, and, except when he wished it, no particular notice was taken of him. It may be added that quite a number of interesting works of art relating to the Bonapartes are possessed by the club, and are kept in the visitors' drawing-room.

The Army and Navy Club contains what amounts to quite a collection of pictures, statuary, and works of art, some acquired by purchase, others gifts of various members of the club. In the first category is a colossal bust of Queen Victoria, by Alfred Gilbert, R.A., which is a replica of that exhibited in the Royal Academy in 1887—the Jubilee year. Another bust executed for the club, to replace one of plaster which had been broken, is that of Field-Marshal H.R.H. the Duke of Cambridge, the President of the club. This bust was executed by Admiral H.S.H. Prince Victor of Hohenlohe

(Count Gleichen), R.N., who was for many years, and until within a short time of his death, a member of the club. Two portraits in the inner hall—one of Queen Victoria, the other of the Duke of Wellington—were purchased by subscription.

Two interesting marble busts of T.R.H. the Prince and Princess of Wales were presented by Admiral Sir Arthur Cumming, K.C.B. The late Captain J. S. Manning, 1st Dragoon Guards, made some liberal gifts to the club, including the clock and marble case on the centre chimney-piece in the coffee-room. This member also gave several portraits, including one of the first President of the club, H.R.H. the Duke of Cambridge, and of Lord Nelson. Two silver snuff-boxes and a picture of the Battle of Camperdown were likewise presented by him.

In the coffee-room, panelled with portraits of distinguished officers, are two fine busts of Wellington and Nelson, both presented by members. A particularly interesting relic in the possession of the club is a miniature portrait of Lady Hamilton, which was found in Lord Nelson's cabin after his death at Trafalgar, and which was presented to the club by J. Penry Williams, Esq., late 1st Royals. The club also possesses autograph letters of Lord Nelson and of the first Duke of Wellington.

The Army and Navy started with a smoking-room at the very top of the house, but in course of time gave up first one and then a second strangers' coffee-room to lovers of tobacco. A lift has now been constructed to convey visitors to the original smoking-room upstairs. A determined effort was made a few years back to allow smoking in the beautiful morning-room facing Pall Mall, but this was defeated by a small section of the older but fast-diminishing set opposed to smoking.

A curious feature of the Army and Navy Club is the position of a fireplace in the entrance hall, where it is under a short flight of stairs leading to the main staircase. At first sight one is puzzled to imagine where the outlet for the smoke can be. In the same club-house is another fireplace situated directly beneath a window—a most unusual but agreeable position.

In 1862 the only service clubs existing in London were the United Service, Junior United Service, and Army and Navy, which were all full. To meet the want of another, a service club—the Naval and Military—was founded in March of that year by a party of officers chiefly belonging to The Buffs, then quartered at the Tower of London. These officers were : Major W. H. Cairnes, The Buffs ; Captain W. Stewart, The Buffs ; Lieutenant F. T. Jones, The Buffs ; Captain L. C. Barber, R.E. ; and H. H. Barber, Esq., late 17th Lancers.

The club commenced with 150 members, at an entrance fee of £15 15s., a home subscription of £5 5s., and a supernumerary subscription of 10s.

The first club-house was at No. 18 Clifford Street. Soon, however, it was found too small, and at the end of 1863 a move was made to more commodious premises at No. 22 Hanover Square, where the club remained until the end of 1865. Cambridge House, full of Palmerstonian associations, was taken in 1865, and opened in April of the next year.

On the renewal of the lease in 1876, it was determined to make the house as perfect as possible. Alterations were carried on from December of that year till April 1878, during which time the original house was entirely renovated. The structure was also enlarged, a new dining-room, billiard-rooms, offices, and cellars being added on the site of the stables and other offices.

The upper smoking-room, in which hangs a portrait of General Sir W. Nott, G.C.B., and some engravings after Hogarth, was once Lord Palmerston's bedroom, from which formerly a small semi-secret staircase led to Whitehorse Street, by which it is said foreign spies and other desirable or undesirable persons were admitted. The present card-room was Lady Palmerston's bedroom, opening into her boudoir — the octagon room, which retains a beautiful ceiling.

Mr. Gladstone used to say that Lord and Lady Palmerston once formed a Ministry in this octagon room.

The present library was the ball-room, and the State apartments were *en suite*.

The Duke of Cambridge — tenth child of George III—lived at Cambridge House till his death in 1850, the year in which Queen Victoria, who had gone to inquire after his health, was struck with a cane by Robert Pate, a retired officer, just as the royal carriage was driving out of the gate. Her bonnet was crushed over her forehead, and her cheek hurt.

Pate was transported for seven years.

A number of portraits and busts are in the Naval and Military—the Duke of Wellington ; Napoleon ; Nelson, after Hoppner ; Queen Victoria, by Winterhalter ; and George III, by Beechey. Some fine heads presented by members also decorate this club, which is one of the most comfortable and best managed in London.

An interesting feature is the roll of honour in the corridor. This bears the names of members who have lost their lives in the service of their country since the foundation of the club.

The Junior Naval and Military club, almost next door to the Naval and Military, was founded about ten years ago, and has a large membership, mostly drawn from officers of junior rank. The club-house is one of the few modern buildings in London which have a façade of excellent though restrained design. The exterior of this club affords an agreeable contrast to most buildings of recent years, being quite free from the superabundance of decoration which now disfigures so many West End thoroughfares.

The Guards' Club was established in 1813 at a house in St. James's Street, next Crockford's. The present club-house, however, was erected only as far back as 1848 ; it was built from the designs of Mr. Henry Harrison. Established for the three regiments of Foot Guards, it seems originally to have been conducted on a military system. Billiards and low whist were the only games indulged in. The dinner was, perhaps, better than at most clubs, and considerably cheaper.

The Guards' club-house in St. James's Street fell down on November 9, 1827, in consequence, it was said, of the walls being undermined in the preparation for building a foundation to the new subscription house about to be erected next door by Mr. Crockford. The following epigrammatic verses were written on this occasion :

> " ' Mala vicini pecoris contagia lædunt.'
>
>> What can these workmen be about ?
>> Do, Crockford, let the secret out,
>>> Why thus your houses fall.
>> Quoth he : ' Since folks are not in town,
>> I find it better to pull down,
>>> Than have no pull at all.'

> " See, passenger, at Crockford's high behest,
>> Red-coats by black-legs ousted from their nest ;
>> The arts of peace o'ermatching reckless war,
>> And gallant Rouge undone by wily Noir !

> " ' Impar congressus ' . . .
>
>> Fate gave the word—the king of dice and cards
>> In an unguarded moment took the Guards ;
>> Contriv'd his neighbours in a trice to drub,
>> And did the trick by—turning up a club.

> " ' Nullum simile est idem.'
>
>> 'Tis strange how some will differ—some advance
>> That the Guards' club-house was pulled down
>>> by chance ;
>> While some, with juster notions in their mazard,
>> Stoutly maintain the deed was done by hazard."

The Guards' Club, it should be added, is considered as a guard-house, and can be used by officers on duty.

In St. James's Square is the East India United Service Club, which was founded in 1849. The present club-house really consists of two mansions —Nos. 14 and 15—which were formed into one commodious and handsome building by the skill of the architect—Mr. Adam Lee. The East India United is of course an essentially Anglo-Indian club, and many distinguished officials—civil as well as military—have been members.

A number of pictures and prints are in this club-house, most of the portraits of famous Anglo-Indians being copies of originals in the India Office, National Portrait Gallery, and elsewhere.

An interesting piece of plate here is a silver vase presented by the Patriotic Fund at Lloyd's to Commodore Sir Nathaniel Dance, H.E.I.C., upon the occasion of his defeating a French squadron on February 15, 1804. This was lent to the club in October 1895, by the great-nephew of the Commodore, G. W. Dance, Esq., B.C.S.

A quite modern military club, which has prospered exceedingly, is the Cavalry, which was started in 1895 for officers who had served in the various mounted arms, English and Indian cavalry, Royal Horse Artillery, and Imperial Yeomanry. Unlike several other clubs started about the same time, it flourished, and has a membership of 1,300. Here there is a dining-room to which ladies are admitted as guests, which has no doubt contributed to the success of the club.

During the last year the comfortable club-house in Piccadilly was enlarged, and it is now capable of accommodating a larger number of members than before.

Little is ever heard of the Royal Naval Club—

one of the oldest in the world, for it originated about 1674. Many great Admirals have belonged to this convivial dining club, including Nelson, who is generally supposed to have belonged to no club. At one time these dinners were held in the large dining-room at the Thatched House, in St. James's Street, on the walls of which hung the portraits of the Dilettanti Society, illuminated by wax candles in fine old glass chandeliers.

During the present year yet another military club—the Junior Army and Navy—has opened its doors at the Clock House, Whitehall, which was originally built for Lord Carrington.

The Caledonian, in Charles Street, St. James's, also occupies a mansion which was once in private hands. The largest house in the street, it was erected in 1819 for Pascoe Grenfell, and subsequently became the property of the Beresford family, from whom it was acquired by the Caledonian Club.

The Junior Athenæum, at the corner of Dover Street, Piccadilly, like the Caledonian, was not intended for a club, having been built some sixty years ago, at a cost of £30,000, for Mr. Henry Thomas Hope, whose initial still remains upon the elaborate cast-iron railings of French design.

CHAPTER X

OF the many convivial dining clubs which once
abounded in London few now survive, though the
famous and venerable Dilettanti Society happily
still flourishes. Its dinners are held at the Grafton
Galleries, and certain quaint old usages are still
maintained. A member who speaks of the Society
as "the club" has to pay some petty fine, whilst
the secretary when reading the minutes puts on
bands. The presence of these somewhat ecclesias-
tical additions to costume in one of the beautiful
portraits belonging to this club once caused the
late Mr. Gladstone to take the picture for that of
a Bishop—which aroused some merriment.

The Society was founded about 1734 by a number
of gentlemen who had travelled much in Italy, and
were desirous of encouraging at home a taste for
those objects which had contributed so much to
their intellectual gratification abroad. Accordingly
they formed themselves into a Society, under the
name of Dilettanti (literally, lovers of the fine
arts), and agreed upon certain regulations to keep
up the spirit of their scheme, which combined

friendly and social intercourse with a serious and ardent desire to promote the arts. In 1751 Mr. James Stuart ("Athenian Stuart," as he was called) and Mr. Nicholas Revett were elected members. The Society liberally assisted them in their excellent work, "The Antiquities of Athens." In fact, it was in great measure owing to the Dilettanti that, after the death of the above two eminent architects, the work was not entirely relinquished, and a large number of the plates were engraved from drawings in possession of the Society. It was mainly through the influence and patronage of the Dilettanti Society that the Royal Academy obtained its charter. In 1774 the interest of £4,000 three per cents. was appropriated by the former for the purpose of sending two students, recommended by the Royal Academy, to study in Italy or Greece for three years.

In old days the funds of the Society were greatly increased by the fines. Those paid "on increase of income, by inheritance, legacy, marriage, or preferment," were very odd—for instance, 5 guineas by Lord Grosvenor, on his marriage with Miss Leveson Gower; 11 guineas by the Duke of Bedford, on being appointed First Lord of the Admiralty; 10 guineas compounded for by Bubb Dodington, as Treasurer of the Navy; 2 guineas by the Duke of Kingston, for a colonelcy of Horse (then valued at £400 per annum); £21 by Lord Sandwich, on going out as Ambassador to the Congress at Aix-la-Chapelle, and $2\frac{3}{4}$d. by the same nobleman, on becoming Recorder of Huntingdon; 13s. 4d. by the Duke of Bedford, on getting the Garter, and 16s. 8d. (Scotch) by the Duke of Buccleuch, on getting the Thistle ; £21 by the Earl of Holderness, as Secretary of State ; and £9 19s. 6d. by Charles James Fox, as a Lord of the Admiralty.

The general toasts originally proposed and adopted by the Society were " *Viva la Virtù*," " Grecian Taste and Roman Spirit," and " Absent Members." To these was added, by a minute of March 7, 1744½, " *Esto præclara, esto perpetua*." On March 29, 1789, it was resolved to add the toast of " The King," which was to precede all others. This addition was no doubt due to the outburst of loyalty which took place when the King resumed his authority, after his recovery from his first attack of insanity, on March 10 of the same year.

Walpole was very severe upon the Dilettanti. " The nominal qualification for membership," said he, " is having been in Italy, and the real one, being drunk ; the two chiefs are Lord Middlesex and Sir Francis Dashwood, who were seldom sober the whole time they were in Italy." Were the owner of Strawberry Hill to attend a meeting of the Society at the present time, he would be surprised to observe the sobriety which now prevails.

In the distant past, some of the more juvenile members occasionally did behave in a riotous manner. On January 30, 1734, for instance, a party of young men, seven of whom (Harcourt, Middlesex, Boyne, Shirley, Strode, Denny, and Sir James Gray) were members of the Dilettanti, met to celebrate the birthday of one of the company present, by a dinner at the White Eagle Tavern in Suffolk Street. The disorder caused by their drunken revels attracted a crowd of people, who were led to believe that the dinner was held to commemorate the execution of Charles I. on that day, and that a calf's head had been served at table by way of ridicule. A bonfire was lit, and on the diners appearing at the windows they were stoned by the mob, in spite of their protestations of fidelity to the Government and the King. It ended in a riot, stirred up by a Catholic priest, which the newspapers converted into an event of historical importance.

The Dilettanti Society has never lost sight of the main objects for which it was founded, and in 1855 a project was started for reproducing by some process of engraving the whole of the Society's collection of portraits. Sir Richard Westmacott, R.A., communicated with Mr. George Scharf, jun. (afterwards Director of the National Portrait Gallery), and received from him an estimate of the cost of engraving on wood the thirty-one portraits in question. The cost, however, was probably the reason which deterred the Society from proceeding in the matter.

The Society once met at the Star and Garter Tavern in Pall Mall, but in 1800 transferred its meetings to a great room in the Thatched House Tavern in St. James's Street.

The ceiling here was painted to represent the sky, and was crossed by gold cords interlacing one another, from the knots of which hung three large glass chandeliers.

The room formed an admirable setting for the Society's pictures, the most remarkable of which are, of course, the three painted by Sir Joshua Reynolds.

The first of these is a group in the manner of

A DINNER OF THE DILETTANTI SOCIETY AT THE THATCHED HOUSE.
From a drawing by T. H. Shepherd.

Paul Veronese, containing the portraits of the Duke of Leeds, Lord Dundas, Constantine Lord Mulgrave, Lord Seaforth, the Hon. Charles Greville, Charles Crowle, Esq., and Sir Joseph Banks. Another group in the same style contains portraits of Sir William Hamilton, Sir Watkin W. Wynne, Richard Thomson, Esq., Sir John Taylor, Payne Gallwey, Esq., John Smythe, Esq., and Spencer S. Stanhope, Esq. The portrait of Sir Joshua shows him in a loose robe, wearing his own hair.

It should be added that earlier portraits in the possession of the Society are by Hudson, Reynolds's master.

Some are in eighteenth-century costume, others in Turkish or Roman dress. There is a convivial spirit in these pictures. Lord Sandwich, for instance, in a Turkish costume, is shown casting an affectionate glance upon a brimming goblet in his left hand, while his right holds a flask of great capacity. Sir Bourchier Wrey is seated in the cabin of a ship mixing punch and eagerly embracing the bowl, of which a lurch of the sea would seem about to deprive him; the inscription is, *Dulce est desipere in loco.* The Dilettanti possess a curious old portrait of the Earl of Holderness in a red cap, as a gondolier, with the Rialto and Venice in the background; there is Charles Sackville, Duke of Dorset, as a Roman senator, dated 1738; Lord Galloway in the dress of a Cardinal. A curious likeness of one of the earliest of the Dilettanti—Lord le Despencer—portrays him as a monk at his devotions, clasping a brimming goblet for his rosary, and with eyes not very piously fixed on a statue of the Venus de'

Medici. Some of these pictures, indeed, recall the Medmenham orgies, with which some of the Dilettanti were not unfamiliar.

In 1884 the two groups by Sir Joshua Reynolds and the portrait of himself were lent by the Society to the Grosvenor Gallery for an exhibition of the collected works of the great master. In March, 1890, on the Society's removing from Willis's Rooms, the two fine groups by Sir Joshua were once more deposited on loan with the Trustees of the National Gallery, until the whole collection of pictures was removed and rehung in the Society's new room in the Grafton Gallery.

During recent years the Society has from time to time added to its pictures.

In January 1894, a portrait of Mr. William Watkiss Lloyd, painted by Miss Bush, was received by the Society from his daughter, Miss Ellen Watkiss Lloyd, having been bequeathed to the Society by her late father, who had for many years been one of its most active and respected members. After the death of Lord Leighton, President of the Royal Academy, in January 1896, the Dilettanti, being anxious to obtain a portrait of one of the most illustrious of their body, decided to have a copy made of the portrait painted by Lord Leighton of himself for the Uffizi Gallery at Florence. The work was entrusted to Mr. Charles Holroyd (now Keeper of the National Gallery of British Art), and completed before the close of the same year. In February 1896, on the resignation by Mr. (now Sir) Sidney Colvin of his post as secretary and treasurer of the Society, the Society ordered that a portrait of that gentleman should be added to their collection. Sir Edward Poynter undertook to paint the portrait of Mr. Colvin, which was, by permission of the Society, sent to the Royal Academy Exhibition of 1897. Another modern portrait of interest is Sir Edward Ryan, by Lord Leighton.

The Dilettanti, the membership of which at the present day is largely composed of high legal and Government officials, generally have six dinners a year, and sometimes more, at the Grafton Galleries. The ancient ceremonies, including the appointment of a functionary known as the Imp, are retained. The father of the club at the present day is Mr. W. C. Cartwright, who was originally introduced by the late Lord Houghton.

The Thatched House Tavern, in the large room of which the members of the Dilettanti Society were once wont to assemble, was for a time also the meeting-place of another somewhat similar society, the Literary Club. This is now represented by The Club, which is perhaps the most exclusive institution in Europe. So little known is the existence of this society that at the foundation of the Turf Club it was at first proposed to call it The Club ; and, indeed, it was some time before the discovery that the name had been long before appropriated placed the adoption of such an appellation out of the question. The membership of The Club is limited in the extreme, which may be realized when it is stated that since its foundation, in 1764, not 300 members have secured election. Forty, according to the regulations, is the extreme limit of membership. Amongst distinguished men who have been members appear the names of Dr. Johnson, Boswell, Garrick, Sir Joshua Reynolds, Oliver Goldsmith, Burke, Fox, and Gibbon. In more modern times many prominent personalities have been members— amongst them Mr. Gladstone, Lord Leighton, Professor Huxley, Lord Salisbury, Lord Rosebery, Lord Goschen, the Duke of Argyll, Lord Herschell, Lord Dufferin, Lord Wolseley, Sir Mountstuart Grant Duff, Mr. Arthur Balfour, Lord Peel, Mr. Asquith, Sir Edward Poynter, and many others whose names are well known in legal, political, artistic, and literary circles.

The club was founded in 1764 by Sir Joshua Reynolds and Dr. Samuel Johnson, and for some years met on Monday evenings at seven. In 1772 the day of meeting was changed to Friday, and about that time, instead of supping, they agreed to dine together once in every fortnight during the sitting of Parliament. In 1773 The Club, which soon after its foundation consisted of twelve members, was enlarged to twenty; March 11, 1777, to twenty-six; November 27, 1778, to thirty; May 9, 1780, to thirty-five; and it was then resolved that it should never exceed forty. It met originally at the Turk's Head, in Gerrard Street, and continued to meet there till 1783, when their landlord died, and the house was soon afterwards shut up. They then removed to Prince's, in Saville Street; and on his house being, soon afterwards, shut up, they removed to Baxter's, which afterwards became Thomas's, in Dover Street. In January 1792, they removed to Parsloe's, in

St. James's Street; and on February 26, 1799, to the Thatched House, in the same street.

The club received the name of Literary Club at Garrick's funeral.

In the early days of The Club, Dr. Johnson was exceedingly particular as to the admission of candidates, and would not hear of any increase in the number of members. Not long after its institution, Sir Joshua Reynolds was speaking of the club to Garrick. " I like it much," said the great actor briskly; " I think I shall be of you." When Sir Joshua mentioned this to Dr. Johnson, the latter, according to Boswell, was much displeased with the actor's conceit. " He'll be of us!" growled he; " how does he know we will permit him?"

Sir John Hawkins tried to soften Johnson, and spoke to him of Garrick in a very eulogistic way. " Sir," replied Johnson, " he will disturb us by his buffoonery." In the same spirit he declared to Mr. Thrale that, if Garrick should apply for admission, he would blackball him. " Who, sir?" exclaimed Thrale, with surprise: " Mr. Garrick— your friend, your companion—blackball him?" " Why, sir," replied Johnson, " I love my little David dearly—better than all or any of his flatterers do; but surely one ought to sit, in a society like ours,

'Unelbowed by a gamester, pimp, or player.'"

By degrees the rigour of the club relaxed; some of the members grew negligent. Beauclerk lost his right of membership by neglecting to attend.

Nevertheless, on his marriage (with Lady Diana Spencer, daughter of the Duke of Marlborough, and recently divorced from Viscount Bolingbroke), he claimed and regained his seat in the club. The number of the members was likewise augmented. The proposition to increase it originated with Goldsmith. " It would give," he thought, " an agreeable variety to their meetings ; for there can be nothing new amongst us," said he : " we have travelled over each other's minds." Johnson was piqued at the suggestion. " Sir," said he, " you have not travelled over my mind, I promise you." Sir Joshua, less confident in the exhaustless fecundity of his mind, felt and acknowledged the force of Goldsmith's suggestion. Several new members therefore were elected ; the first, to his great joy, was David Garrick. Goldsmith, who was now on cordial terms with the great actor, zealously promoted his election, and Johnson gave it his warm approbation.

The meetings of the Literary Club were often the occasion of much discussion between Edmund Burke and Johnson. One evening the former observed that a hogshead of claret, which had been sent as a present to the club, was almost out, and proposed that Johnson should write for another in such ambiguity of expression as might have a chance of procuring it also as a gift. One of the company said : " Dr. Johnson shall be our dictator." " Were I," said Johnson, " your dictator, you should have no wine ; it would be my business ' cavere ne quid detrimenti respublica caperet.' Wine is dangerous ; Rome was ruined by luxury." Burke replied : " If you allow no wine as dictator, you shall not have me for master of the horse."

Dr. Johnson for a time completely dominated the club, and once, in his usual grandiloquent manner, said to Boswell : " Sir, you got into the club by doing what a man can do. Several of the members wished to keep you out ; Burke told me he doubted if you were fit for it. Now you are in, none of them are sorry." *Boswell :* " They were afraid of you, sir, as it was you proposed me." *Johnson :* " Sir, they knew that if they refused you they would probably have never got into another club—I would have kept them all out."

At last, owing to his ill-temper and rudeness, the great lexicographer's influence in the club sensibly decreased.

The club possesses a very valuable collection of autographs of former distinguished members, and amongst its memorials is a portrait of Sir Joshua Reynolds, with spectacles on, similar to the picture in the Royal Collection ; this portrait was painted and presented by Sir Joshua, as the founder of the club.

Another club which was once the resort of many clever and distinguished men was the Cosmopolitan, in Charles Street, Berkeley Square. This ceased to exist not very many years ago. The house in which it held its meetings had been pulled down, and though the Cosmopolitan migrated to the Alpine Club, it did not long survive the change. Its meetings were held twice a week, in the evening, no meals whatever being served, though light refreshments were supplied. The house in Charles Street had previously contained the studio of Watts the painter, and a great feature of the club-room was a very large picture representing a scene from the "Decameron," which had been painted by that artist. This is now in the Tate Gallery. When the Cosmopolitan was dissolved, a certain sum of money remained, and this, on the suggestion of a former leading member, is gradually being spent in dinners at which former members from time to time foregather.

A dining club which for a time attracted considerable attention was the Roxburghe, which originated under the following circumstances : The Duke of Roxburghe was a noted bibliophile; the sale of his library, which excited great interest in 1812, lasted for forty-two days, and on the evening when the sale had been concluded the club was formed by about sixteen bibliomaniacs, after a dinner at the St. Albans Tavern, Lord Spencer being in the chair. The Roxburghe consisted mostly of men devoted to rare books. Tomes containing alterations in the title-page, or in a leaf, or in any trivial circumstance, were bought by these collectors at £100, £200, or £300, though the copies were often of small intrinsic worth. Specimens of first editions of all authors, and editions by the early printers, were never sold for less than £50, £100, or £200. So great became this mania that, in order to gratify the members of the club, facsimile copies of clumsy editions of trumpery books were reprinted. In some cases, indeed, it became worth the while of unscrupulous people to palm off forgeries upon the more credulous of these collectors.

The club issued various publications, but its

costly dinners attracted more attention than anything else. On one occasion the bill was above £5 10s. per head, and the list of toasts included the "immortal memory" not only of John, Duke of Roxburghe, but of William Caxton, Dame Juliana Berners, Wynkyn de Worde, Richard Pynson, the Aldine family, and " The Cause of Bibliomania all over the World." In one year, when Lord Spencer presided over the club feast, the " Roxburghe Revels " thus recorded the fact : " Twenty-one members met joyfully, dined comfortably, challenged eagerly, tippled prettily, divided regretfully, and paid the bill most cheerfully."

The bill of one of the dinners of the Roxburghe Club held at Grillion's Hotel has been preserved. Its curious phraseology is due to the French waiter who made it out :

DINNER (*sic*) DU 17 JUIN, 1815.

	£	s.	d.
20	20	0	0
Desser	2	0	0
Deu sorte de Glasse	1	4	0
Glasse pour 6	0	4	0
5 Boutelle de Champagne	4	0	0
7 Boutelle de harmetage	5	5	0
1 Boutelle de Hok	0	15	0
4 Boutelle de Port	1	6	0
4 Boutelle de Maderre	2	0	0
22 Boutelle de Bordeaux	15	8	0
2 Boutelle de Bourgogne	1	12	0
[Not legible]	0	14	0
Soder	0	2	0
Biere e Ail	0	6	0
Por la Lettre	0	2	0
Pour faire une prune	0	6	0
Pour un fiacre	0	2	0
	55	6	0
Waiters	1	14	0
	£57	0	0

Amongst the curious old clubs of the eighteenth century, the Kit-Kat, founded about 1700, deserves attention. This was composed of thirty-nine noblemen and gentlemen zealously attached to the House of Hanover, among them six Dukes and many other peers. The club met at a small house in Shire Lane, by Temple Bar, where a famous mutton-pie man, by name Christopher Katt, supplied his pies to the club suppers and gave his name to the club, although it has been stated that the pie itself was called "kit-kat."

The extraordinary title of the club is explained in the following lines :

> " Whence deathless Kit-Kat took its name,
>   Few critics can unriddle ;
>   Some say from pastrycook it came,
>   And some from Cat and Fiddle.

> " From no trim beaux its name it boasts,
>   Grey statesmen or green wits,
>   But from the pell-mell peck of toasts
>   Of old cats and young kits."

A feature of the club was its toasts. Every member was compelled to name a beauty, whose claims to the honour were then discussed ; and if her name was approved, a special tumbler was consecrated to her, and verses to her honour engraved on it. Such of these tumblers as still survive must be very rare. When only eight years old, Lady Mary Wortley Montagu enjoyed the honour of having her charms commemorated on one of these "toasting tumblers." Her father, afterwards Duke of Kingston, in a fit of caprice proposed "The Pretty Little Child" as his toast. The other members, who had never seen her, objected, but, the child having been sent for, found her charming, and yielded. The forward little girl was handed from knee to knee, petted and caressed by the assembled wits. Another celebrated toast of the Kit-Kat, mentioned by Walpole, was Lady Molyneux, who, he says, died smoking a pipe.

Several of the more celebrated of these "toasts" had their portraits hung in the club-room.

The character of the club was political as well as literary, but its chief aim was the promotion of culture and wit. The members subscribed the sum of 400 guineas to offer as prizes for the best comedies written.

This club at one period of its existence had a room built for the members at Barn Elms (now the highly prosperous Ranelagh Club). This was hung with portraits painted by Kneller, which, being all of one size, originated the name "Kit-Kat," which is still in use.

A prominent member of the Kit-Kat Club was the famous Court physician, Dr. Samuel Garth, who, while dining one evening, protested that he must leave early, as he had many patients to visit. Nevertheless he lingered on hour after hour. Sir Richard Steele, who was present, reminded him of his professional duties, when Garth produced a list of fifteen patients. "It matters little," he cried, "whether I see them or not to-night. Nine or ten are so bad that all the doctors in the world could not save them, and the remainder have such tough constitutions that they want no doctors."

A celebrated early eighteenth-century literary

club was the Royal Society, instituted by a number of literary men who met in Dean's Court, there to dine on fish and drink porter. One of these gatherings expanded into the Club of Royal Philosophers, or, as it came to be called, the Royal Society Club. They dined together on Thursdays, usually to the number of six, but sometimes more. A favourite dining-place was Pontack's, the celebrated French eating-house in Abchurch Lane, City; and they also dined at the Devil Tavern, near Temple Bar, and at the Mitre Tavern, in Fleet Street. In 1780 the club, as it had become, went to the Crown and Anchor Tavern, in the Strand; and here they remained for sixty-eight years, only removing to the Freemasons' Tavern, in Fleet Street, in 1848. Finally, when the Royal Society was installed at Burlington House in 1857, the club held its meetings at the Thatched House, in St. James's Street, which they frequented until that tavern was demolished.

As time went on, the cost of the club dinner gradually rose. It began at 1s. 6d. per head, then went to 4s., including wine and 2d. to the waiter, and was afterwards increased to 10s. The wine was laid in at £45 the pipe, or 1s. 6d. per bottle, and charged by the landlord at 2s. 6d. This club was sometimes known as Dr. Halley's, for Halley was said to have been its founder.

An eccentric member was the Hon. Henry Cavendish, commonly called the "Club Crœsus." Though wealthy, he seldom had enough money in his pockets to pay for his dinner, and his manners were extraordinary. He picked his teeth with a

fork, carried his cane stuck in his right boot, and
was very angry when anyone else hung his hat
on the peg he preferred in the hall. Yet he was
not unsociable ; he is said to have left a large legacy
to a fellow - member — Lord Bessborough — in
gratitude for his pleasant conversation.

Cavendish was rather a misogynist. One evening
a pretty girl chanced to be at an upper window on
the opposite side of the street, watching the philosophers at dinner. She attracted notice, and one
by one they got up and mustered round the window
to admire the fair one. Cavendish, who thought
they were looking at the moon, bustled up to them
in his odd way, and, when he saw the real object of
their study, turned away with intense disgust, and
grunted out " Pshaw !"

The President of the Royal Society was always
elected president of the club. Princes, Ministers,
men of high rank, and Ambassadors were entertained
together with men of science, great ecclesiastics,
and distinguished soldiers and sailors ; Franklin,
Jenner, John Hunter, Sir Joshua Reynolds, Sir
Thomas Lawrence, Gibbon, Wedgwood, Turner,
De la Beche, and Brunel were amongst these.

The modern Royal Societies Club, in St. James's
Street, has no connection with the ancient institution just mentioned. It was founded in 1894, and
its members either belong to learned societies,
Universities, and institutions of the United Kingdom, or are well known in the spheres of Literature,
Science, and Art. The committee possesses the
right of granting the use of certain rooms in the
club-house for lectures or for meetings of any of

the societies or institutions recognized by the constitution of the club. This club has a somewhat peculiar subscription, town members—that is, those residing within a radius of twenty miles—paying eight guineas, country members six, and colonial and foreign members two.

A club which has done much to promote a knowledge and appreciation of art in London is the Burlington Fine Arts, now at 17 Savile Row. This was founded in 1866, when the Marquis d'Azeglio, then Sardinian Minister in London, and a well known connoisseur, was chairman. In the early days there were 250 members, and the club premises were at No. 177 Piccadilly. At that time the Fine Arts Club was still in existence, and most of its members joined what was called the Burlington Fine Arts Club, on account of its premises being opposite Burlington House, into which the Royal Academy had just moved. Exhibitions of considerable importance were held in the rooms in Piccadilly, the first chiefly of French etchings, and the last (in 1870) of original drawings by Raphael and Michael Angelo. In that year the club moved to Savile Row, where was built the present gallery, which has been the scene of a series of annual exhibitions.

The membership of this flourishing association of art-lovers is now 500, and since the foundation of the club its annual exhibitions have gathered together many priceless works of art in the club-house. This, however, contains no furniture or *objets d'art* calling for mention, with the exception of an Italian sixteenth-century mirror boldly carved out of walnut wood in the style of Michael Angelo. The present chairman is Lord Brownlow, whilst the secretarial duties are most ably performed by Mr. Beavan.

The foremost modern literary club in England is of course the Athenæum, which was first established in 1824, under the name of The Society. The latter appellation was, however, changed to the Athenæum at an inaugural dinner given at No. 12 Waterloo Place.

Three years later the committee, having obtained possession of a more convenient site, part of which had been occupied by the recently demolished Carlton House, entrusted Decimus Burton with the task of building a suitable club-house. In the course of its construction Croker insisted that the Scotch sculptor, John Heming, should contribute a frieze designed as a reproduction of that of the Parthenon—an ornamentation at the time characterized as an extravagant novelty. In spite of a good deal of opposition, Croker carried the day, and the construction of an ice-house, which had been advocated by several members, was abandoned in order to afford funds for the classical decoration.

In connection with this was written the epigram:

> " I'm John Wilson Croker,
>   I do as I please:
> They ask for an Ice-house,
>   I'll give 'em—a Frieze."

The new Athenæum club-house was formerly opened in February 1830, some soirées being given, to which ladies were admitted, though not without protest. The building, which is of some architectural interest, was erected on the west end of the courtyard of old Carlton House, the smoking-room being exactly under what was the Prince Regent's dining-room.

In the finely-proportioned hall eight pale primrose pillars on broad bronzed bases, copied from the Temple of the Winds at Athens, support the panelled waggon roof, the Pompeian ornamentation being of an original design. The two statues in niches, " Venus Victrix " and " Diana Robing," were chosen by Sir Thomas Lawrence, who also designed the club seal.

On the right of the hall is the morning-room, redecorated in 1892, when the ceiling was elaborately painted by Sir Edward Poynter. The bust of Milton in this room was bequeathed by Anthony Trollope ; in the adjoining writing-room hangs a portrait of Dr. Johnson by Opie, the gift of Mr. Humphry Ward. The drawing-room up-stairs, one of the finest rooms in London, has no fewer than eleven windows. But the chief glory of the Athenæum is its library, the view from which embraces the pretty garden, where a rookery once existed. The annual expenditure on books since 1848 has averaged about £450. The Athenæum library is by far the finest and most important club library in the world, all departments of foreign as well as English books being represented by rare and complete examples. Moreover, there is on its shelves one of the best collections of reference books in England, and the bookcases are stored with valuable volumes—rare tomes dealing with history, topography, and archæology, as well as

sumptuously - bound books on art. Of these a
number were obtained under a legacy of the
Rev. Charles Turner, and others were left by the
late Mr. Felix Slade. The collection of English
pamphlets is also singularly complete, and includes
21 volumes collected together by Sir James Mackintosh, 43 by Dr. Nasmith the antiquary, 139
volumes by Morton Pitt, 23 volumes by Gibbon
on historical and financial subjects, 23 volumes
devoted to foreign and colonial affairs, and 52
volumes of smaller publications relating to America.
Amongst literary matter of a lighter description
preserved in this library are 26 portfolios containing
newspapers and caricatures collected during the
siege of Paris and the Commune. In a case is
preserved a large number of proof engravings, most
of them after portraits of members. These were
executed by George Richmond, R.A., who presented the collection. An interesting relic of
Thackeray is the original manuscript of " The
Orphan of Pimlico," in the great novelist's beautiful
handwriting.

A portrait of George IV was formerly over the
fireplace. Sir Thomas Lawrence, its painter, was
engaged in finishing the sword-knot and orders
only a few hours before his death. He intended
to present it to the club, but, as his executors
declined to part with it, the painting was eventually
purchased for £128 10s. This portrait is now in
the museum of the Royal Pavilion at Brighton,
having been handed over to the Corporation of that
town in 1858. Busts of Dr. Johnson (presented by
Mr. Percy Fitzgerald) and of Pope (a bequest) are

here, together with the carved armchair used by Dickens at Gad's Hill, in which, on the day of his death, the great novelist had been sitting at work on "Edwin Drood." Many will remember "The Empty Chair" which appeared in the then newly-founded *Graphic* in June 1870. Macaulay's corner, near the books on English history, is a well-known feature of this library, which the late Mark Pattison said he thought the most delightful place in the world, especially on a Sunday morning. At the table in the south-west corner Thackeray used constantly to work. A great habitué of the library in the early days of the club was Isaac Disraeli, who, as befitted the author of the " Curiosities of Literature," was one of the earliest members—indeed, one of the founders of the club. His invariable costume consisted of a blue coat with brass buttons, a yellow waistcoat, and knee-breeches. A similar fashion was followed by another member —Dr. Booth—as late as 1863.

One evening, in or about the year 1830, a non-member, young Benjamin Disraeli, in defiance of the club rules, coolly walked upstairs to the library, and there proceeded to confer with his father. He was duly requested to withdraw, and it is perhaps not extraordinary that the future Prime Minister should have been blackballed in 1832. The reason given at the time for this rejection was that his proposer or seconder had rendered himself particularly unpopular.

It was not until thirty-four years later that the great statesman became a member of the Athenæum, to which he was admitted under the rule allowing the committee to elect annually a limited number of persons "who have attained to distinguished eminence." As Lord Beaconsfield he seems to have used the club but little, although, according to tradition, he abstracted from the library his own "Revolutionary Epick," written in 1834.

In a corner of the Athenæum library the late Cardinal Manning, who had been elected at a time when he was attending the Vatican Council, used to sit quietly reading. At one time he used the club a good deal, as did another venerable ecclesiastic, Dr. Tatham, noted for eccentricity and long sermons. Yet another divine well known at the Athenæum was the nonagenarian Bishop Durnford, of Chichester. Bishops have always been more or less abundant at this club, for which reason, when an unusually large number were collected together for Convocation, Abraham Hayward is said to have grumbled out : " I see the Bishops are beginning to swarm : the atmosphere is alive with them ; every moment I expect to find one dropping into my soup."

There was a great storm amongst the Bishops when Bishop Colenso visited England, and, as can be imagined, his admission to the Athenæum as an honorary member was violently opposed.

Samuel Wilberforce, Lord Lytton the novelist, Abraham Hayward (the Vernon Tuft of Samuel Warren's "Ten Thousand a Year," still remembered by some), and many other celebrated characters, were frequenters of this peaceful room. Here, too, Theodore Hook dashed off much brilliant

work. This spontaneous and volatile wit at one
time used the club a great deal. He it was who
wrote the lines :

> " There's first the Athenæum Club, so wise, there's not a
> man of it
> That has not sense enough for six (in fact, that is the plan
> of it);
> The very waiters answer you with eloquence Socratical,
> And always place the knives and forks in order mathe-
> matical."

Hook dined much at the Athenæum—often, it
was said, " not wisely, but too well." The name
of his favourite spot in the dining-room—" Tem-
perance Corner "—is still preserved. Here he used
to call for toast-and-water and lemonade, which the
waiters quite understood was his humorous way of
indicating the various alcoholic beverages of which
he was so fond. Hook loved to sit long over his
meals, in which respect it is interesting to remember he was quite unlike Dickens, who often lunched
standing, off sandwiches.

It was at the foot of the Athenæum staircase
that the author of " Pickwick " ended his unfortunate estrangement from Thackeray, being inter-
cepted by the latter and forced to shake hands.

Intellect rather than love of comfort formerly
distinguished most members of the club, and for
this reason, perhaps, the Athenæum has never been
noted for its cooking. "Asiatic Sundays" was the
name given to the Sabbaths, on which curry and
rice always appeared on the bill of fare. Another
Athenæum dinner was known for its marrow-bones
and jam roly-poly puddings. Sir Edwin Landseer

once denounced an Athenæum beefsteak in a terse manner: "They say there's nothing like leather; this beefsteak is." A boar's head on the sideboard was described by a witty member as the head of a certain member who had at last met with the thoroughly deserved fate of decapitation.

Kinglake, the historian, lived almost entirely at the Athenæum, even when aged, infirm, and terribly deaf. People used to say that, when they talked to him, everybody in the room heard except Kinglake. Like many deaf men, he was given to shouting in people's ears, and on one occasion was heard screaming to Thackeray at the top of his voice: "Come and sit down; I have something very private to tell you: no one must hear it but you." Another distinguished soldier, equally deaf, used to select the smoking-room of his club for confidential conversations with members of his staff, putting momentous questions and receiving answers which were given in such a loud tone that everyone heard his official secrets.

The Athenæum has never been very favourable to the stage. Some of the great actors of the past, however, belonged to it, notably Sir Henry Irving, who was a most popular member.

Other actor members were Charles Mathews the elder, Macready, Charles Mayne Young, Charles Kemble, Charles Kean, and Daniel Terry.

Considering the partiality of literary men for tobacco, it seems curious that the only smoking-room in this club used to be in the basement. To supply a pressing need, an upper floor was a short time ago constructed at the top of the building;

and smokers can now be conveyed by a lift, put in at the time of the alterations in 1900.

Membership of the Athenæum would seem to favour a man's chances of living to a green old age, and certain members have belonged to the club for an extraordinary number of years. Mr. Lettsom Elliot, for instance, who died in 1898, had been a member since 1824, when he was elected at the first committee meeting of the club. Mr. Elliot had kept a copy of the first list of members, and in 1882 he had a reprint of this produced, which forms a record of considerable interest. On this committee were Chantrey, the sculptor; John Wilson Croker; Sir Humphry Davy; Sir Thomas Lawrence; Sir James Mackintosh; Tom Moore, the poet; Sir Walter Scott; together with some others. Amongst distinguished ordinary members have been Benjamin Brodie; Mark Isambard Brunel, the engineer; Dibdin; Isaac Disraeli; Lord Ellenborough; Michael Faraday; John Franklin; Henry Hallam; James Morier, the diplomatist, and author of "Haji Baba"; Samuel Rogers; Sir John Soane, who bequeathed to the nation the Soane Museum in Lincoln's Inn Fields; Joseph Turner; Charles Kemble; Charles Mathews the elder; Westall, the artist; David Wilkie; Henry Holland; Blanco White, a friend of Coleridge's; Whately; Newman; Jekyll, the wit; John Stuart Mill; and Herbert Spencer.

The last-named was fond of playing billiards in the club, where he is said to have made the famous remark to a very skilful antagonist: "Though a certain proficiency at this game is to be desired, the skill you have shown seems to argue a misspent youth."

A club which somewhat resembled the present Athenæum in character was the Alfred, founded in 1808 for men of letters, travellers, and the like. It was first started at a house in Albemarle Street, when it appears to have been a very solemn institution. A member, indeed, not in sympathy with its tone, called it the " dullest place in the world, where bores prevailed to the exclusion of every other interest, and one heard nothing but idle reports and twaddling opinions. It is," said he, " the asylum of doting Tories and drivelling quidnuncs."

Lord Byron, however, called it " a pleasant club—a little too sober and literary, perhaps, but, on the whole, a decent resource on a rainy day."

In 1811, three years after its foundation, there were no fewer than 354 candidates for six vacancies, but this happy state of affairs did not last.

Sir William Fraser described the Alfred as having been " a sort of minor Athenæum," which perhaps caused a wag to say the title should be changed from Alfred to " Halfread."

Lord Alvanley, who was a member, once said at White's: " I stood the Alfred as long as I could, but when the seventeenth Bishop was proposed I gave in ; I really could not enter the place without being put in mind of my Catechism." The Bishops, it is said, resigned the club when a billiard-table was introduced. In the course of time the Alfred languished, and was finally dissolved in 1855.

Hatred of tobacco, it is said, caused the end

of the Alfred. A certain influential section of members persistently opposing any improvement in the smoking-room, which was at the top of the house and stigmatized as an "infamous hole," the committee would make no concession, and so the club was eventually closed.

When it was evident that the Alfred could not maintain an independent existence (though perfectly solvent), a sort of coalition was formed with the Oriental. A large number of members were admitted to the latter without entrance fee, but most of the Alfred members joined other clubs, especially the Athenæum.

A flourishing little literary club of modern origin is the Savile, in Piccadilly. This possesses a very curious table, which was purchased some years ago. It would appear to have been made during the mid-Victorian period, and is embellished with a number of curious designs in various woods— masterpieces of the inlayer's art. Amongst these is a portrait of the late Queen Victoria.

CHAPTER XI

THOUGH various London clubs possess a certain number of pictures and *objets d'art*, the Garrick stands alone in the ownership of a unique collection. This, however, has been described so frequently that any detailed treatment would be superfluous.

The Garrick was originally started at 35 King Street, Covent Garden, in 1831, " for the purpose of bringing together the ' patrons ' of the drama and its professors, and also for offering literary men a rendezvous."

The club-house had been a family hotel. It was comfortable enough when it was first transformed into the home of the Garrick Club, but in course of time the building was found insufficient for the increased number of members, and in 1864 the club removed to a new house built for them a little farther west than the old one, in the then newly-made Garrick Street—a classic region associated with the old club-house.

The new Garrick was built by Mr. Marrable, who cleverly surmounted certain difficulties connected with the back of the building.

The bulk of the Garrick Club collection consists

of the gallery formed by the elder Mathews, who had a passion for collecting theatrical portraits, and who purchased most of the pictures owned by Mr. Harris, the old lessee of Covent Garden.

Mrs. Mathews, the actor's wife and biographer, describes how the pictures were saved from the swindling tenant who robbed them of their rent in the King's Road cottage. Mathews's "giant hobby," as she calls it, was then (1814) in its infancy; but the Mr. Tonson who succeeded them in the cottage begged to be allowed to retain the pictures, which were at that time hanging in one small room. Mathews, who would as soon have left behind him an eye or a limb as these his treasures, managed to retain them. Later on he built at his house at Hampstead a special gallery for his pictures, which had then considerably increased in number. Many writers came there to see them, all of whom were not equally appreciative. When, however, Mathews found a real judge of art, he called it "receiving a dividend," and would launch out into all sorts of disquisitions as to his treasures, enlivened by anecdotes and imitations of the persons portrayed. Inquisitive people, who came to see the actor as a celebrity rather than to inspect his pictures, irritated and exasperated him by their behaviour and their mistakes, which were often absurd. Harlowe's fine picture of Mrs. Siddons as Lady Macbeth was taken for a portrait of Mrs. Mathews; Dewilde's exquisite portrait of Miss De Camp—Mrs. Charles Kemble—in male attire, in "The Gentle Shepherd," was praised as being Master Betty. One individual, who had evidently never entered a London theatre, asked why there was no portrait of Milton. Eventually all the pictures were exhibited in Oxford Street, and there still exists a catalogue of this exhibition, to which a characteristic article of Charles Lamb's, which appeared in the *London Magazine*, is prefixed.

During Mathews's lifetime the collection was removed to the Garrick Club. It then practically passed into the possession of a member, Mr. John Durrant, who eventually gave the pictures to the club.

There are many good portraits of Mathews at the Garrick, of which the most remarkable is, perhaps, the one by Harlowe, who depicted him in four perfectly different and distinct characters —a tribute to the actor's versatility. The four characters are those of Fond Barneyl, the idiot newsvendor of York ; another weak-minded simpleton catching a fly; Mr. Wiggins, an extraordinarily stout man, in a farce called "Mrs. Wiggins"; and Mathews himself in ordinary day dress. Another good portrait, by Clint, A.R.A., shows Liston and Mathews in "The Village Lawyer," the former as Sheepface, the latter as Scout. Liston impressed people on casual acquaintance with an idea of inveterate gravity ; as Sheepface he fairly amazed Mathews, and in this part made him laugh so much that he was hardly able to go on.

Two of the finest pictures in the Garrick are those representing Garrick and Mrs. Pritchard in "Macbeth," and Garrick and Mrs. Cibber in "Venice Preserved." Zoffany, who excelled in theatrical portraiture, painted both of these.

Another portrait by him shows the great actor as Lord Chalkstone.

The fine picture of Macbeth is highly interesting on account of Garrick's costume. Though a stage reformer, he did not dare to discard old traditions of dress, and played the Highland thane in a long-skirted blue coat with crimson cuffs, and a full-bottomed wig of the Georgian period. Occasionally he acted Macbeth in the costume of a fashionable gentleman of the day—a suit of black silk, with silk stockings, and shoes, buckles at the knees and feet, a full-bottomed wig, and sword.

Benjamin West once asked Garrick why he adhered to this ridiculous usage, to which he replied that he was afraid of his audience, who would have thrown bottles at him if he had dared to change. John Philip Kemble, when stage-manager at Drury Lane, finally corrected the absurdities of stage costume, although Henderson appears to have preceded him in this respect. In Romney's picture of Henderson as Macbeth, which is in the club, the chieftain appears as a medieval warrior wearing body armour, with arms and legs bare. In 1772 Macklin played Macbeth at Covent Garden in the dress of a Highlander, but, being a clumsy old man, he is said to have looked more like a Scotch piper than a warrior. Kemble, oddly enough, first played Othello in the full uniform of a British General—as Macbeth he wore a hearse-like plume in his bonnet; whilst Mrs. Crough, the singer, who played the First Witch, wore powdered hair and the fashionable costume of her day.

Garrick excelled in the art of facial expression.

When he sat to Gainsborough, he paid, it is said, no fewer than sixteen visits to his studio, and on each occasion wrought a change in his features. At length the painter, declaring he could not paint a man with such a " Protean phiz," threw down his brush in despair. Garrick sat to Hogarth as Fielding, after the novelist's death, when the painter wished to paint a posthumous likeness of the great writer. Dressed in a suit of Fielding's clothes, the actor cleverly assumed his features, look, and attitude. Small wonder that Johnson, when he heard that Garrick's face was growing wrinkled, exclaimed : " And so it ought, for whose face has experienced so much wear and tear as his ?"

At times this great actor would indulge in very unconventional behaviour. Acting in a tragedy in which a Mr. Thomas Hurst—who was a brandy-merchant—took a part, Garrick, conceiving Hurst too tame to support him, reproved him publicly on the stage. " Mr. Hurst," said he, " if you will put MORE *British spirit* into your *acting*, and LESS in your *brandy*, you may send me *two gallons* to-morrow morning." Whether the brandy-merchant was offended or not, history does not relate ; but he took care to remember the order, which he sent the following day, writing at the bottom of the bill of parcels : " As per your order last night, on the stage of Drury Lane Theatre."

Garrick once set up a man in a snuff-shop, and actually recommended his snuff, known as " No. 37," from the stage, as a result of which the snuff-merchant realized an ample fortune.

Garrick, as is well known, was not devoid of

vanity, and was at times fond of praising himself. During one evening at the Sublime Society, he remarked that so many manuscript plays were sent him to read, that in order to avoid losing them and hurting the feelings of the poor devils the authors, he made a point of ticketing and labelling the play that was to be returned, that it might be forth-coming at a moment's notice. " A fig for your hypocrisy !" exclaimed Murphy across the table. " You know, Davy, you mislaid my tragedy two months ago, and I make no doubt you have lost it." " Yes," replied Garrick ; " but you forget, you ungrateful dog, that I offered you more than its value, for you might have had two manuscript farces in its stead."

Amongst the many fascinating actresses of other days who smile from the Garrick walls, some mention must be made of Mrs. Oldfield—Pope's Narcissa. Mrs. Oldfield was supposed to be the daughter of a Captain Oldfield. Her early years were passed with an aunt, who kept the Mitre Tavern in St. James's Market. At this resort she attracted attention for her recitation of one of Beaumont and Fletcher's comedies, and Rich, the celebrated manager, gave her an engagement at Drury Lane. Starting at a small salary, she quickly rose to speaking parts, and soon became the leading lady on the stage of that day. She went to the theatre in a chair escorted by two footmen, and, seldom mixing with her fellow-actors, enjoyed a unique position in spite of a by no means severe morality. She had one son by Arthur Mayn-waring, and afterwards lived under the protection of General Churchill, a brother of the great Duke of Marlborough. It is said that Queen Caroline remarked to her one day: "I hear that you and the General are married." "Madam," replied the actress discreetly, "the General keeps his own secrets." Mrs. Oldfield's children married well; her granddaughter became the wife of Lord Walpole of Wolterton, and was the direct ancestress of the present writer. The American novelist Mr. Winston Churchill is, I believe, a descendant of the sprightly actress.

From time to time the original collection at the Garrick Club has been largely increased, and some of the additions are notable. One of the most admirable modern portraits in the club now hangs over the morning-room mantelpiece. It represents the late Sir Henry Irving in morning dress, and was painted and presented by Sir John Millais. Another good portrait of the veteran Phelps as Cardinal Wolsey, in scarlet robes, is the work of that talented artist and actor—Mr. Forbes-Robertson. Mr. Henry Neville, who died but recently, was painted as Count Almaviva, by Mr. W. John Walton; and Sir Squire and Lady Bancroft are represented in marble statuettes, done by the late Prince Victor of Hohenlohe. A picture of Sir John Hare in one of his most successful creations —Benjamin Goldfinch in " A Pair of Spectacles "— has recently been added.

In the Garrick are preserved some small silver candlesticks, formed of little figures representing harlequins and the like. These were presented by the writer's great-uncle, Edward Walpole, known as Adonis Walpole on account of his good looks. The rest of the set is in the possession of Lady Dorothy Nevill.

There have been many "characters" amongst Garrick members in former days, of whom, perhaps, the most original was Tom Hill, who was an authority upon most things—grave or gay.

Born in 1760 at Queenhithe, he became a dry-salter, but, having sustained financial losses in 1810, retired about that year to rooms in the Adelphi, where he lived comfortably enough. A great collector of books, chiefly old poetry, and theatrical relics, he was very well known in literary and stage circles.

Hill is said to have been the original of Paul Pry, but this is doubtful. The great joke in connection with him was his age. James Smith once said that it was impossible to discover his age, for the parish register had been burnt in the Fire of London; but Hook capped this: "Pooh, pooh!" —Tom's habitual exclamation—"he's one of the Little Hills that are spoken of as skipping in the Psalms."

Till within three months of his death, Hill usually rose at five, took a walk to Billingsgate, and brought the materials for his breakfast home with him to the Adelphi. At dinner he would eat and drink like a subaltern of five-and-twenty, and one secret of his continued vitality was that a day of abstinence and repose uniformly followed a festivity. He then nursed himself most carefully on tea and dry toast, tasted neither meat nor wine, and went to bed by eight o'clock. But perhaps the grand secret was the easy, imperturbable serenity of his temper, which, when he died in 1841 at the age of eighty-one, enabled him to look twenty years younger. It was probably due to this fact, also, that his cheerfulness remained unimpaired, in spite of the comparative poverty of his later years.

Hill's collection of old English poetry was dispersed in 1810, whilst other rarities and memorials which he had got together took Evans, of Pall Mall, a week to sell by auction. These included some very interesting autograph letters, and among the memorials were Garrick's Shakespeare cup, a vase carved from the Bard's mulberry-tree, and a block of wood from Pope's willow at Twickenham.

The late sittings for which the Garrick was formerly renowned seem to have become more or less things of the past.

Supper at the Garrick some twenty-five years ago was, especially on certain nights, a regular institution. The late Sir Henry Irving and Mr. Toole were regular attendants, often sitting very late at the long table in the smaller dining-room, where the supper-table was regularly laid. Many of those who assembled round the festive board have now, like the before-mentioned theatrical stars, joined the great majority.

At that time, except for lunch, the Garrick Club was not, during the day, used by so many members as at present, nor was the club-house so comfortable or the pictures and relics displayed to such advantage. Those desirous of smoking were also hampered by restrictions, which have since been removed. As a result of the enlightened policy pursued in recent years, this club is now one of the most sociable and agreeable in London, whilst its membership is still largely composed of men well known in the literary and theatrical worlds.

The Arts Club, now in Dover Street, was formerly located at 17 Hanover Square. "Sweet Seventeen,' as it came to be called, was a fine old Georgian house, with marble mantelpieces and ceilings painted by Angelica Kauffmann. Some of the rooms were originally panelled, and the staircases were of old oak ; but all these fine things are now dispersed, and the house has been pulled down. At the time when it was occupied by the Arts Club the walls were further adorned by pictures which were lent for exhibition, and which completed a *tout ensemble* of singular charm.

Another club of which much has been written is the Savage, started in 1855. This Bohemian institution has always had a number of celebrities on its list. In its early days the membership included George Cruikshank, J. L. Toole, Paul Bedford, Shirley Brooks, Dion Boucicault, and George Augustus Sala. Sala's name appears in the first list, and he served on the first committee, but although he twice joined the club he was not a "Savage" when he died. Other notable members of those days were "Mike" Halliday, Arthur Sketchley, Sir Squire Bancroft, Sothern, Henry S. Leigh, "Tom" Robertson, Lord Dunraven (then Lord Adair), Joseph Hatton, Kendal, George Henty the war - correspondent (who won great fame as a writer of boys' books), W. S. (now

Sir William) Gilbert, and Arthur Sullivan the composer.

In connection with Bohemian clubs, some mention of the Players' Club, at 16 Granmercy Park, New York, may not be out of place. The club in question was opened on the last night of 1888 by the late Mr. Edwin Booth, who, having purchased the building, remodelled and furnished it as a club-house, and presented the title-deed to the members as a free gift.

Membership of the Players', like that of the Garrick, is not confined to actors alone. It also resembles the latter club in that it contains many prints and mementoes of great theatrical stars who have passed away, including a priceless collection of costumes and properties. The memory of Edwin Booth is commemorated firstly by the conservation, in an untouched condition, of the bedroom in which the last years of his life were passed; and secondly by the Booth library, containing a fine collection of volumes bequeathed to the club by the great actor.

The contents of Edwin Booth's bedroom are kept exactly as in his lifetime, even to the last book he read, with a mark on the last page the great actor turned. A chair and skull used by him in " Hamlet " are also here.

On the last night of the old year, club custom at the Players' ordains that about midnight a loving-cup should be passed round amongst members, in order that they may drink to the memory of the founder.

" Ladies' day " is an annual festival of this club,

held on Shakespeare's birthday—April 23rd—on which date a number of ladies, either connected with or interested in the stage, are entertained.

This and "founders' night" are the only two functions held, and consequently invitations are very highly prized. Each member is allowed but two cards of admission.

Another Bohemian New York club is the Lambs. The funds to pay off a mortgage of 36,000 dollars on the club-house in West Thirty-sixth Street were raised in a highly characteristic manner. For the space of one week a company consisting entirely of stars—actors, musicians, and authors—formed themselves into a minstrel troupe and toured through eight cities, with the result that they made 67,000 dollars. Each member of this troupe on its dispersal received one dollar as a souvenir of his services.

The present club-house of the Lambs, at West Forty-fourth Street, cost no less than 300,000 dollars. It is a most luxurious building furnished with every modern convenience, and contains a theatre where the Lambs hold their famous Gambols, and where plays never performed elsewhere are played. Besides their private Gambols, the Lambs give an annual public Gambol at a New York Theatre, to see which the public can obtain tickets through members.

The Lambs are exceedingly charitable to any of their number who may be overwhelmed by misfortune or sickness, and, indeed, membership of the club has been said to constitute an insurance against adversity. Many a stricken actor has had reason to bless the club, which on one occasion, through a benefit performance organized in conjunction with the players, obtained a comfortable annuity for an actor who had been seized by an incurable malady.

Whilst hardly a club in the sense now usually understood, the Jockey Club possesses rooms at Newmarket, and a number of sporting prints are to be seen here. The most interesting relic in the possession of the club, however, is a hoof of Eclipse, formed into an inkstand. On the front are the royal arms in gold in high relief, and on the pedestal is the following inscription : " This piece of plate, with the hoof of Eclipse, was presented by His Most Gracious Majesty William the Fourth to the Jockey Club, May 1832." This hoof was originally given as a prize in a Challenge race (rather like " The Whip ") run on Ascot Thursday. The King gave an additional £200, and there was a £100 sweepstake between members of the Jockey Club. It was run for soon after it was presented, in the year of the great Reform Bill, on the same afternoon that Camarine and Rowton ran a dead-heat for the Gold Cup, and over the same course. One subscriber scratched, and, of the other two, Lord Chesterfield, with the famous Priam (Conolly up), beat General Grosvenor and Sarpedon, ridden by John Day. In 1834 Lord Chesterfield won again with Glaucus (Bill Scott up), beating Gallopade, who had won for Mr. Cosby the year before. Twelve months later the hoof was challenged for by Mr. Batson, but there was no reply. It is much to be regretted that no sporting event is now connected with this historic hoof. Considering how small an interest the contests for the Whip have excited of late years, there is little likelihood of this relic being again run for on Newmarket Heath.

Eclipse is closely connected with the history of the Jockey Club. This race-horse of historic memory lived for twenty-five years, and the years in question just coincided with the period during which the Jockey Club grew into a powerful body. It was also the time of the foundation of the Derby, the Oaks, and the St. Leger. Then it was that the Jockey Club first began to be quoted as a real and powerful authority, and when its rulings were first accepted by racing men. The sentence of "warning off," originally established by precedent, was legally recognized in 1827, when, in the case of the Duke of Portland *v.* Hawkins, a man to whom the Jockey Club objected was successfully proceeded against for trespass on the freehold property of the club.

Although the memory of Eclipse is intimately connected with the history of the Jockey Club, it is a rather remarkable thing that his owner never succeeded in obtaining admittance to that exclusive circle. Colonel O'Kelly's one great grievance, which led him persistently to denounce the Jockey Club, was the stubborn refusal of the members to elect him.

On one occasion, when Colonel O'Kelly was making a contract with a jockey, he stipulated as a special condition that he should never ride for any of the *black-legged* fraternity. The consenting jockey saying "he was at a loss to know who the

Captain meant by the black-legged fraternity," he instantly replied, with his usual energy : " Oh, ——, my dear, and I'll soon make you understand who I mean by the black-legged fraternity ! There's the Duke of Grafton, the Duke of Dorset," etc., naming the principal members of the Jockey Club, " and all the set of *thaves* that belong to the humbug societies and *bugaboo* clubs, where they can meet and rob one another without fear of detection."

Though old O'Kelly was never admitted, his nephew Andrew became a member soon after his uncle's death.

The Jockey Club appears to have been founded about 1752. The first public mention of the new association—which is to be found in Mr. John Pond's " Sporting Kalendar "—evidently assumes the familiarity of his readers with the club ; for it makes the simple announcement for 1752 of " a contribution free plate by horses the property of noblemen and gentlemen belonging to the Jockey Club," and by the May meeting of 1753 two "Jockey Club Plates " were being regularly run for. The list of members as shown by these and similar races run for between this year and 1773, and the date when the " Racing Calendar " was first produced by James Weatherby, " Keeper of the Matchbook," indicate very clearly what were the objects of a club the origin and early history of which are wrapped in considerable obscurity.

Another very exclusive institution is the Royal Yacht Squadron at Cowes, which was originally founded by a number of noblemen and gentlemen (as the old-world phrasing ran) desirous to promote the science of marine architecture and the naval power of the kingdom. Prize cups were frequently given to be sailed for, not only by their own vessels, but by those of other clubs; the pilot and fishing vessels of the Island were not forgotten; and liberality and national utility were the main objects of the club. The result of all this was that great improvement in the construction of ships was absolutely forced upon the Government of that day.

On June 1, 1815, a body of gentlemen met at the Thatched House Tavern in St. James's Street, under the presidency of Lord Grantham, and decided to form a club which should consist only of men who were interested in the sailing of yachts in salt water. These gentlemen nominated themselves with others to the number of forty-two to form a list which should constitute the original members of the club, decided upon a small subscription, and drew up a few simple rules to govern their newly-formed yacht club.

The original idea of the club would seem to have been merely an association of those yacht-owners who frequented Cowes during the summer, and it was to be maintained by a couple of annual meetings—one in the spring at the Thatched House, the other at a dinner at the hotel at East Cowes. There was at first no club-house, and the subscription was only two guineas. The qualification for any future candidate was the possession of a yacht of a certain tonnage, the payment of an entrance fee of three guineas, and the occupation of such a social position as should commend him to the members of the club, who would consider the matter at a general meeting.

The original title was the Yacht Club, and the rules relating to yachting were few and simple. Every member, upon payment of his three guineas to the secretary and treasurer, was entitled to two copies of the signal-book, "and will be expected to provide himself with a set of flags according to the regulations contained therein." That same signal-book was the subject of a great deal of anxious consideration during the next few years. The club paid Mr. Finlaison £45 for printing the first copies, which they soon found to be based upon a wrong system, and appointed a committee to consider the matter, who called in "the well-known skill and experience of Sir Home Popham, K.C.B.," to assist them in devising a new set. A few years later these also were found wanting "as clumsy and inconvenient," by reason of the number of flags employed, when the Yacht Club adopted the code "composed by Mr. Brownrigg, midshipman of H.M.S. *Glasgow*, it being thought that two flags, two pennants, and an ensign are all that can be required."

Members were requested to register the name, rig, tonnage, and port of registry, of their vessels with the secretary, and the club adopted as a distinguishing ensign "a white flag with the Union in the corner, with a plain white burgee at the masthead."

Lord Uxbridge, afterwards the first Marquis of Anglesey, of Waterloo fame, was one of the original founders of the club. He was very proud of the whiteness of the decks of his famous cutter, the *Pearl*, and when he gave a passage to Lord Adolphus FitzClarence, who wore carefully varnished boots which left marks on the deck after a shower, he told off one of his hands to follow the offender with a swab and remove the mark of each footstep.

The first Commodore of the club was the Hon. Charles Pelham, so popular in later years as Lord Yarborough, and as the owner of the two famous yachts called the *Falcon*. Lord Yarborough's memory was so revered among his club-mates that when his son came up for election, nearly half a century later, all the formalities of the ballot were dispensed with, and he was elected with acclamation.

Another original member was Lord FitzHarris, and his official yacht, the *Medina*, of eighty tons, was always to be seen at the earlier functions of the club. "She was the connecting link," wrote his son, "between the ships painted by Van de Velde and those which preceded ironclads. She was built in William the Third's reign, and her sides were elaborately gilded. She was highest by the stern, with such a deep waist forward as to endanger her going down head foremost if she shipped a heavy sea. She had very little beam, and her complement consisted of Captain Love, R.N., the master, and twelve men."

Sir William Curtis, the founder of the present banking house of Robarts, Lubbock and Co., was another member. The Prince Regent often stayed with him upon his luxurious yacht, the *Emma Maria*. Sir William was an amiable and charitable man, of whom many amusing stories were told. He went with George IV to Scotland in 1822, and appeared in complete Highland costume at Holyrood, even down to the knife stuck in his stocking. The King himself appeared in a kilt, and, it was said, was much chagrined to find Curtis the only man in the room similarly clad. The Baronet, on the other hand, was flattered to think that he alone shared the Highland costume with His Majesty, and asked King George if he did not think him well dressed. " Yes," replied that monarch, " only you have no spoon in your hose."

In 1821 the Yacht Club, for some obscure reason, changed the original white ensign and jack with a white burgee to a red ensign and burgee. In 1824 they added the letters R.Y.C. and a crown and foul anchor to the burgee; in 1826 they changed the ensign to a jack with a white border, without any explanation being recorded in the minutes.

In 1824 the club began to feel the want of a meeting-place at Cowes, and a year later the Gloucester Hotel became its first habitation. To meet the increased expenses resulting from the change, we may note that the annual subscription was raised in the year of removal successively to £5 and to £8, the entrance fee to £10, and the tonnage qualification for the boats of new members was raised from 20 to 30 tons.

After the vacation of Cowes Castle by Lord Anglesey, the Governor, the Squadron acquired the old building, and, after a good deal of money had been expended in alterations, the club took up its abode there in 1858. Then began a new era in its history, and, owing to the interest taken by the then Prince of Wales, its importance as an exclusive social institution greatly increased.

One of the most pleasant rooms in the present well-appointed club-house is the library, over which the late Mr. Montagu Guest used to preside. The collection of books here dates from 1835, when members were first invited to increase the number of volumes owned by the club either by donations of money or gifts of books.

In the castle hang a number of pictures connected with the history of the club. These include portraits of Lord Yarborough, the Earl of Wilton, and other notabilities connected with the past history of the Squadron. As a club-house, the old castle is one of the pleasantest in the world. It is an ideal retreat for members tired of town, for whose use a number of excellent bedrooms are provided. The Royal Yacht Squadron is singularly fortunate in its secretary, a retired naval officer of much urbanity and tactful charm.

The Royal Yacht Club, as it was called in the early days of its existence, did much to improve naval architecture, and was without doubt of considerable national utility.

Lord Yarborough's *Falcon* was a very fine vessel, as was the Duke of Norfolk's 210-ton cutter *Arundel*, which was said to be one of the finest and fastest of its kind in the world. Lord Belfast quite put the naval authorities to shame with his brig, the *Water Witch*. Taking the given length of the worst and most despised class of vessels in King William IV's navy—that called the " ten-gun brig "—he declared that he would construct a brig that should not only be superior for the purposes of war, but should actually be made to outsail any vessel in the royal navy—rather a bold declaration this, it must be acknowledged, more particularly as two vessels built upon an improved and scientific plan were to be opposed to him. To work, however, his lordship went, and the product of his labours was the celebrated *Water Witch*, built for him by Mr. Joseph White, of East Cowes, on the model of his former yachts, the *Harriet*, *Thérèse*, and *Louisa*, and precisely the length of the ten-gun brig, which, though incapable of either fighting or running, was, unfortunately, quite capable of going to the bottom.

Lord Yarborough enforced naval discipline on board the *Falcon*, the crew of which were paid extra wages on condition that they submitted to the usual rules in force on British vessels of war. These included flogging under certain circumstances, and it is said that, in consideration of the additional sum paid by Lord Yarborough, some of the crew cheerfully submitted to the occasional application of the cat-o'-nine-tails.

Indeed, before the *Falcon* left Plymouth Sound for a cruise, all hands cordially' signed a paper setting forth the usefulness of a sound flogging in cases of extremity, and their perfect willingness to undergo the experiment whenever it was deemed necessary for the preservation of good order.

In the early days of the club only two instances of blackballing seem to have occurred. One was in the person of a noble Duke who had been scratched off the list on account of not paying his annual subscription, who, when he sought re-election, was excluded as a matter of course. The other individual was the owner of a yacht like a river barge, with a flat bottom, and he was rejected more in joke than otherwise, it being reported that his yacht was two months on her voyage from the Thames to Cowes, and that, moreover, the bulkhead and chimney in the cabin were of *brick!*

The candidates of that day, as may be judged from their almost invariable success in the ballot, were generally of a highly acceptable description. The same, perhaps, can hardly be said of some in recent years, when, in accordance with the spirit of the age, certain individuals, whose only claim to social consideration lay in their wealth, have made attempts to force the Squadron portals.

One of these received what was perhaps the most severe rebuff ever sustained by a candidate, in the shape of no fewer than seventy-eight black balls, which figure, it was said, would have been increased to eighty had his proposer and seconder attended the election. It should be added that the name of the candidate in question had been submitted for election at the instigation of a highly important personage whose suggestions it was impossible to ignore.

A prominent figure at the Squadron from about 1834 to 1882 was the late Mr. George Bentinck, well known as Big Ben. Mr. Bentinck was very bluff and outspoken, and when in Parliament he once administered a violent lecture to both front benches, shaking his finger at the distinguished offenders who sat on both, and saying: " You know

you have all ratted ; the only difference between
you is that some of you have ratted twice."

He was no fair-weather yachtsman, and had the
greatest contempt for people who did not live on
board their vessels, who employed captains or
sailing-masters, and who confined their yachting
to the safe waters of the Solent. He had no
notion, as he said, of a Cowes captain who always
wanted to be ashore with his wife, so he com-
manded his own ships with the strictest discipline,
and with the thorough respect of his crew. When
in harbour, his first officer always knocked at his
cabin door and reported eight bells. " Are the
boats up ?" was Mr. Bentinck's inquiry. " Yes,
sir." " Very well, make it so ;" and after that
hour there was no going ashore for anybody. He
was always delighted to take friends on a sea-
voyage, but could never be induced to give any
particulars as to where bound or the probable
length of the cruise, and very much resented an
inquiry on either point. People, accordingly, who
accompanied him always settled their affairs for
a reasonable period, not knowing when they would
return. One of Mr. Bentinck's trips from Cowes
to Gibraltar took forty-two days owing to bad
weather, and on another voyage he declared that
his yacht, the *Dream*, once shipped twenty tons of
water in the Baltic. A somewhat unflattering
caricature of Mr. Bentinck is preserved in the
club-house at Cowes.

Another well-known member of the Squadron
was Lord Cardigan, of Balaclava fame, who
exhibited considerable eccentricity as a yachtsman.

Whilst out sailing one day, his skipper said : " Will you take the helm, my lord ?"   " No, thank you," was the reply ; " I never take anything between meals."   Lord Cardigan was certainly not much of a sailor, and, according to tradition, was accustomed to appear in a costume which included military spurs.   He was also, according to all accounts, a man of somewhat unconciliatory temper, thoroughly imbued with a high sense of the importance of his great social position.   He was born in the closing years of the eighteenth century, and was at strife with most of his acquaintance throughout his career of seventy-one years.   He was very late in choosing the army as a profession, as he entered the service in 1824, at the age of twenty-seven, and by 1830 was a Lieutenant-Colonel, promotion being easy for a rich nobleman in the days of purchase.

Whilst the Royal Yacht Squadron at Cowes occupies a unique position as the chief yachting club and authority in the United Kingdom, it cannot boast a history dating back as far as an Irish yacht club—the " Royal Cork "—which traces its origin from a very ancient yachting club exist- ing at Cork as far back as 1720.   This would seem to have been a highly convivial institution, for one of the rules ran: " Resolved that no admiral do bring more than two dozen of wine to his treat, for it has always been deemed a breach of the ancient rules and constitution of the club, except when my lords the judges are invited."

At that date the rules and constitutions were described as being ancient, and some of the customs connected with the club (curious records of which are in the possession of the Royal Cork Yacht Club) were picturesque and curious.

Once a year the " Water Club " took part in a ceremony, something like that performed by the Doge of Venice, when he was wedded to the Adriatic. A contemporary writer thus describes this function : " A set of worthy gentlemen, who have formed themselves into a body which they call the ' Water Club,' proceed a few leagues out to sea once a year in a number of small vessels, which for painting and gilding exceed the King's yacht at Greenwich and Deptford. Their admiral, who is elected annually, and hoists his flag on board his little vessel, leads the van and receives the honours of the flag. The rest of the fleet fall in their proper stations, and keep their line in the same manner as the King's ships. This fleet is attended with a prodigious number of boats with their colours flying, drums beating, and trumpets sounding, which forms one of the most agreeable and splendid sights your lordship can conceive."

The rules of this club dealt largely with conviviality. Rule XIV, for instance, laid down " that such members of the club as talk of sailing after dinner be fined a bumper."

In 1737 it was ordered " that for the future, unless the company exceed the number of fifteen, no man be allowed more than one bottle to his share and a peremptory."

The Royal Thames Yacht Club springs from the Cumberland Society which was formed of members who had sailed for the Duke of Cumberland's Cup. His Grace himself was wont to present this cup to the winner at a function of considerable solemnity. The boats of the society were all anchored in line, flying the white flag with the St. George's cross. The captains waited in skiffs, and only boarded their boats when the Duke appeared in his gilded barge and proceeded to the boat of the Commodore of the fleet. The victorious captain was then summoned to that vessel and introduced to the Duke, who filled the cup with claret and drank the health of the winner, to whom he thereupon presented the cup. The winner then pledged the health of His Royal Highness and his Duchess, and the whole squadron sailed to Mr. Smith's tea-gardens at the Surrey end of Vauxhall Bridge, then a pleasant rural spot.

The owner of the gardens in question, Mr. Smith, seems to have held the post of Commodore in the society during the first five years of its incorporation, and a year or two later his establishment took the name of the society's patron, and was thenceforward known as Cumberland Gardens.

It was the rule, after the annual dinner, for members to adjourn to Vauxhall, close by, where they finished a jovial evening.

At the present day there exist a multitude of other clubs, but scarcely any of them come within the scope of this volume—which the writer hopes may prove not unwelcome both as a record of interesting club possessions and as a modest contribution to the history of English social life.

INDEX ERRATA

Cocoa-tree, the, for 1 read 2
Edward VII, King, delete 204
Garrick Club, for 193 read 195 and delete 256
Landseer, Sir Edwin, for 281 read 280-281
Royal Thames Yacht Club, the, for 310 read 309-310
Tatler, the, for 23 read 22-23
Thackeray, delete 211

DELETE references to page 256 under the following entries:

Arthur's
Athenaeum Club
Brooks's
Carlton Club
Guards' Club
Junior Carlton Club

Junior United Service Club
Naval and Military Club
Travellers' Club
Turf Club
United Service Club
White's

INDEX

THE END